Genghis Khan
CONQUEROR OF THE WORLD

Genghis Khan

CONQUEROR OF THE WORLD

LEO DE HARTOG

I.B.Tauris *Publishers*
LONDON • NEW YORK

Paperback edition published in 1999 by I.B.Tauris & Co Ltd
Victoria House, Bloomsbury Square, London WC1B 4DZ
175 Fifth Avenue, New York NY 10010
website: http://www.ibtauris.com

In the United States and Canada distributed by St. Martin's Press
175 Fifth Avenue, New York NY 10010

First published in 1989 by I.B.Tauris & Co Ltd
Originally published in 1979 under the title *Djenghis Khan 's Werelds Grootste
Veroveraar* by Elsevier

Copyright © Leo de Hartog, 1989

ISBN 1 86064 375 2

A full CIP record for this book is available from the British Library
A full CIP record for this book is available from the Library of Congress

Library of Congress catalog card: available

Printed and bound in Singapore by
South Wind Production (Singapore) Pte Ltd

Contents

Preface

The study which forms the basis of this book began in 1941 when I was a prisoner of war in Colditz. That I was able to work in those years on the subject of Genghis Khan and the foundation of the Mongol Empire I attribute with gratitude for the most part to the co-operation I received from the French Red Cross. When I asked if they could send *L'Empire des Steppes*, by René Grousset I received this book with the note: '*L'Empire des Steppes* de Grousset, actuellement introuvable, il vous est spécialement adressé par l'auteur, par notre entremise.' In 1944 Professor Grousset also sent me his book *Conquérant du Monde*.

After the war there was little opportunity for serious historical study. From 1972, however, I applied myself to acquiring knowledge about Genghis Khan and the Mongol Empire. In the early period of my work I gained much useful information from Professor K. E. O. Jahn and Dr Th. Raff. In 1976 I came into contact with Professor J. A. Boyle. During my correspondence with this scholar he regularly supplied me with invaluable advice when I was confronted with problems. It was a great disappointment to me when I heard in 1978 the sad news that he had suddenly died.

Later I communicated with two prominent experts on the subject of the Mongol Empire: Professor Denis Sinor and Professor Bertold Spuler. From them I was informed of books and articles that had escaped my attention

Finally I am grateful to Dr R. H. Poelmeijer who was prepared to read the translated typescript and offer comments on it.

As the book is primarily addressed to the general reader, the common spelling Genghis has been used, instead of the more scholarly 'Chinggis'.

March 1989

Yesügei	Shiban
Genghis Khan (Temüjin) d. 1227	Möngke d. 1259
Qasar	Qubilai d. 1294
Temüge d. c. 1247	Hülagü d. 1265
Jochi d. 1256	Böchek
Chaghatai d. 1242	Mö'etüken d. 1221
Ögödei d. 1241	Baidar
Tolui d. 1232	Güyük d. 1248
Orda	Köten d. c. 1247
Batu d. 1256	Qadan
Berke d. 1266	Büri d. c. 1253

Genealogy of principal persons relevant to the text

1
Mongolia on the eve of the birth of Asia's greatest son

GEOGRAPHY AND CLIMATE

Until the beginning of the thirteenth century the natural configuration of the country isolated that part of Central Asia which was the cradle of the Mongol Empire from the rest of the Asiatic continent. In the west lay two enormous mountain masses converging on each other, the Altai and the Tien Shan mountains, both of which made access to Mongolia difficult from the west. In the south the Gobi Desert formed another barrier. In the north extended the vast Siberian forests. The Mongolian plateau, largely shut off from the rest of Asia, lies at a height of about 1,200 to 1,800 metres; it is broken by a number of mountain ranges: the Sayan, the Hangay, the Yablonovy mountains and the Greater Khingan range.

In the region between the forests and the steppes, the moist slopes and deep valleys were covered with trees such as fir, cedar and beech. Growing more densely in a northern direction, in the border region they usually followed the course of the rivers. Where the forests thinned out, the mountain meadows became thinner in places subjected to the dry winds from the Gobi Desert. The steppes changed their appearance each season. In spring, when plant growth began, they were covered with an immense green carpet, which blossomed with magnificent flowers later in the season and in early summer. The months of July and August brought a scorching heat that turned this colourful scene to that of the arid expanses of the steppes, which in October, when the snow began to fall changed to oppressive white mountain masses and plains where life was difficult for man and beast. In November all streams and rivers froze; it was not until the thaws of April that life began to stir again. In general the weather was characterized by extremes. In summer the temperature could climb to over 38 degrees centigrade and in winter it could drop to below −42 degrees. Unexpected changes in the weather occurred frequently. John of Plano Carpini records that on 29 June 1246 snow fell in the country of the Naiman.[1] Throughout the year violent gales would suddenly rise, causing snowstorms or driving the burning sand before them. There were no barriers against the ice-cold winds from Siberia and the desert storms from the Gobi.

The inhabitants – human and animal – of these regions were hardened by the circumstances in which they had to live, and were accustomed to a merciless struggle for existence.

THE TRIBES

Mongolia is the most easterly part of the Eurasiatic belt of steppes. These steppes have always been inhabited by various nomadic tribes – such as the Turks, the Mongols and the Tungus. These tribes, in many ways related to each other, were members of the same national and linguistic community, the Altaic.[2]

There is very little known about the tribes in Mongolia that first became famous with the rise of Genghis Khan.[3] The history of the Mongols before Genghis Khan is unknown, and unlikely ever to become known.[4]

The Mongol tribes consisted of two groups: the pastoral-nomads, who moved from one steppe pasture to another; and the forest-hunters, who also engaged in fishing.[5] These contrasting ways of life explain why the most important region for the Mongol tribes lay on the border between the Siberian forests in the north and the steppes stretching south to the Gobi Desert.

In general the forest-hunters did not go further than the country around Lake Baikal, the source of the Yenisey and the upper reaches of the Irtish. The pastoral-nomads occupied the territory south of this region in the foothills of the Altai mountains to Buyr Nor.[6] The division between forest-hunters and pastoral-nomads was not so sharp as the names might suggest. Some tribes of forest-hunters also kept cattle, and the pastoral-nomads could not exist without hunting. In principle all Mongols took part in hunts, which they regarded as a refined pleasure.[7] In addition to individual hunting, *battues* were organized. They could become large-scale events and were carried out according to a previously prepared plan of war. Most of them were indeed a form of military manoeuvre, the wild animals functioning as the enemy. (The *battue* as a military exercise will be discussed in chapter 5.)

Although cattle raising was all-important to the pastoral-nomads, they also hunted. On the endless steppes, armed with bows and arrows or lassos, they pursued antelope, boar and wild donkeys.[8] The pastoral tribes kept cows, sheep, goats and horses. They also used cows as beasts of burden and draught animals. Sheep provided them with meat, leather and wool. At the end of the autumn or early in winter the animals were slaughtered. The meat was then prepared and frozen.[9] The pastoral-nomads moved several times a year from one mountain pasture to another; the distances they travelled depended on the size of the herds and flocks. As they did not lay up stores of fodder, they had to choose their camp sites carefully in the winter, the difficulty being that the horses and sheep, which constituted the majority of the animals, required different foodstuffs.[10] Very few camels were kept before the days of Genghis Khan in the region around the Tuula, Onon and Kerulen rivers because the terrain was too mountainous.[11]

With the uncertainties of life in these regions, the tribes sometimes temporarily abandoned their usual activities and took up others.[12] In general the tribes living in the forests remained more barbarous than those living on the steppes, who were able to maintain some contact with the culture of the neighbouring peoples: Uighurs, Khitan and Jurchen.[13] During the founding of the Mongol Empire in the beginning of the thirteenth century, the forest-hunters increasingly had to give ground to the pastoral-nomads. Gradually their territory became smaller as the pastoral-nomads settled in certain forest areas, compelling the hunters to conform to their way of life.

The basic element in Mongol society between the eleventh and thirteenth centuries was the clan, a unit based on the patriarchate. The clan, divided into a number of sub-clans, was exogamous and consisted of agnates.[14] The members of a clan were not permitted to intermarry, the young men having to choose their brides from a different clan.

Polygamy was normal, although the first wife was at all times the most important. The Mongols needed many women from other clans and the abduction of women was not unusual. This frequently caused wars between the clans.[15] The stories of the lives of Genghis Khan and his father Yesügei reveal where this exogamy could lead.

A peculiarity of the society was that the father's estate on his death passed to his youngest son by his chief wife. This son was regarded as the guardian of the possessions originally belonging to the clan, a position which gained him the title of *otchigin*: keeper of hearth and home.[16]

Before Genghis Khan assumed power, the Kereit and the Naiman were the most important tribes. It is accepted that the centre of the region occupied by the Kereit must be sought along the upper reaches of the Orkhon River; in the east their territory was bordered by the Tuula and in the south by the Ongiin River.[17] Although it is thought that the Kereit were of Turkish origin, they had been subjected to strong Mongol influences. According to the Syrian Bar Herbraeus, the Kereit were converted to Nestorianism about the year 1000.[18] West of the Kereit lived the Naiman, at that time the most powerful tribe; they can be considered as Mongolized Turks.[19] It is likely that their territory extended between Ubsa Nor in the north and the Kara Irtish River in the south, and from Lake Zaysan in the west to the upper course of the Selenga River in the east.[20] It is significant that the Naiman had adopted the culture of their southern neighbours the Uighurs, who, it is thought, also influenced them in their conversion to Nestorianism.[21]

At the end of the twelfth century the Merkit and the Tatars were equally powerful tribes.[22] The Merkit, who lived on the lower Selenga, south-east of Lake Baikal, were forest-hunters.[23] In the east, south of Buyr Nor, there was a Mongol tribe called the Tatar. They were formidable and warlike soldiers and for a long time formed a serious threat to the Chinese, who often supported the tribes living west of the Tatars in their wars against their quarrelsome neighbours. From this Chinese involvement Genghis Khan derived advantage in his war against the Tatars.

In the period between the eighth and twelfth centuries the Tatars wielded great influence because of their bellicosity. It is not unlikely that in that period all tribes speaking a Mongol language were called Tatars; this was especially so with the Chinese.[24] The name Tatar remained in use even after the rise of the Mongols under Genghis Khan.[25] Europeans travelling to the Mongol Empire often used the name Tatar,[26] but were told by the Mongols that the Tatars were a tribe they had conquered.

Although they were not of much consequence in the beginning of the thirteenth century, mention must be made of the Kirghiz and the Oirat. The Kirghiz, a Turkish tribe, drove the Uighurs out of Mongolia in 840. They caused much misery during the ninth century by their unscrupulous behaviour. In the early tenth century they were driven away by the Khitan, and settled around the upper Yenisey.[27] From that time the Kirghiz played no role of any importance. West of Lake Baikal there was a Mongol tribe, the Oirat, who lived in the forests. In the twelfth and thirteenth centuries they were of little account, but after the fall of the Yüan dynasty in China in 1368 they were the dominating tribe in West Mongolia.

Between the Onon and the Kerulen rivers lived the Mongols. This tribe would later give its name to all those who spoke a Mongol language. The Mongol tribe consisted of the Borjigin and the Taijut clans.[28] The Borjigin, who lived between the Onon and the Kerulen, were steppe nomads. The Taijut, the outstanding Mongol clan before the emergence of Genghis Khan,[29] stayed in the region of the confluence of the Onon and the Ingoda, where the steppes met the forests. They were partly pastoral-nomads and partly forest-hunters.

Some other tribes are of importance in the history of Genghis Khan. The Unggirat, who were nomads,[30] lived south-east of Buyr Nor. The Jalair, probably a defeated Turkish tribe who had undergone strong Mongol influences, had settled between the Selenga and the Onon.[31] The Ongut, Turkish nomads, who had been more or less converted to Nestorianism,[32] were to be found south of the Gobi Desert in the vicinity of north China. The Chinese called them White Tatars.[33]

Although they did not live in Mongolia and by 1200 were of no great significance, the Uighurs should be mentioned here, for their influence on the later Mongol Empire was not without importance. In about the year 745, the Turkish Uighurs settled in what is now Mongolia. There they established a great and powerful kingdom, which extended as far as East Turkestan and Tibet. The capital, Ordu Baliq (Qara Balghasun),[34] lay on the Orkhon River, close to the place where later Qaraqorum was built. The ruins which have been found show that the Uighur capital was even bigger than that of the Mongols.[35] The Uighurs, a nomadic tribe, tried to combine the life of the steppes with town life. In about 840 their kingdom was destroyed by the Kirghiz, who came from the west. Two smaller Uighur states then came into being, the eastern one in present-day Kansu and Alashan; it was conquered by the Tangut in about 1030. The western state was situated on the north-east boundary of the Tarim Basin and established itself in towns already standing there. It remained in existence until it was absorbed into the Mongol Empire in the thirteenth century. The head of this Uighur state bore the title of *idiqut* (sacred majesty).[36]

The western state reached a high stage of advancement. The influence of these Uighurs on the surrounding tribes was considerable, particularly on the Naiman, who came to be the most highly developed tribe in the region of what is now Mongolia.[37] Originally the Uighurs were followers of Manichaeism; in 763 this system became their state religion.[38] Shortly after the tenth century it disappeared to make way for Buddhism and Nestorianism, both of which were tolerated by the Uighurs. After the second half of the eleventh century Manichaeism disappeared entirely.

The Uighurs had taken their alphabet from the Sogdians, an east Iranian people who came from the region of Samarkand and Bukhara.[39] This alphabet, originally Semitic,[40] is known in history as the Uighur script. As his own people had no written language, Genghis Khan introduced it as the official script of the Mongol Empire. Thereafter it became very widely known.

MONGOL SOCIETY

Religion

The shamanism that formed the main element in the religious life of the Turkish and Mongol tribes rested on the Turkish–Mongol animism, which was more or less influenced by the Chinese and by Mazdaism.[41] This religion, in which public worship played no part, expressed itself in all kinds of formalities, oracles, exorcisms and the magic of images. The absence of any services of worship and prayers gave travellers to Mongolia the impression that the Mongols had no religion. However, they had their religious doctrines. They believed in one god, Tengri (Eternal Heaven).

A number of Mongol customs had their origin in the old animism with its cult of mountain tops and river springs. The Mongols climbed to the tops of sacred mountains to approach Tengri and to call upon him. As a sign of their submission to him they took their hats off and threw their belts over their shoulders. As they believed that springs represented higher powers, water was not permitted to be fouled.[42] Washing the body, clothes, cooking utensils or dishes was strictly forbidden on religious grounds,[43] a practice that resulted in the complete absence of any form of hygiene among the Mongols. After the conquests of Genghis Khan there were frequent difficulties about the use of water with the subjected Islamic tribes, who were accustomed to washing themselves ritually.

The sun, in particular the rising sun, was an object of worship to the Mongols. The south played an important part in their lives because it was connected with their worship of the sun.[44] Homage to the sun was expressed by a number of genuflexions made facing towards the south. There were other customs of a religious import. It was forbidden to touch fire, which was also an object of worship, with a knife. Sacrifices of drink were made by throwing a full cup in the air while certain sentences were uttered. An oath (*anda*) taken to solemnize friendship or treaties was accompanied by the drinking of blood from a cow's horn in which lay a gold piece. This oath was sometimes confirmed by hacking a stallion and a mare in half.[45]

Through neighbouring tribes the Mongols came in contact

with Nestorianism (the Kereit, Naiman and Ongut), Buddhism (Uighurs), Taoism (the Chinese) and Islam (merchants from South-west Asia). Such contacts with other religions made them doubt to some extent whether Tengri was indeed the only and almighty god. They began to take account of the existence of other gods, and judged it wise not to hinder too much worshippers of other religions in the practise of their religious duties. This point of view resulted in a remarkable tolerance which was unusual in a barbarous people and was one of the characteristics which favourably distinguished the Mongols. Nevertheless, after the foundation of their empire the Mongols accepted that Tengri had granted them the domination of the world and that the Great Khan had been given the task of carrying out this purpose.

Death

Before the moment when a person died, all family members left the bedside.[46] The deceased person was buried in a place that he or she had been especially fond of when living. Eminent Mongols chose their burial place during their lifetime.

The bodies of the dead were buried with many valuable possessions. To prevent violation of the bodies or robbery from the tombs, the location of the graves of chiefs and later the lords of the Mongol Empire were kept secret.[47] To ensure that the place remained secret it was not unusual for slaves who had assisted at the burial to be executed on the spot.[48] Another method of preventing the discovery of a grave was to arrange the burial at night. Often large numbers of horses were driven over the site of the grave; when it became overgrown with vegetation it would be impossible to find. This was one of the reasons why the Mongols raised no burial mounds.[49] The graves of the common Mongols however were not concealed. On such graves a pole was placed and on it was hung the skin of the dead person's horse.

The eras of the Mongol-Turkish tribes were marked by cycles of animals. They consisted of twelve years, each indicated by the name of an animal.[50] The sequence was: Rat, Ox, Tiger, Hare, Dragon, Snake, Horse, Sheep, Monkey, Hen, Dog, Pig.

Dwellings

The distinction between the forest-hunters and pastoral-shepherds was also apparent in their dwellings. The most rudimentary huts of the forest-hunters were made of birch bark. The tents of the pastoral-shepherds and those of the hunters living where the forests joined the steppes were of various kinds.[51] The hunters had simple low tents made of linen.

The pastoral-nomads used circular felt tents, called *jurt*, the framework of which consisted of a large number of thin wooden stakes and slats. This means that these tribes lived in the vicinity of forests.[52] In the middle of the jurt stood the main support, which at all costs had to be carefully erected in view of its most important function. If this central pole collapsed the whole jurt was often destroyed, with unhappy consequences for the family concerned. The walls and the roof were of felt. In the middle of the roof was a round opening on which there was a short chimney.[53] Under this was the fireplace, used for warmth and the preparation of food. The entrance to the hut faced south.[54] Apart from the fact that the Mongols usually orientated themselves towards the south, there was another reason for this: the prevailing cold winds came from the north.

Originally the jurts had to be completely taken down when the nomads moved, and erected again on the new pastures. It was probably early in the thirteenth century that the Mongols began to build the jurts on wooden carts, so that it was unnecessary to take them down, and there was little work to do on the new site. The carts were usually pulled by oxen, their number depending on the size of the jurt. This method of transport, which was used most extensively in the first decades of the Mongol Empire, disappeared completely after the fall of the empire.

Food and drink

Impressed by the considerable differences between Mongol eating and drinking habits and those of contemporary Europeans, travellers from Europe wrote a great deal on the subject. The Mongols' nomadic existence necessitated a diet consisting mainly of meat,[55] while milk was the chief drink.

They ate flesh of any animals they could catch during the hunt:[56] dogs, wolves, fox, rats, mice, marmots and rabbits. For them there were no religious inhibitions to eating flesh. Only animals hit by lightning could not be used for food.[57] Horse flesh was a favourite food of the Mongols, while cows and sheep usually provided the meals for festive occasions.

Only in emergencies was flesh eaten raw, after it had been put under the saddle of a horse which was ridden until it became tender. This, however, was exceptional treatment. Usually meat was boiled or roasted.[58] At meals everybody ate from a common pot. Meat left-overs were kept in leather bags. No attention was paid to hygiene. Everything points to the conclusion that the Mongols had what we would regard as filthy eating habits, largely as a result of the law that water should not be fouled. It is known that the Mongols in dire need ate human flesh.[59] Ancient Chinese texts confirm that there was some question of anthropophagy among the Mongols.[60]

Although they drank fresh milk, *qumys*, the fermented milk of mares, was the favourite drink of the Mongols. In the winter they made a kind of light wine from rice, wheat, millet and honey.[61] It was a drink that often caused drunkenness, which was common enough among the Mongols, although it never led to quarrels or fights. Drunkenness was nothing to be ashamed of among the Mongols; on the contrary it was a matter of honour.[62] They saw it as an expression of a particularly male virtue.[63] The descendants of Genghis Khan were no exception in this respect.[64]

Women

The attitudes of the Mongols regarding women were by no means uniform. In spite of the polygamy that was customary among them, women played an important role in Mongol social life.[65] The tribal chiefs often sought the opinion and advice of their wives, a habit that was continued by the later rulers of the Mongol Empire.[66] The wives of the tribal and clan chiefs frequently accompanied their husbands during actions against enemies. Later, when the campaigns of Genghis Khan became long and extensive, several wives went with the army. It was their duty to take over during the battles the work normally done by their husbands.

Although women did not generally play a subordinate role in Mongol society, it is striking how easily they submitted if, after an abduction, they had to accept a new husband from a different clan. It is likely that some women were abducted in this way more than once; this method of acquiring wives was not unusual. The new husband did not object when the first-born of his wife was not his own child.

Women, like the men, rode horses. Draught animals pulling carts were always driven by women. They milked the cows and goats, made clothes and sewed the felt tents. The men made bows, arrows, saddles and bags in which the qumys was kept. Milking the mares was also a job for the men.[67]

In addition to the characteristics already mentioned – tolerance, unhygienic habits and frequent drunkenness – the Mongols possessed other personal qualities. As with all nomads in Central Asia, they were remarkably carefree and easygoing, an attitude which resulted from their life-style: they were quite unfamiliar with regular and continuous work.[68] But their powers of endurance were exceptional. In times of famine the food that was available was honourably divided.

The killing of human beings seemed to present no problems of conscience to them. They did not steal from each other, but they were very covetous and often tried to take with them more spoils of war than they could carry. When there was no war booty, they were not above taking or extorting possessions from non-Mongols.[69] The tribal chiefs displayed their greed in an authoritarian way: they considered that they had the right to avail themselves of the goods of their subordinates.[70]

2

The rise of a young chief of the Borjigins

THE EMERGENCE OF AN OBSCURE TRIBE

One of the more important of the heads of the Borjigin clan was Yesügei. It is indisputable that he was no more than a *baghatur* (man of valour).[1] Yesügei won some successes against the Tatars. He was helped by the Kereit, who aimed at hegemony over the Mongol and Turkish tribes. To achieve this, the Kereit had first to conquer the powerful Tatars. In their turn, however, the Kereit were attacked by the Naiman, who chased away Toghril, the khan of the Kereit. With Yesügei's support Toghril managed to restore his damaged reputation. After this success Toghril and Yesügei swore eternal friendship.[2]

During a falconry trip Yesügei, with the help of his two brothers, abducted the young wife of a distinguished member of the Merkit tribe.[3] Hö'elün, as she was called, came from the Unggirat tribe. Yesügei took Hö'elün with him to his jurt and made her his wife.[4] From this marriage four sons and a daughter were born. The sons, in order of birth, were: Temüjin, Qasar, Qachi'un and Temüge; the daughter was the youngest.[5] Yesügei had another wife, Qo'aqchin[6] who had two sons, Belgütei and Begter.[7]

There are conflicting accounts of the events of the year when Yesügei's eldest son Temüjin was born. The great Persian historian Rashid al-Din (1247–1318) says it was 1155.[8] Chinese and Mongolian sources[9] give 1162, which is currently accepted in Mongolia to be the official year of birth. Relying on Chinese sources from 1340, the French orientalist Paul Pelliot claims that Temüjin was born in 1167.[10] All these suppositions, however, have little solid evidence to support them. In this book I have taken the date of birth to be 1162.

Temüjin's birthplace is the present Deliüm Boldog, on the right bank of the Onon River. On 31st May 1962 a monument ten metres high was unveiled, when the People's Republic of Mongolia commemorated the birth of the great Mongol at this place 800 years before.[11]

There is some indication that Temüjin owed his name to the following circumstances. It was a Mongol custom to name a newly born child after a recent important event, or after a person who attracted the attention of the mother after the birth.[12] When Hö'elün had given birth to her eldest son, Yesügei returned from a successful attack in the country of the Tatars, in the course of which he had slain a Tatar chief named Temüjin. Yesügei therefore called his son Temüjin.[13] The name means 'smith'.[14]

When Temüjin was nine years of age, he accompanied his father on a visit to his mother's tribe, the Unggirat, to choose a bride.[15] The choice fell on Börte, a year older than Temüjin and the daughter of Dei Sechen, a prominent member of the Unggirat tribe.[16] Yesügei left his son with the Ungirrat and started back to his own people. Tradition has it that during this journey he passed through the territories of the Tatars and incomprehensibly accepted food from some members of this tribe (his greatest enemy). Three days later he reached his jurt, showing symptoms of poisoning. Shortly after his return he died.

Hö'elün was left with five children and two stepsons. Temüjin was brought back from the Unggirat by Münglig, a friend of Yesügei. There followed a hard time for the bereaved family. It was understandable that the Borjigins found Temüjin too young to accept him as the head of the clan. The circumstances in which the Mongols lived were too rigorous for a boy to be able to lead them. It is not clear why the Borjigin clansmen deprived Hö'elün's family of a large part of their possessions and then left them behind when the clan moved elsewhere. Yesügei's abandoned family had to try to survive in the country around the source of the Onon by hunting and fishing.

The leadership of the Mongols was taken over from the Borjigins by the Taijut; Tarqutai Kirlituq now became the chief.[17] The young Temüjin quickly displayed original methods of tackling problems which he faced. A quarrel with his half-brother Begter led him, with the help of his brother Qasar, to kill Begter. Temüjin had a loyal companion in the physically very strong Qasar (who was two years younger).[18] Tarqutai Kiriltuq, who had not anticipated that the eldest son of Yesügei could hold his own for long, took him prisoner to eliminate him as a future rival. Temüjin succeeded in escaping, thanks to his ingenuity, daring and perseverance, although he was also helped by an old man named Sorqan Shira and his two sons Chila'un and Chimbai.[19] These three later became loyal supporters of the young Mongol they had liberated.

Hö'elun's little family had in the meantime gathered together a few possessions. It was therefore a heavy blow for them when thieves ran off with eight of their nine horses. Temüjin set off in pursuit on his own, but was followed by a youth named Bogorju from the Arulat tribe. The young men managed to get the stolen horses back.[20] Temüjin and Bogorju started what was to become an enduring friendship; Bogorju was destined to be one of the future world conqueror's most intimate and valued helpers.

At the age of eleven Temüjin was a friend of Jamuqa, a boy of the same age of the Jajirat tribe.[21] The two became brothers bound by oath (anda-brothers). Jamuqa, who like Temüjin was of aristocratic origin,[22] later rose to be head of the Jajirat.

When he was a few years older, Temüjin considered that Börte, the young woman he had married as a child, should now come to live with him. He therefore journeyed to the Unggirat with Belgütei to claim her.[23] Then he and his family left the Onon source region for the upper reaches of the Kerulen River.[24]

This move was the apparent cause of what followed. Temüjin offered his services to Toghril, the khan of the Kereit. Toghril welcomed this son of his dead anda-brother, Yesügei, as an intimate subordinate, and the young Mongol naturally acquiesced to this role without difficulty. Returning from his visit to Toghril, Temüjin met a young man of the Uriangqat tribe who offered him his services. Jelme, as he was called,[25] was to become one of the most loyal comrades of Genghis Khan.

Temüjin – who, thanks to the help of Toghril, had again become head of the Borjigins – met with a misfortune which was not unusual for this country. A band of the Merkit tribe overran his camp. Temüjin himself was able to escape, but not without difficulty. With him his mother, sister, brothers, Bogorju and Jelme managed to find a hiding-place in the Hentey mountains, on the mountain called Burqan Qaldun.[26] His young wife Börte, however, fell into the hands of the Merkit. The leader of the attackers took her as his wife. The Merkit also abducted the second wife of Yesügei.[27]

The fact that the Burqan Qaldun had saved him, his family and his comrades was sufficient reason for Temüjin to hold this mountain in honour. 'The mountain has saved my poor life,' he said; 'I shall not forget it.' He voiced his gratitude in the Mongol manner: the belt over the shoulder, bareheaded and with nine genuflexions towards the south.[28] With the help of Toghril, but chiefly with the help of his anda-brother Jamuqa, the Merkit were defeated at the confluence of the Khilok and the Selenga rivers. Börte was freed and resumed her position as Temüjin's first consort.[29] Belgütei's mother was not taken back. She remained voluntarily with the Merkit who had taken her as his wife.[30]

The abduction of Börte had a sequel. After the reunion with Temüjin her first son was born on a date that left in doubt the paternity of this eldest son, who was named Jochi.[31] Conforming to Mongol custom, Temüjin raised no difficulties about his uncertain paternity, and there are no indications that he treated his eldest son differently from his other children. Nevertheless the uncertainty was not without results. Jochi's descendants, although they formed the oldest branch of the Genghisids, were never considered for the succession of the empire. The descendants of Genghis Khan's other sons apparently exploited the uncertainty so well that Jochi's branch of the family remained permanently ineligible in the election for Great Khan.

The friendship between Temüjin and Jamuqa led to co-operation between the two anda-brothers. This partnership lasted one and a half years without any notable problems.[32] During this period Temüjin met various heads and leading

men of other tribes. From this time dates his friendship with
Muqali of the Jalair, later one of his greatest generals. He
attached great importance to any advice given by Muqali.[33]

After Temüjin and Jamuqa had left the meadows on the
banks of the Onon, Jamuqa said to his friend: 'If we encamp
near the mountains it will be to the advantage of the horse
keepers. If we encamp by the mountain stream it will be to the
advantage of the shepherds.' Temüjin, who did not understand
the remark, discussed it with Hö'elün and Börte. Strangely
enough it was Börte in particular, who had been freed from the
hands of the Merkit with the help of Jamuqa, who set Temüjin
against Jamuqa. The same night the two men separated.[34]

The clans which had been united during the partnership of
Temüjin and Jamuqa separated into two groups. In the group
which followed Temüjin there were a few descendants of the
first khans, who had in earlier times created unity among the
Mongols. These, each of whom was a pretender to the
leadership of the Mongols, declared Temüjin to be khan in
about 1195. They promised to serve him faithfully 'and they
raised Temüjin to the rank of khan with the title of Genghis
Khan'.[35]

The meaning of Genghis is not known and was for a long
time a point of discussion.[36] It is likely that the adoption of the
name Genghis originated in the ambitions of the young
Temüjin. Although Temüjin himself was not superstitious, he
wished for political consideration to create the impression by
this change of name that he had been chosen by Tengri. In this
connection we should recall his association with the influential
shaman Kököchü, who played a significant role in the choice of
the name.[37] The suggestion that it is associated with a might of
the shamanism of those days and that it was chosen to confirm
the impression that Genghis Khan had been elected by Tengri,
might be possible.[38]

After his elevation Genghis Khan named his two loyal
friends, Bogorju and Jelme, as his supreme counsellors.[39] One
of the qualities that contributed to Genghis Khan's strong
position, particularly in the early years, was his skill in
organization. It is no exaggeration to claim that his genius lay
primarily in his talent as a general, his knowledge of men and
his ability in organization. These three qualities were to make

him one of the greatest leaders in the history of the world.

One of the first measures taken by the new lord was the creation of an organization for the place where he and his followers were staying at a given time. Genghis Khan knew from experience that the nomadic life was attended by many risks. Marauding expeditions and raids were common. He took the standpoint that, if he wanted to remain in power, it was necessary to have available a central position on which his subordinates could fall back and from which radiated the essential unifying strength. For this purpose Genghis Khan formed a guard which, although it was then still small numerically, was composed of selected archers and swordsmen. This guard had to remain always near him. Other measures to which he gave particular attention were the protection of subsidiaries following a military unit with food and equipment, and the training of horses. These were important matters to nomads living in the steppes. He made strict demands upon those in his immediate neighbourhood; he accepted there only those whose presence he valued highly. He demanded the swiftest execution of all his orders.[40]

THE BEGINNING OF THE ELIMINATION PROCESS

Shortly after his nomination as Genghis Khan, his first confrontation with Jamuqa took place. The sources contradict each other on this. According to one source Jamuqa was victorious in the battle and ordered 70 Mongol prisoners to be boiled alive in an iron cauldron. There is even a suggestion that Jamuqa afterwards ate his victims.[41] There is a different version: Genghis Khan was the conqueror and he executed 70 of Jamuqa's men in this way.[42]

Toghril began to be concerned about the increasing solidarity among the Mongols and the rise of his young vassal. Genghis Khan for his part needed Toghril's support. Confronting Genghis Khan there was still Jamuqa, who he apparently at first saw as his greatest rival. Moreover, among his own ranks there were still a number of pretenders to the leadership of the Mongols, namely the descendants of the first khans. Genghis Khan therefore gave Toghril no cause for suspicion. Further, he had a good opportunity to demonstrate his loyalty towards his old suzerain. Toghril was deposed by his brother Erge Qara, who was supported by the khan of the Naiman, Inancha Bilge.[43] Toghril fled first to the Qara Khitai and moved later to the Gobi Desert, where he called for Genghis Khan's aid. Genghis Khan received the deposed khan of the Kereit near the source of the Kerulen, and not only accorded Toghril all the honour to which he was entitled, but also helped him to regain his dignity among the Kereit.[44]

Shortly afterwards a chance came to take vengeance upon the Tatars. Muqali had told Genghis Khan of the need to punish this tribe for the death of his father. The Chin emperor made Toghril and Genghis Khan a request to join him in an attack upon the Tatars, who regularly plundered the north Chinese border districts. This offer presented an opportunity to eliminate a troublesome and formidable rival.[45] While the Chin attacked the Tatars from the south-east,[46] Toghril and Genghis Khan penetrated the western defences. The khan of the Tatars was captured in 1196 and executed.[47] The emperor at Peking showed his gratitude by giving Toghril the honorary title of *Wang* (prince).[48] Toghril remained known in history as Ong-Khan, which he was subsequently called (the Mongol pronunciation of wang was ong). Genghis Khan received a lower title: *Ja'utquri* (keeper of the frontier).[49] This difference indicates that the Chin emperor at that moment saw Genghis Khan as no more than a vassal of Toghril. The fact that they both accepted a title from the Chin reveals that they acknowledged the might of this empire.

While they were plundering a Tatar camp the Mongols found a small boy. Genghis Khan took the boy and gave him to his mother, Hö'elün, who adopted him as her son. She called the boy Shigi Qutuqu.[50] There is another version of the story. The child was taken by Genghis Khan in 1182–3, after a raid against the Tatars. He and Börte had at that time no children. He gave the young Tatar to Börte, who brought him up as an adopted son.[51] This conflict led to the confusion that exists about the status of Shigi Qutuqu. Some call him a stepbrother of Genghis Khan, others his adopted son. Shigi Qutuqu, who was very intelligent, later became lord chief justice of the Mongol Empire.

The struggle against the Tatars gave Genghis Khan a good opportunity to disembarrass himself of a number of the descendants of the first Mongol khans, who were competitors for his position as leader. They had declined to participate with their contingents in the war against the Tatars.[52] Genghis Khan marched against them, defeated them near Köde'ü aral, a plain on the left bank of the upper reaches of the Kerulen River, and put them to death.[53]

Meanwhile Inancha Bilge, the Khan of the Naiman, had died. His territories were divided between his two sons who were both jealous of the other: Taibuqa, who dominated the region of the lakes south-east of Ubsa Nor; and Buyruq, who possessed the mountainous part of the Altai. The quarrel between the two brothers started when Taibuqa (the younger) took one of the favourite wives of his father. Buyruq considered that as the elder son he was entitled to her. Apparently this wife's name was Gübersü; she later became one of the women in Genghis Khan's harem.[54]

In 1199 Genghis Khan and the Ong-Khan took advantage of this dissension to attack one of the brothers, Buyruq.[55] Buyruq withdrew to the Urungu River, on the southern slopes of the Altai. He probably later fled to the region of the upper course of the Yenisey.[56] He left the greater part of his army behind in the hands of his deputy commander Kökse'ü Sabraq. When Genghis Khan and the Ong-Khan withdrew in an easterly direction, Kökse'ü Sabraq laid an ambush. The attack was so successful that the Ong-Khan quickly retreated during the night without warning Genghis Khan. By lighting fires in his camp the Ong-Khan gave the impression that the Kereit were still there.[57] Genghis Khan managed to extricate himself from his difficult situation without excessive losses.[58] But the army of the Kereit was not yet safe. A part of it, which was under the command of Jaqa Gambu and Senggüm (the brother and the son of the Ong-Khan), was surprised by Kökse'ü Sabraq and was defeated.[59] In his desperation Toghril made an appeal to his vassal. Genghis Khan sent four of his best commanders: Bogorju, Muqali, Boroqul and Chila'un. They defeated the Naiman and restored a part of the possessions which had been plundered.[60] Qasar, Genghis Khan's brother, brought this war to a close with a resounding defeat of the Naiman.[61]

In 1200 the Ong-Khan and Genghis Khan carried out an attack on the Taijut. The Taijut were defeated and their tribal chief, Targutai Kiriltuq (who had earlier taken the young Temüjin prisoner), was killed.[62] The successes of the Ong-Khan and Genghis Khan roused a spirit of emulation among the other tribes in Central Asia and for this reason they joined forces. The first alliance against the ever-growing might of the two leaders was made between the Qatagin and the Saljut; the Taijut, the Tatars and the Unggirat also joined this alliance. Genghis Khan, warned by his father-in-law Dei Sechen, wasted no time: he attacked the united tribes near Buyr Nor and scattered them.[63]

In 1201, however, a real threat to the Ong-Khan and Genghis Khan emerged. A large number of tribes resolved to try to break the power of the allies. For this purpose the Merkit, the Taijut, the Naiman of Buyruq, the Jajirat, the Unggirat and the Saljut all assembled on the banks of the Argun. It is doubtful whether this great gathering formed a co-ordinated combination capable of marching effectively into battle. There was too much mutual dissension between the tribes. The only thing that bound them together was their fear of the growing might of their opponents. The *quriltai* (an assembly of the tribal chiefs and the main military commanders) met by the river Ken (a tributary of the Argun).[64] Jamuqa was appointed leader and took the title of Gur-Khan (this title was used by both the Muslims and the Mongols; it meant khan of khans, or universal and mighty khan).[65]

The fact that Jamuqa was chosen to lead this great alliance indicates not only that he was a capable figure, but also – because Jamuqa was his direct opponent – that Genghis Khan was recognized as the greatest danger. Even though Genghis Khan was not yet the more important man in the opposing camp, it was clear that the coming struggle would decide who was to be the future leader of the Mongol and Turkish tribes in Central Asia: Genghis Khan or Jamuqa.

Genghis Khan received early intelligence about the alliance from a source in Jamuqa's camp. The story of this man's journey from the Argun to Genghis Khan's camp near the Kerulen[66] gives the impression that he was more a spy than a deserter. Genghis Khan decided to anticipate his rival. In 1201 he set off northwards with the Ong-Khan but arrived in a snowstorm which was so violent that neither side was apparently able to join battle. Both armies withdrew, and Jamuqa's alliance disintegrated.[67]

Soon after the failure of this campaign, Genghis Khan made his final assault on the Taijut.[68] The attack (carried out without the aid of the Ong-Khan) reveals many similarities with the subsequent campaign against the Tatars in its aims and execution. During the battle against the Taijut, Genghis Khan was wounded so severely in a jugular vein that he lost consciousness. Thanks to the great sacrifices of his loyal companion Jelme, he survived.[69] Genghis Khan's horse, which he had been particularly fond of, was killed by an arrow. It was a chestnut horse with a white muzzle and looked like the one on which he had fled as a youth when he escaped from imprisonment by the Taijut. The Taijut were totally defeated. Genghis Khan put a number of them to death. The rest submitted to him and were enlisted into the Borjigins. Unity among the Mongol tribe had thus been restored, even if it had only been achieved at the cost of heavy losses.

Among the prisoners there was a young man, Jirqo'adai, who probably belonged to the Besüt, one of the sub-clans of the Taijut.[70] When he was brought before Genghis Khan he admitted that he had killed the horse of his conqueror. Genghis Khan, who took a liking to the young Besüt (who was an excellent archer), granted him mercy and took him into his service. Genghis Khan never regretted his clemency. He called his new servant Jebe (Arrow) in commemoration of what had happened.[71] Jebe was destined to become one of the greatest generals in the Mongol Empire.

There was still a tribe with whom Genghis Khan wished finally to settle accounts – the Tatars. It is not likely that this was done in order to punish the murderers of his father; vengeance for the death of his father had been taken in 1198. The far-seeing Genghis Khan had another motive. As long as the warlike Tatars were not destroyed, they formed a threat to Genghis Khan in the east. He foresaw even then that a confrontation between him and the Ong-Khan (his western neighbour) could not be avoided much longer. He had first defeated the Taijut in the north and reduced their numbers; the remainder were incorporated into his own troops. A similar fate awaited the Tatars. Throughout his life Genghis Khan eliminated his opponents one by one. He never neglected to bear in mind the ever-changing balance of power with which he was regularly threatened. Moreover, he possessed the patience to bide his time.

In 1202 Genghis Khan (again without the support of the Ong-Khan) launched his assault against the Tatars. After they were defeated, the conquerors began an appalling slaughter of the male population. A number of prisoners managed to escape before the massacre of the men began, having been informed by Belgütei of the instructions of his half-brother. After this Genghis Khan temporarily relieved Belgütei of his right to participate in councils of war.[72] The survivors were divided among the various clans who at that time recognized the overlordship of Genghis Khan. The Tatar tribe had ceased to exist.[73] Genghis Khan took two Tatar sisters, the young and beautiful Yesüi and Yesügen, as his wives.[74] In accordance with nomadic custom each wife was given her *ordu* (residence) and attendants.

The struggle against the Tatars had a sequel. Three descendants of the first Mongol khans (relatives of Genghis Khan) had ignored Genghis Khan's orders not to plunder for personal profit.[75] Genghis Khan sent Jebe and Qubilai after them to bring back the booty.[76] When the three were called upon to answer for their disobedience, they resolved to try their luck with the Ong-Khan. That they fled to that quarter was highly significant.

Circumstances in Central Asia were undergoing a drastic change at the beginning of the thirteenth century. The Turkish and Mongol tribes who in the twelfth century were constantly warring, began to unite into a few confederations. Of these the Ong-Khan and Genghis Khan undoubtedly formed the most powerful combination. In addition there were in western Mongolia a number of important tribes which had little connection with each other: the Naiman were the most influential of these. The others were the Merkit, the Oirat and the Kirghiz. The remnants of a few tribes which had formerly suffered defeat, and which found a livelihood by wandering from place to place, in a sense constituted a further group. However, these tribes did not form an indivisible association. From time to time they did indeed unite to carry out some attack, only to separate when it was over. They were extremely mobile bands who carried out a kind of guerrilla warfare in the region enclosed by the Altai mountains and the Greater Khingan range.[77] Genghis Khan was not mistaken: after the elimination of the most powerful tribes, the Kereit and the Naiman, the other groups were compelled to submit to him.

3
Ruler of all tribes living in felt tents

THE FINAL OVERTHROW OF THE ONG-KHAN

The relationship between Genghis Khan and the Ong-Khan would soon become threatened. The Ong-Khan was getting old and sought a successor; he thought the obvious person for this position was Genghis Khan. His opinion aroused the jealousy of Senggüm, the son of the Ong-Khan.[1]

To further his ambition and to increase his prestige, Genghis Khan wished to marry his eldest son Jochi to a daughter of the Ong-Kahn;[2] he offered one of his daughters as the bride of one of the sons of Senggüm.[3] However, Senggüm considered that the daughters of the Ong-Khan were of too high birth to marry Jochi. The rejection of his proposal grieved Genghis Khan deeply.

There was more, however, to Senggüm's refusal than appeared on the surface. Jamuqa had fled to the Kereit for refuge and become the close friend of Senggüm. Both of them, the Ong-Khan believed, distrusted Genghis Khan. They accused Genghis Khan of preparing a treacherous attack.[4] The descendants of the first Mongol khans, who had also fled to the Kereit, missed no opportunity to inflame the suspicions fostered by Senggüm. Toghril, now an elderly man, had no enthusiasm for going to war with his young and formidable vassal. Reluctantly he followed the advice of his son. In 1203 the break between the two allies became final. Genghis Khan, who until this time had played a secondary role in the alliance, had now to begin the struggle for hegemony in Central Asia.

Senggüm tried to steal a march on his opponent. He first invited Genghis Khan to attend a conciliatory meeting at which the proposed marriages were to be solemnized.[5] When this trick failed (Münglig, the former friend of Yesügei, had warned Genghis Khan), Senggüm decided to make an attack, which was rashly carried out, on the Mongols. Two shepherds, Badai and Kishiliq, who overheard a sub-commander of the Ong-Khan talking about the forthcoming attack, went as quickly as possible to inform Genghis Khan.[6] We may assume that these shepherds were spies Genghis Khan had commissioned; he had already learned that he must have a good intelligence if he wished to remain a step ahead of his enemies. Genghis Khan, who had barely enough time to prepare his departure, fled to the foothills of the Greater Khingan range and went to ground in the neighbourhood of the Khalka River. Half way there he left behind a small security detachment under the command of Jelme.[7] Although the approach of the enemy pursuit troops was reported in good time by this detachment, the task facing Genghis Khan was not easy.

The old Toghril had given Jamuqa command of the army of the tribes, who had joined the Kereit.[8] The battle that now followed was particularly fierce. Some of Genghis Khan's sub-commanders, Quyildar and the veteran Jurchedei, showed great courage and self-sacrifice.[9] The superior numbers of the Kereit, however, were too much for them. Genghis Khan was obliged to take advantage of the coming darkness to break off the battle and withdraw. When he considered it safe to halt, he found that not only his son Ögödei, but also his sub-commanders Bogorju and Boroqul were missing. Suddenly Bogorju arrived. His horse had been killed and he was riding a captured Kereit horse. Then came Boroqul, with the seriously wounded Ögödei hanging over his saddle-bow. The father wept when he saw his son.[10]

Genghis Khan realized that he could do nothing against the numerically greater army united under the Ong-Khan. He therefore decided to gain time by withdrawing to Buyr Nor. Around the Khalka River lived the Unggirat, the tribe from which his mother and his wife Börte had come. He succeeded in getting some assistance from them. During the time that he stayed in this region, he attempted to break up the league that had formed against him. He dispatched to various groups all kinds of reports and offers in order to spread mutual suspicion among them. Senggüm could see the danger of this propaganda campaign, but his father began to doubt the justice of the war they had started against Genghis Khan. The irresolute Ong-Khan, influenced by the friendly messages he received from Genghis Khan,[11] became less and less inclined to use his stronger position to destroy his opponent.[12]

Genghis Khan still thought it wiser to avoid the enemy and to let time work in his favour. He marched away in a north-easterly direction along the Kerulen and Sengur rivers[13] and set up camp on the banks of the Baljuna Lake.[14] During the summer of 1203 he went more or less into hiding there. Those who had accompanied him had to suffer much privation. Genghis Khan referred to his comrades of those days as 'the men who drank turbid water with me'.[15]

Genghis Khan had made a sound estimation of the situation. The confederacy led by Ong-Khan was one of nomadic tribes; it was very difficult for them to stay together voluntarily for any length of time. The suspicions sown by Genghis Khan threatened the unity of the different groups. Jamuqa and three partisans attempted to assassinate Toghril.[16] The Ong-Khan, alerted in time, surprised the conspirators who fled as hastily as possible to the Naiman.

By autumn the state of affairs had considerably improved for Genghis Khan. He resolved to take the initiative himself and therefore moved in the direction of the Onon. The family of Qasar had fallen into the hands of the Kereit.[17] Genghis Khan sent a messenger to the Ong-Khan to ask if Qasar could join his family. This request was meant to give the impression that, if Genghis Khan allowed his brother to return, there was no question of warlike intentions. In the footsteps of the messengers he sent two men to reconnoitre the road to the camp of the Kereit. The unsuspecting Ong-Khan agreed with the coming of Qasar. Genghis Khan now decided to act. With the two scouts as guides, the Mongol cavalry carried out a night march which had been kept strictly secret. The army of the Ong-Khan was trapped in a defile between the sources of the Kerulen and the Tuula. The Kereit defended themselves bravely for three days and three nights, but found no way to avoid defeat. On the third day of the battle it was Muqali who, at the head of his hand-picked troops, stormed the Ong-Khan's camp.[18] The first great victory of Genghis Khan was achieved. This success, which opened the way for his hegemony over Central Asia, showed clearly the military talent the future world conqueror possessed.

The old Toghril and his son Senggüm escaped in a westerly direction, towards the territories of the Naiman. The Ong-Khan was beheaded by a Naiman who had not recognized him.[19] Senggüm fled in the hope of finding protection among the Uighurs. In the neighbourhood of Kucha he also was killed. The deaths of the Ong-Khan and his son took place in the autumn of 1203.[20] The Kereit were dealt with mercifully. After their defeat there was no massacre of the people. But the independent existence of this great tribe could at a later date have led to revolt; so Genghis Khan decided to distribute the majority of the tribesmen among the clans who served him already. Thereafter the Kereit proved to be loyal followers.

A small part of this tribe remained independent under Jaqa Gambu, who had lived in constant discord with his brother Toghril. Jaqa Gambu received a number of privileges, but had to surrender two of his daughters. Genghis presented one of these, Sorqaqtani, to his youngest son Tolui. This was a most important marriage; from it were born four sons, Möngke, Ariq Böke, Qubilai and Hülagü, each of whom was to play a significant role in the Mongol Empire. Genghis Khan took Jaqa Gambu's other daughter, Ibaqa Beki, as his own wife but later, when he was rewarding the heroes of the conquest over the Kereit, gave her to the valorous Jurchedei. The two shepherds, Badai and Kishiliq, received the entire possessions of the Ong-Khan.[21]

WEST MONGOLIA YIELDS TO THE NEW RULER

After the subjugation of the Kereit, Genghis Khan held the eastern part of what is now Mongolia in his power. The most important tribes outside this area were the Naiman, the Oirat, the Merkit, and the Ongut who lived south of the Gobi Desert. Moreover, Jamuqa and his Jajirat had still not been wholly eliminated. Together with a few less influential tribes, such as the Kirghiz and the Tumat, small surviving groups of the Tatars, the Kereit and the Saljut were still active.

Before and during the coming struggle for absolute power in
Mongolia, Genghis Khan set to work on the organization of his
empire and his army. These matters, which were such
important elements in the Mongol Empire, are considered in
separate chapters.

After the defeat suffered by Buyruq at the hands of Genghis
Khan, Buyruq's brother Taibuqa had become the most
prominent ruler of the Naiman. He assumed the title *Tayang*
(prince) and those who felt themselves to be threatened by
Genghis Khan, grouped themselves around him. The most
important of these men were Qutuqa Beki and Toqto'a Beki,
the khans of the Oirat and the Merkit respectively, and Jamuqa
with the remainder of his Jajirat. Taibuqa attempted to win the
Ongut to his side. But the khan of this tribe, Alaqush Tegin,
realized that in his isolated position he would be an easy victim
of the ever-growing might of Genghis Khan. He therefore chose
Genghis Khan as his ally and warned him of the coming attack
from the west.

To deal with this threat Genghis Khan called a quriltai in
1204, at which his family members and his commanders were
present. Following the advice of his brothers Temüge and
Belgütei, in the spring of that year he launched his attack
against the Naiman.[22] He wished to anticipate his opponent but
in so doing ran the risk of advancing with horses that were still
insufficiently well nourished so early in the year.

The two armies marched against each other. The Mongol
vanguard was under the command of Jebe and Qubilai. The
reconnaissance troops made contact with each other on the
western foothills of the Hangay mountains.[23] The Mongol army
was numerically smaller than that of Taibuqa and to confuse
the enemy on this point, Genghis Khan ordered extra camp
fires to be lit at night.[24] Taibuqa began to hesitate; he thought
it better to retreat slowly to the Altai mountains and there, in
familiar terrain, ambush Genghis Khan's army in the defiles.
This would have been a good plan: for Genghis Khan, who had
been obliged to cover long distances with ill-fed horses, would
have had to take great risks in pursuing the Naiman if they
withdrew to the Altai. However, Taibuqa's son Küchlüg and
his sub-commander Korisü Beshi (who had always faithfully
served Taibuqa's father, Inancha Bilge) wished to mount a

direct attack upon the Mongols.[25] Küchlüg rejected his father's proposal in a somewhat insulting manner, calling it a cowardly plan. Taibuqa followed the advice of his son and of Korisü Beshi; he demanded, however, that Küchlüg should turn his bold words into deeds.[26]

Battle was joined near the place later called Qaraqorum. Genghis Khan, as supreme commander, led his army personally. A particularly fierce struggle followed in which Qasar, who commanded the centre of the Mongol army, showed himself to be an especially capable leader.[27] Temüge organized the protection of the reserve horses.[28] Taibuqa was carried off the field, mortally injured. Korisü Beshi stayed with him for a while, but when he saw that Taibuqa was dying, he no longer wished to live. At the head of a few loyal followers he rushed into battle and fought until he found death. Large numbers of the Naiman were killed; of those who tried to flee under cover of darkness, many fell to their deaths from the rocks.[29]

The result of the battle was a great victory for Genghis Khan. Jamuqa, fearful of the might of the Mongol army, left the ranks of the Naiman accompanied by small groups of the Jajirat survivors.[30] He sent Genghis Khan a message in which he not only said that he had deserted the Naiman, but in which he showed he had contempt for Taibuqa.[31] Why he did this is not clear. Küchlüg and Toqto'a Beki retreated with small groups in the direction of the Kara Irtish.[32] Later Jamuqa also joined this force. They hid in the region between Lake Zaysan and the Tarbagatai mountains. The main body of the Naiman and the Merkit submitted to Genghis Khan. Like the Kereit, they were distributed among the other tribes. With these two tribes, the Unggirat, the Saljut and the Qatagin also came totally under the sovereignty of the Mongols.[33]

After the battle against the Naiman and the Merkit, Genghis Khan acquired two new wives. He took possession of Gübersü, Taibuqa's wife,[34] even though she had earlier called the Mongols 'stinking savages'.[35] Toqto'a Beki's successor as head of the subjected Merkit gave Genghis Khan his daughter Qulan, who was a much-celebrated beauty.[36]

Genghis Khan resolved to offer his scattered enemies no opportunity to gather their forces together. He pursued the fugitives, but had to call off the hunt in the winter of 1204–5. In the spring of 1205 he renewed the pursuit. The first victim was Buyruq, who was attacked and killed in 1206.[37] After 1207 Genghis Khan resumed his conquest of west Mongolia, but to a large extent left operations to his sub-commanders.[38]

In that year he sent his eldest son Jochi to the country lying west of Lake Baikal to subjugate the tribes living in the forests there. Qutuqa Beki, the khan of the Oirat, surrendered without battle and offered his services.[39] Many tribes recognized that they had no alternative but to acknowledge the overlordship of the mighty khan of the Mongols. Not only the Kirghiz, who lived along the upper reaches of the Yenisey, but also the Buriat, the Barqun, the Ursut and the Tubas subjected themselves to Jochi. When he returned from his campaign, Jochi received the proud approval of his father for his achievements as a military commander.[40]

In the autumn of 1208 Genghis Khan decided personally to put an end to the risings of those enemies who had fled from the earlier battlefield. On the banks of the Kara Irtish, Küchlüg and Toqto'a Beki were defeated. Küchlüg escaped westwards to the Qara Khitai; Toqto'a Beki was killed,[41] and both his sons appealed to the Uighurs for protection.[42]

After the death of Toqto'a Beki the moment had arrived for a quick settling of accounts with his arch-enemy Jamuqa. Jamuqa's status had now declined to that of the leader of a wandering gang of robbers. His confederates do not appear to have been over-loyal, for they handed Jamuqa over to Genghis Khan. Without mercy Genghis Khan ordered the faithless followers to be put to death. Genghis Khan wanted to spare his enemy, who was once his anda-brother, but Jamuqa himself asked to be put to death – he considered himself no longer worthy to live. Genghis Khan therefore ordered his execution by the method reserved for princes – without blood-letting.[43]

The campaigns in the west were continued for some time. In 1211 the Mongol general Qubilai conquered the area west of Lake Zaysan.[44] Arslan, the khan of the Turkish tribe of the Qarluq (who lived south of Lake Balkash) joined Genghis Khan.[45] The sons of Toqto'a Beki, who had fled with the survivors of the Merkit to the country of the Uighurs, took up their positions there.[46] The Mongol general Sübedei (who belonged to the Uriangqat tribe) defeated the Merkit in 1218 (see pages 88–90).

While Jochi was subduing the Oirat and the Kirghiz, a powerful prince came to offer his services to Genghis Khan, namely Barshuq, the idiqut of the Uighurs.[47] The idiqut first sent an ambassador, but in 1209 went himself to Genghis Khan to make known that he acknowledged him as his suzerain.[48] As a token of respect Barshuq was given one of Genghis Khan's daughters as a wife.[49] Barshuq's change of camp contributed significantly to the increasing authority of Genghis Khan in Central Asia. Like Arslan (the khan of the Qarluqs) who went over in 1211 to Genghis Khan, Barshuq was originally a vassal of the Qara Khitai. Unrest was disturbing the eastern areas of this once-powerful kingdom (see pages 82–4).

In their actions to subdue the west of Mongolia, the Mongols on one occasion met heavy resistance when Boroqul marched against the Tumat in 1217. The Mongols ran into an ambush and during the subsequent fighting the faithful Boroqul was killed. Furious at the loss of his friend and lieutenant, Genghis Khan dispatched a force to avenge his death. The Tumat abandoned further resistance and surrendered.[50]

POWER AND SUSPICION

In the spring of 1206 (the year of the Tiger), before he had conquered all the Mongol and Turkish tribes in Mongolia, Genghis Khan called a quriltai.[51] During this gathering he named himself the ruler of 'all tribes who live in felt tents'.

The clan of Genghis Khan, the Borjigin, had brought the Mongol tribe to greatness and glory; it was this clan that would lead the Mongols in the future. The Borjigins formed the basis of the new kingdom: 'Mongol ulus'. The collective name of 'all tribes who live in felt tents' became 'the Mongols'. The conquered tribes, even the great ones like the Kereit and the Naiman, thereafter called themselves Mongols. After several victories Genghis Khan would destroy the tribal unity of his victims by distributing the defeated tribes among other tribes. Those which surrendered voluntarily, such as the Unggirat and the Oirat, he often left intact. A Mongol nation was beginning to emerge. Although the Turkish influence was unmistakable, since many Turkish tribes had been overcome, the Turkish supremacy which had existed for centuries in Central Asia was now being replaced by Mongol domination.

During the quriltai of 1206 Genghis Khan undoubtedly kept in mind the customs that were characteristic of the aristocracy of the steppes: their preference was for a strong leader who would not only unite them, but guarantee many victories and plenty of booty. They were prepared to follow any lord who would see to it that under his leadership they could live an agreeable and comfortable life.[52]

Just as he did during Genghis Khan's earlier elevation, the shaman Kököchü (Teb Tengri) played a part in this quriltai. How influential a part, is not known exactly. Genghis Khan allowed the shaman to make certain declarations so that his power would be as unassailable as possible from religious and political points of view. Kököchü said for example that he had ridden into heaven on a dapple-grey horse and spoken to Tengri. The Eternal Heaven had then appointed Genghis Khan as his representative on earth. Genghis Khan had therefore received his omnipotence from the Eternal Heaven. This religious basis formed a fundamental principle of the empire of Genghis Khan (see chapter 4).

There are differences of opinion about the moment when Temüjin began to call himself Genghis Khan. In the official Chinese source, Yüan-shih,* Temüjin was only called Genghis after the quriltai of 1206.[53] On the other hand the two important Persian historians, Juvaini (1226–1283)† and Rashid al-Din (1247–1318), write that this occurred after the conquest of the Kereit in 1203.[54] The thirteenth-century Mongol source, the Secret History of the Mongols,‡ has no doubt on this matter: Temüjin called himself Genghis even before 1200 (see page 2).

---

* The Yüan-shih, the official history of the Mongols in China, was assembled in less than a year because of the fall of the Yüan dynasty in 1368. (See Krause, 1922.)
† Ala al-Din Juvaini (see Boyle, 1958).
‡ The Secret History of the Mongols was first written in 1228, after which a partial revision took place in the second half of the thirteenth century. (See Cleaves, 1982, and Haenisch, 1948.)

These discrepancies arise presumably from the fact that the organization and consolidation of Genghis Khan's empire took place in the period 1196–1206; the change of name from Temüjin to Genghis was a part of this process. To all appearances the quriltai of 1206 simply proclaimed what had become an established fact during the preceding ten years. At the moment of the change of name he was, however, not greater than the khans of the other tribes, such as the Kereit and the Naiman. He did not at that time see himself as their superior. This is clear from the message that he sent (after he had begun to call himself Genghis) to the Ong-Khan, who he addressed as 'My king and father'.[55]

During the quriltai of 1206 Genghis Khan's standard was raised; it was white, with nine yak tails. The nine tails were (on the flying part of the standard) placed as pennants among each other.[56] The white standard with the nine pennants marked the place where the genius of the family of Genghis Khan (the Golden Family) resided, a genius that would protect his troops and lead them to victory.[57]

During the formal proclamation of the empire, Genghis Khan rewarded not only many of his meritorious generals, such as Bogorju, Muqali, Jurchedei, Qubilai, Jelme, Boroqul, Quyildar, Jebe and Sübedei, but also a number of his other servants: Münglig, Shigi Qutuqu, Sorqan Shira, the shaman Kököchü, the shepherds Badai and Kishiliq, and the khan of the Ongut, Alaqush Tegin.[58] The faithful Muqali received in 1217 the hereditary title of Gui-Ong, which corresponds to prince of state.[59]

After he had successfully led the quriltai of 1206 in the right direction for Genghis Khan, the shaman Kököchü believed that he was now in a strong position. He was moreover the son of Münglig, a trusted friend of Yesügei and later of Genghis Khan. In order to be able to exert more influence upon Genghis Khan, Kököchü decided to eliminate some family members of the new ruler of whom he disapproved. The first victim was Qasar who, because of his generally independent behaviour, might have aroused doubts in the mind of his elder brother.

Kököchü declared that the Eternal Heaven had confided in him that Qasar would eventually seize Genghis Khan's place for himself. Genghis Khan, who was given to suspicion when his own position was threatened, deprived his brother of all his functions and then agreed to have him imprisoned. Genghis Khan, with his gift for assessing men at their true value, undoubtedly recognized Qasar's great capacity as a military commander. Kököchü's accusation had the desired effect: arousing suspicion in the new ruler. The indignant old mother of the two brothers accused her eldest son of gross ingratitude; he had always made use of the brave Qasar and as overlord he had no right to treat him in such a way. Influenced by Hö'elün's appeals, Genghis Khan released his brother and reinstated him in his functions. He could never, however, repress a certain distrust of Qasar.[60]

Kököchü was not to be put off. He insulted and degraded Temüge. It was now Börte's turn to speak her mind: she realized what dangers the shaman might bring. She warned her husband that Kököchü would eventually accuse their own sons. Genghis Khan, who valued Börte's advice highly, decided to get rid of Kököchü. When Temüge and Kököchü again fell out in Genghis Khan's ordu (the quarrel was probably provoked by Temüge), Genghis Khan ordered both to settle their dispute outside. Kököchü was then seized by three hired murderers who broke his back, killing him. Münglig declared after the death of his son that he would continue to serve Genghis Khan loyally.[61] Genghis Khan appointed Usun, the oldest member of the Ba'arin clan, to succeed Kököchü. The new supreme shaman stirred up no problems.

4
The Yasa: Genghis Khan's code of laws

Shaman Kököchü, probably at Genghis Khan's instigation, had raised the status of the future world-conqueror to legendary heights: Genghis Khan had been sent by the Eternal Heaven to rule over the world. After Kököchü's death, Genghis Khan himself saw to it that this myth was kept alive. 'Heaven has ordered me to rule over all men,' he said; 'the protection and the help of the Eternal Heaven has enabled me to destroy my enemies and attain this high dignity.'[1] With the death of Kököchü the only man who could have frustrated his designs was eliminated and there was nobody else, not even any religious figure, to equal Genghis Khan.

Thus consolidated, his position was strong enough to permit him to create a powerful aristocratic regime. Just as a family or clan stood at the head of a tribe, so Genghis's family (the Golden Family) with its vassals and helpers, stood at the head of 'all people who live in felt tents'. The head of the Golden Clan was the khan of the Mongols. Genghis Khan never saw himself as the head of a people: he was the head of the Mongol aristocracy which he had united. Nor did he ever address himself to his inferiors, but always to his brothers, his sons and his main military commanders.[2] Not only Genghis Khan, but also his successors considered themselves as the representatives of Tengri on earth. Their orders were Tengri's orders and opposition to them was opposition to divine will.

The organization of the Mongol state rested upon the feudal relationships of Mongol and Turkish society which had been established by Genghis Khan. In it the Turkish element was strongly represented. The severely aristocratic structure of the state did not affect the social coherence which existed among the tribes and clans. The power of the aristocracy of the steppes had, however, considerably increased. Personal loyalty to the ruler of the state formed the bond between the various groups. At the outset Genghis Khan's ambitions were curbed by the unruly conditions prevailing among the tribes he had subdued. At that time the Mongols were a largely backward people, even in comparison with other tribes such as the Kereit and the Naiman. Before attacking the more educated countries it was therefore necessary to establish order at home. The first to exert any influence in this connection were Muslim traders, who visited Mongolia just before 1203.[3]

One of the most important decisions taken by Genghis Khan, in the organization of the government of his realm, was the introduction of the Uighur script as the official alphabet. The Mongols had no script of their own. After his conquest of the Naiman in 1204 Genghis Khan took the Uighur Ta-ta-T'ong-a, keeper of the seals of the slain Taibuqa (the tayang of the Naiman), into his own service in the same function. This was in essence the beginning of the process that was to lead to the establishment of a Mongol state. Ta-ta-T'ong-a was charged with the preparation and co-signature of the official instruments. We have unfortunately little information about the seal or seals used by Genghis Khan; but it is assumed that there were two – the scarlet seal and the blue seal.

Although himself illiterate, Genghis Khan was shrewd enough to realize that his sons and leading officials would have to learn to read and write. Ta-ta-T'ong-a was therefore given the position, in addition to keeper of the seals, of tutor to the sons of the new overlord. Other members of his court were also given lessons. Among these was the young Tatar Shigi Qutuqu, who seems to have been an intelligent pupil.

That Genghis Khan's gifts were not limited to the selection of his military commanders is shown by his choice of Shigi Qutuqu as supreme judge of the Mongol Empire. The Tatar fulfilled his function in an exemplary manner. His decisions served as models for others. He contributed little to the inhumanity sometimes practised by the Mongols and seems often to have reduced it.[4]

Even before the time of Genghis Khan the Mongol tribes possessed a common law, which was unwritten and showed some variation among the various tribes. As the overlordship of Genghis Khan extended, the need arose for laws applying to the whole empire and with it the need for a binding legal code. The Yasa was a codification of ancestral traditions, customs, laws and ideas of the Mongols, to which Genghis Khan added further laws of his own devising.[5]

The composition of the Yasa was not settled immediately. There is no doubt that it took a long time to complete. In all probability its first edition appeared shortly before or during the quriltai of 1206.[6] In 1218 a revised version was prepared.[7] Work on it continued throughout the lifetime of Genghis Khan.[8]

In the Mongol state whatever was laid down in the Yasa had to be followed to the letter. Civil and military disobedience were equivalent to common crime. This resulted in an unusually strong discipline, which in turn determined the life pattern of the Mongols over a long period. The Franciscan monk John of Plano Carpini, who visited Mongolia in 1246, was greatly impressed by the discipline. According to him the Mongols showed more submission and obedience than the clergy in Europe. Disputes and differences were always settled amicably.

Through the Yasa and the demand for strict obedience, Genghis Khan had a profound effect upon the morality of the Mongol people who, before his time, had lived in the greatest confusion. In another respect too he influenced the mentality of his people. The greatness which they attained under his leadership gave the Mongols a certain pride.

In the presence of a personality such as Genghis Khan's it was impossible for others to exercise any power. If they did, it was only as his representative. Genghis Khan, however, retained the practice of the Mongol-Turkish tribes of endowing his sons and other family members with apanages. The eldest son Jochi was given the territories of the tribes subdued by himself in 1207 and 1208 between the Selenga and the Yenisey rivers. After the great expansion that Genghis Khan's empire underwent in the course of the years, Jochi's appanage (Ulus of Jochi) came to lie in the outermost north-west: 'as far as the hooves of our horses have been'.[9]

No manuscript of the Yasa survives, nor has any document describing its contents yet been discovered. Assumptions about this book of laws must therefore be treated with caution, for

there can be no real certainty about what was written in it.
There exist only a few fragments written about the Yasa by
Persian, Arabian and Syrian historians; all of whom lived after
the death of Genghis Khan. The most important of them was
undoubtedly the Persian writer Juvaini, and it is not impossible
that he was the source of the information about the Yasa given
by others. It is unlikely that any of these historians ever saw a
copy of the Yasa, which was written in Mongolian in the
Uighur script.[10]

Furthermore the fragments of information which have come
down to us do not reflect Genghis Khan's wording. Some refer
to Yasas of the successors of the great conqueror or later
inventions. In addition to commands and laws there were
maxims issued by Genghis Khan on special occasions, to which
he probably attributed the same legislative binding. We may
assume that there were recollections of such maxims and the
quotations which have come down to us represent no more than
references in such recollections.[11]*

Although a start was made on a written record of Mongol law
in 1206,[12] the rapid growth of the Mongol Empire (first parts of
China, then the Qara-Khitai kingdom followed by the
Khwarazm sultanate) resulted in the flowering of what was
originally a nomadic state into an Asiatic empire. The Yasa
had, therefore, to be augmented to cater for the demands upon
the law by the growing state. China's high cultural standard
exerted a natural influence upon the primitive tribes. This was
probably also the case in matters of law. As the Mongols were
remarkably tolerant in relgious matters, they had no hard and
fast rules governing the slaughter of animals. There was no
standard method among the Mongol tribes and for this reason
they could not have objected to ritual killing practised by the
Muslims.[13] The Mongols allowed the Chinese, Persian and

---

* An interesting view on the Yasa is given by D. O. Morgan: 'It [the Yasa] may
well have been no more than the recollection of those of Chingiz Khan's
utterances, or alleged utterances, that were more or less legislative in character:
utterances to which he or his descendants attributed binding force . . . There was
probably believed to be a "Great Yasa of Chingiz Khan", derived in part from
Chingiz himself and perhaps in part from earlier Mongol custom. But this was
not written down in any coherent form, and it was therefore possible to attribute
to it a wide variety of provisions, as was thought or desirable.' (Morgan, 1986*a*,
pp. 169, 170.)

Russian law to remain valid. The governors of these regions, however, were expected to take the Yasa into account and to know its contents.[14]

An important point for which provision had to be made was the position of the Golden Family. The new lord of Central Asia had to develop his nomadic possessions into a strictly aristocratic state with an imperial family. The Yasa was based on the belief that Genghis Khan had been granted the task of conquering the world; potential enemies were therefore rebels. The status of those exercising the highest authority was laid down in the Yasa; any ruler of the Mongol Empire had to be one of Genghis Khan's descendants. The new Khan had to be designated at a quriltai consisting of members of the Golden Family, the supreme commanders, and the heads of the tribes and clans. Later the question of the observance of the Yasa was to dominate in large measure the opposing factions which arose in the Mongol Empire. In the imperial family, which was destined to split into various mutually hostile branches, the members of one branch constantly tried to show that the infringements which were increasing everywhere were perpetrated by an opposing party, while they themselves carefully observed the decisions made by Genghis Khan.[15]

The Mongols knew very many cruel punishments, which were often nothing other than forms of torture. When a member of the Golden Family or of another princely house was condemned to death, no blood was permitted to flow. Strangulation by bowstring or asphyxiation under a pile of carpets were but two of a large number of ingenious methods of execution while avoiding the shedding of royal blood. Conviction might mean that the entire family of the victim (including women and children) were also executed, being considered accessories to the crime.

It is clear that the Yasa, which was applied with merciless rigour, affected daily life in Genghis Khan's empire to a considerable degree. Among the nomadic tribes adultery, robbery, plunder and murder were exceptional. Before Genghis Khan's time, however, such crimes were common. Furthermore, the Yasa upheld an aristocratic regime, which laid a heavy burden on the common people. The position of slaves was often aggravated and their conditions of life made more inhuman by the Yasa. Their numbers increased as the Mongol wars of conquest met with more and more success. Genghis Khan's aim was to make the Yasa inviolable. In order that it should be kept intact and maintained after his death, he appointed his second son, Chaghatai, as its guardian. Genghis Khan could not have made a better choice: Chaghatai was a stubborn and severe supporter of the principles of his father's system.[16]

The Yasa, as a general code of law for all nomadic tribes in the Mongol Empire, did not survive for long. By the end of the thirteenth century its influence was already beginning to diminish, a process which was hastened by the breaking up of the empire. Among the Khanates, as they grew increasingly independent, either Buddhism or Islam prevailed.[17] A few ordinances, however, remained applicable for a long time; most of these had originated directly from the authority of Genghis Khan. Furthermore, in the various parts of the disintegrating empire, the only legitimate rulers were considered to be those who could trace their ancestry back to Genghis Khan. This requirement, of course, did not apply to China after the fall of the Yüan dynasty in 1368.

One of the institutions protected by the provisions of the Yasa, for it was among the most important of the Mongol Empire, was the mounted courier service (*Yam*). It is likely that Genghis Khan began organizing the Yam after the quriltai of 1206.[18] The idea of such a service, probably originated in China.[19]

Along a number of routes covered by couriers of the intelligence service, a series of stages were established where the couriers could obtain fresh horses, food and rest. At these posts horses had to be maintained continuously for the service of the couriers travelling to and from Genghis Khan. The efficient functioning of the Yam was closely dependent upon the rigid discipline throughout the Mongol Empire. The discipline brought a large measure of security with it. As the Mongol Empire grew, the Yam not only grew with it, but also acquired a new significance. Each inhabitant of the empire was obliged if necessary to put the interest of the Yam before his own. Thanks to this system couriers were able to cover 2–300 kilometres daily. Sometimes they rode for hours on end, swathed in extra cloth strips. As they approached a staging post they announced their arrival by ringing a bell. There were some couriers who would ride 2,000 kilometres with only short pauses for rest. Probably many horses fell dead at the end of the stage.[20]

Military commanders and governors, irrespective of where they found themselves, had orders to report every unusual event as speedily as possible to Genghis Khan and later to his successors. Thanks to the Yam the overlord was continuously aware of all that happened in the empire. Towards the end of Genghis Khan's life, the Yam had become an impressive organization. In order to continue to fulfil its purpose, as a result of the rapid and enormous expansion of the Mongol Empire, the service had to satisfy increasing demands.[21]

Foreign ambassadors also made use of the Yam and were even accorded certain privileges in this respect. Originally merchants were also allowed to use it, without charge. When, however, it became clear that this favour was being abused, the Great Khan Möngke (1251–9) decided that the traders should be compelled to pay for using the Yam staging posts.[22] All profited, however, from the security existing along the routes. The stages grew into settlements having large numbers of horses, sometimes as many as twenty.[23] For the couriers of the Great Khan a few horses had always to be saddled.

The Yam greatly impressed European travellers who visited Mongolia during the time of the world empire. From John of Plano Carpini, William of Rubrouck, Marco Polo and Odoric of Pordenone, we possess fairly precise descriptions of this service, which are mentioned several times in their travel accounts. The Yam, one of the pillars upon which the Mongol world empire rested, is still regarded as an exceptional achievement of organization.[24]

5
The Mongol army

'All who live in felt tents' were combined by Genghis Khan into a military organization; the army formed the foundation of his empire. The feudal principles which applied to the Mongol state were also operative in the army.

The organization of the army was based numerically on the decimal system. The largest unit of 10,000 men (*tümen*) was divided into 10 *mingghan*, each consisting of 1,000 men; these in turn contained 10 *jaghun* each of 100 men; while this last unit was divided into 10 *arban*. Such an arrangement was not Genghis Khan's own but an ancient organizational method among the nomads of Central Asia whose historical origin cannot be traced.[1]

Foreign models (probably Chinese) also influenced the form of the Mongol army.[2] It is an established fact, however, that Genghis Khan himself played a unique role in creating it; his brilliant gift for organization was largely responsible for the reputation of invincibility acquired by the Mongol army among the Eurasian peoples for nearly half a century. The new element in the governing principles laid down by Genghis Khan was the clearly defined demand that commander and subordinate should serve each other loyally and obediently. The solidarity of the units was achieved by an absolute prohibition against transfers from one unit to another. Any man who attempted to do this on his own initiative risked the death penalty; the commander who accepted him was also heavily punished.[3]

Genghis Khan's administrative arrangements for Central Asia, which was the core of his empire, were influenced by his ideas on military organization. The various clans and tribes were divided in such a way that the jaghuns and mingghans could be formed in the shortest possible time. At the head of each unit he appointed men whom he knew personally and trusted. These were in general members of the same tribe or clan as those they commanded. This plan ensured that the clan acquired a military framework which prevented its disintegration. Men who had demonstrated in every possible way that they were loyal to their ruler were placed at the head of the clans.[4]

In his army Genghis Khan wanted to have at his disposal commanders whom he appointed personally on the strength of what he knew of their abilities. This applied particularly to his guard. The jaghuns, the mingghans and the tümens were commanded by the highest members of the Mongol aristocracy, the *noyans* (commanding officers) and the baghaturs. Genghis Khan had found his youngest son Tolui to possess great military qualities; for this reason he became one of his father's supreme military advisers. The title Great Noyan, which Tolui was given by virtue of his position, was apparently posthumous.[5] Like the younger brothers of Genghis Khan, Temügeotchigin and Belgütei, Tolui had the title of noyan.[6] The freemen commanded the lower units; they had the right to keep war booty and any game they shot themselves during the hunt. Some of them were promoted for their services to baghatur or even to noyan.[7]

Discipline in the Mongol army was maintained by the most uncompromising methods. Superior officers were obliged to carry out without reservation every order brought to them by Genghis Khan's runners. Execution was not unknown as punishment for neglect. The plundering of enemy territories could only begin when Genghis Khan or one of his generals gave permission. Once it had started the commander and the common soldier had equal rights, except that beautiful young women had to be handed over to Genghis Khan and the generals could make special arrangements in regard to the division of the booty.[8]

In accordance with a long-standing custom in the steppes, the troops of Genghis Khan were divided into three main groups.[9] The centre, in which the guard was positioned, was under the orders of Naya'a; the left or eastern flank was commanded by Muqali; and the right or western flank was commanded by Bogorju.[10] As the Mongols were oriented to the south, east signified their left and west their right.[11] Qubilai was charged with all matters concerning the army;[12] in effect his function was that of chief of staff.

Genghis Khan took the first steps in the organization of the guard – which played such a dominating and influential role after the conquest of the Kereit in 1203, when he became the most powerful ruler in east Mongolia. The guard had a fairly complex organization. The bodyguard was formed of 70 men for the day-watch and 80 men for the night-watch. Included in the guard were archers, table servants, sentries posted at the entrance of Genghis Khan's ordu, and messengers. The khan's household was conducted by six *chärbi* (chamberlain). A unit with special responsibilities was the elite guard of 1,000 baghaturs who ensured the safety of Genghis Khan during battles.[13]

The subsequent drastic reorganization of the guard took place during or directly after the quriltai of 1206. The numbers of the various groups were considerably increased. The night-watch was first raised to 800 and later to 1,000 men; the day-watch to 1,000; and the archers first to 400, then to 1,000. The elite guard, in addition to its already existing 1,000 baghaturs, was strengthened by 6,000 men. This means that in its later formation the total guard was 10,000 men strong.[14]

Genghis Khan decided when and where this guard, which was the nucleus of his army, should be employed.[15] He had a thorough knowledge of the dangers and unexpected turns of events which accompanied the nomadic life. He knew that he had to protect himself with a foolproof and permanent security system, providing a terrible and ever-ready striking force. The bodyguard and the elite guard could always be reinforced by the rest of his guard, if it became necessary.

The organization of the guard was not, however, entirely directed at the safety of Genghis Khan and his court. He wished to have available a military school from which he could select trusty and skilled helpers. These picked men were given various tasks according to their abilities. All the members of his guard had to be of aristocratic birth.[16] The sons of the commanders of the different units formed the basis of the guard. The son of a commander of a mingghan had to bring with him, when he entered the guard, a younger brother and ten other men suitable for service in the guard. The son of a commander of a jaghun or of an arban had similar obligations: the former had to bring with him a younger brother and five other men; the latter had to bring a younger brother and three others.[17]

The commander of the elite guard was Chaghan, a young Tangut whom Genghis Khan had adopted as his stepson.[18] In my view this thousand-strong guard formed the main element of the military school from which Genghis Khan chose his future officers for the army, a choice which he made with astonishing insight into human character. Moreover, he appointed all of them with almost infallible precision to the post for which they were best suited.[19] In the choice of his generals, age played no part. Young men were often entrusted with the most responsible assignments. He showed constant personal interest in those he sent to places far removed from his main forces.

The bodyguard was divided into four sections, each of which in turn was responsible for the three day-watches and the three night-watches. The off-duty sections had at all times to remain in the vicinity of Genghis Khan. During the hours of darkness nobody was permitted to approach the neighbourhood of this residence, without being accompanied by the bodyguard. Whoever attempted to do this, risked the death penalty.[20] The guard enjoyed various privileges and was highly respected; in some circumstances its members were given precedence, even above those who were of higher rank.[21]

THE MONGOL CAVALRYMAN AND THE METHOD OF WARFARE

The most important account available to us of the equipment of the Mongol cavalryman is that of the Franciscan monk John of Plano Carpini. Whenever the Mongol was not bound for battle, he wore a fur hat with ear-flaps, felt boots and a fur coat reaching below the knee. The skin of the fur coat was turned outside. In battle he wore a helmet, of which the upper part was made of metal; the part falling over the neck and ears was made of leather. His armour consisted of strips of strong but supple buffalo leather, several layers thick; the garment had a front and back part, two shoulder-plates and protective pieces for the arms and legs.[22]

The Mongol cavalryman carried on his mount a large number of weapons and tools. Two bows, three quivers (there were two kinds of arrows: light ones for use over long distances and heavy ones for close combat),[23] and a lance with a sickle-shaped hook behind the point with which an enemy rider could be pulled off his horses. The commanders had a slightly curved sabre, sharp on one side. Each rider also carried an axe, a lasso made from horsehair, a kettle, a sharpening stone for the arrowheads and a whipstock used to strike the horse's legs if necessary.[24] Stirrups were essential for fighting on horseback. The equipment was completed with a leather bag, used to carry a quantity of reserve water, and also to keep clothing and weapons dry during river crossings.[25]

Emergency rations consisted of about ten pounds of curdled milk dried in the sun. When required about half a pound was dissolved in water until it had the consistency of syrup.[26] In case of dire need the Mongol cavalryman opened his horse's jugular vein, sucked the blood out and then closed the wound.[27] Since this custom is also recorded by Marco Polo, it was apparently still practised at the end of the thirteenth century.

The Mongols had learnt riding and archery as small children. Their proficiency was such that when mounted, they could hit a man at distances of between 200 and 400 metres.[28] If necessary they slept sitting on their horses. Each man had one reserve horse and sometimes as many as three or four. This is the secret of the speed with which the Mongols could cover very great distances.[29]

The horse, which was also partly armoured, was accustomed to the harsh climate and geographic environment. It was a squat animal and unattractive in appearance. It had a strong neck and a thick skin. It gave excellent service on account of its spirit, strength, stamina and frugality. This small horse, without any doubt, made possible the remarkable achievements of the Mongols in very difficult mountain country and in sometimes cruel weather conditions. It may be assumed from the attitude of the Mongol cavalryman of those times, that his horse got little attention during campaigns. The military power of the Mongols rested not only on the excellence of their mounts and the military skill of their soldiers, but also on the number of the horses they could count upon. The steppe could produce horses in great numbers.[30]

The Mongol army consisted entirely of cavalry. Later Genghis Khan and his successors used infantry, who were, however, not Mongols but auxiliary troops, often Chinese or Tangut. The Mongols followed the military tactics employed for centuries by the nomads of the steppes. This method of warfare had been developed from raids and robber expeditions against the border territories of the adjoining civilized countries and from battues against wild animals. In these drives they had learnt to send out scouts who, while they themselves remained unseen, had to observe what beasts lay ahead.

In order to give the impression of a greater strength than it really had, the force advanced on a broad front. As soon as the enemy attempted to stand and fight at a given place, the Mongols withdrew and disappeared. If the foe committed the error of pursuing the withdrawing Mongols, they lured him into unfavourable terrain, surrounded him and finished him off.

The light cavalry was put on the flanks and in the vanguard. Its task was to inflict casualties on the enemy using archery. It could do this over considerable distances; each man released three or four arrows in rapid succession. The group which had shot its arrows rode off to the flanks, to be replaced by the next group which repeated the manoeuvre. The Mongols used this technique also when they were retreating.[31] In this way they could withdraw for several days if it became necessary. The moment of attack was kept secret for as long as possible. During the approach the warriors obeyed signals and advanced at a trot, maintaining a terrifying silence.

As soon as the enemy had been manoeuvred into an awkward position, the heavy cavalry in the centre moved to the attack. They fought with sabre and lance. Their physical strength, their appearance and the stink of men and horses produced fear in the enemy ranks; the Mongols knew exactly how to take advantage of this. At the moment of the charge the heavy cavalry hurled itself with loud shrieks upon the enemy.[32] According to Plano Carpini the Mongols tried as far as possible to avoid hand-to-hand fighting;[33] Marco Polo shares this opinion. If the enemy defended himself resolutely after the charge, the Mongols opened their ranks to offer him a chance to escape. If the offer was accepted, he was pursued and defeated. To make their numbers appear greater, the Mongols made man-size puppets which they mounted on the reserve horses[34] and which, seen against the horizon, looked very realistic. This device often had a particularly demoralizing effect upon defenders at the beginning of a siege. Such deceptions were not only suitable for sieges, however. The Mongols frequently spread rumours ahead of their advancing armies, giving the impression that they were twice as numerous as they really were. To strengthen this impression, prisoners marching in order of battle were made to accompany the army. In the hours of darkness the Mongols had another trick. Each man lit three to five torches at some distance from each other. In this way the enemy was left in doubt about the real strength of the Mongols, as each torch could represent one warrior.[35]

During their wars of conquest the Mongols took first the undefended areas, the villages and the unprotected towns. The mostly defenceless inhabitants were robbed of all their wealth and many were taken prisoner. After becoming the masters of the undefended part of a country, the Mongols turned against the walled towns.[36] The siege of towns presented them with many problems when they first attempted this in China. At first their cavalry troops were only capable of starving a town out; this could take a long time. A method much used for storming defended fortresses, was to drive prisoners forward in front of the attackers. The defenceless prisoners had to choose between death from their compatriots in front or from the Mongols behind.

From the Chinese they learned the use of siege machines, such as catapults, battering-rams, naphtha-barrel throwers, kedges, and also how to undermine fortress walls.[37] Later they adopted siege equipment as used by Islamic peoples. After the fall of a town a cruel fate awaited the citizens. Usually the artisans were first set apart; then a large part of the rest of the people were killed. Young men and those fit for combat had to accompany the army as prisoners, following the mounted Mongols on foot. Those unable to keep up were put to death. Likewise, if the number of accompanying prisoners was so great that they hindered the progress of the army, some of them were killed. This also happened when the prisoners were of no more use.

The mass slaughter of populations was largely because the Mongols were in most cases numerically inferior to their opponents. They therefore had to avoid any threat from their rear at all cost. Before Genghis Khan attacked the Kereit, he destroyed the Taijut and the Tatars, so that they could not stab him in the back. Later in China and in the Khwarazm sultanate, being so far from his own base, he could not risk the survival of forces among the defeated peoples sufficient to rise against him. The inhabitants of a town who offered to surrender without resistance when the Mongol army approached, in the hope of being spared, still ran the risk of partial massacre. The Mongols, who in view of their relatively small numbers could leave behind only small occupying detachments, assumed that even in the towns which had capitulated without battle subsequent revolt was possible.

John of Plano Carpini has described how the Mongols crossed wide rivers. They put their clothes and other possessions into a leather sack. The sack was then tied up tightly, forming a rounded cushion. The saddle was placed on this sack and the rider sat on top of it. The horses were driven into the water and one or more swimmers guided them to the other side. The riders sitting on the sacks could hold on to the tail of the swimming horse or row across with the help of one or two oars.[38] Marco Polo gives an almost identical account of river crossings.

The rapidity of the marches carried out by the Mongol army were remarkable for those days. A distance of 700 kilometres could be covered in a fortnight and if necessary 300 kilometres in three days.[39] In emergency, the Mongols were able to march for ten days without any cooked food.[40]

Before undertaking a campaign Genghis Khan tried to gather as much information as possible about the political and military situation of the enemy country, chiefly by means of spies. We must assume that observation and sense of direction were unusually highly developed in the Mongols, otherwise it is not possible to account for their movements over enormous distances without maps.[41] Special officers had the task of leading the movements of the army and of fixing the position of camps.[42] Cavalry forces of the size used by the Mongols in their major campaigns could not be moved at short notice. It seems certain that careful planning preceded each of the major military campaigns.

Once the Mongol armies embarked on the execution of a plan which would set hundreds of miles between the various wings of the operating armies, it became imperative that they should adhere to the pre-established timetable.[43] The conduct of a battle was controlled by means of mounted orderlies and signals given by flags or trumpets.[44] An important source of income for the army was the often huge amount of war booty. This formed, certainly in the early years, a large part of the Mongol state income.[45]

In view of the dominant place occupied by the hunt in the life of the Mongols, the rules governing its conduct were included in the Yasa.[46] Not only did the great wild-animal round-up play an important part in the provision of food and as a social event, it was also, because of the manner in which it was carried out, a military occasion. A battue could last between one and three months. It was an opportunity to manoeuvre troops and to practise the use of weapons, the maintenance of discipline and the enduring of hardship. As a large number of tümen took part, it was in effect a massive military exercise. It is understandable then, that the Yasa laid down rules for the hunt. If they were breached or neglected severe punishment followed, even the death penalty.[47] Genghis Khan made his eldest son Jochi responsible for the supervision and conduct of the hunt.[48]

Early winter was the best time for large-scale hunts. Orders were sent in advance to the troops who were to be employed. Genghis Khan's relatives were requested to be present. The region where the battue was to take place was reconnoitred to ascertain the numbers of animals it contained. The participating military units were deployed around the region, which was sometimes thousands of square kilometres in area. The generals were each given a sector to control and in turn these sectors were divided among sub-commanders. Each unit placed its beaters as if on a military operation: scouts to the front, behind them the main body, with left and right flank sections. Once it had been closed, the enormous circle of troops was maintained with great accuracy. Each general and each commander was held responsible if any animals escaped. An inquiry was held to determine the guilty parties, who were severely punished, sometimes with death.[49]

Before the troops began their enclosing march, the imperial procession would arrive with Genghis Khan, his family members, wives and concubines. The procession would stop at a place selected for its good viewpoint. Food and drink would be carried up for the royal party. The enormous circle of men then began to move inwards to drive the animals into an area with a perimeter of about 15 kilometres, and Genghis Khan was kept constantly informed of progress. When the beating troops had enclosed the actual hunting ground, ropes to which felt cloths were attached were stretched between the various groups.

The Persian historian Juvaini who attended a battue gives a moving description of the behaviour of the animals enclosed within the ring:

The ring is now filled with the cries and commotion of every manner of game and the roaring and tumult of every kind of ferocious beasts; all thinking that the appointed hour of 'and when the wild beasts shall be gathered together' is come; lions becoming familiar with asses, hyenas friendly with foxes, wolves intimate with hares.[50]

It was Genghis Khan's privilege, and later that of his successors, to open the hunt. Nobody was permitted to kill any animal before he did so. After Genghis Khan, his family members were given the opportunity of hunting. Then it was the turn of the commanders and their subordinates, each according to his rank. This slaughter of animals lasted for a number of days. Finally a group of old men approached Genghis Khan to beg him to spare the lives of those animals that were not yet killed. This request was granted and the surviving beasts were allowed to escape. The slaughtered game was counted and each hunter received his share.

THE STRENGTH OF THE MONGOL ARMY

It is not easy to assess the strength of Genghis Khan's army. Indeed estimates of this kind have always presented a problem in the writing of military history. In most cases the historian can only make rough approximations, which are often on the high side. The number of units is used as a basis, but this does not take account of the possibility of the units being below strength, because of losses or other reasons.

In Genghis Khan's time the core of the Mongol army still consisted of Mongol and Turkish warriors. It is difficult to say whether the Turkish element was bigger than the Mongol. As the Mongol army advanced, those of the defeated tribes, who could be of some use for their knowledge or skill, were compelled to join them. In particular nomads or semi-nomads of Turkish origin were 'recruited'. Some joined voluntarily, eager for booty.[51] It is this pattern of recruitment which makes assessment of the strength of the Mongol army so difficult. The units forming the nucleus of the army were not reinforced by the 'recruits' – this was to avoid any disturbance of the tribal unity which Genghis Khan considered so important. Doubtless the raw recruits were incorporated into units composed of their kinsmen; whether these were always up to full strength is not known. Presumably the Mongol army included more units at the end of a campaign than at the beginning, but whether the total strength was greater is doubtful.

Auxiliary troops consisting of various nationalities, only the commanders being Mongols, were called *tama*.[52] It seems likely that in the tamas the soldiers of a jaghun came from the same tribe. Although the Mongol army of 1227 was not exclusively recruited from the Mongol and Turkish tribes, we may assume that, as Genghis Khan waged war primarily with cavalry, they did in fact constitute the nucleus of his army. In estimating the strength of the Mongol army, the number of inhabitants in the territories occupied by the Mongol and Turkish tribes is therefore an important key.

The Mongol population was never numerous. In 1967 there were in the People's Republic of Mongolia 1,200,000 Mongols, and in Inner Mongolia (excluding the Chinese living there) 1,500,000 Mongols.[53] We may estimate the Mongol population in 1967, including the Mongols living around Lake Baikal, to be approximately 3 to 3.25 million. The living conditions of the people and the enormous losses among the population as a result of the continuous wars justifies the conclusion, that the present population has increased since 1227 by 5–600 per cent.

Between the years 1202 to 1227 Genghis Khan was at war without respite, frequently far from Mongolia. The growth of the population in Mongolia during that quarter of a century was probably small. The total population in 1227 cannot have been more than 4–500,000. The contingent from Mongolia was apparently never more than 70–80,000 strong and perhaps even this is a liberal estimate. Including auxiliary troops from the defeated and incorporated countries, a figure of about 120,000 (taking into account losses during the battles in China, Khwarazm and south Russia) would not be too small for the total strength of the Mongol army in 1227.[54]

The Russian orientalist Barthold writes that Genghis Khan in 1219 marched on the Khwarazm Sultanate with an army of about 150–200,000 men.[55] I find this an unbelievably high figure. If true, the total Mongol army would have approached 250,000 men as Muqali had a contingent in China and troops naturally remained behind in Mongolia. The strength given by Barthold implies that Genghis Khan began his campaign against the mighty Khwarazm empire with an army consisting largely of auxiliary troops, which I think would have been an unjustifiable risk (see page 98). Genghis Khan knew that if things went wrong in this campaign, the superior numbers of the auxiliaries would present a real threat. Genghis Khan was certainly not reckless when preparing his war plans and he usually conducted his campaigns cautiously.[56]

Both in north China and later in Khwarazm, deserters were accepted in large numbers after the enemy's army had been decimated by heavy losses and the Mongol losses made it necessary to bring the units up to strength. As long as the enemy remained unsubdued, large numbers of deserters were dangerous: if there was a set-back the possibility of double treachery by these former enemy troops could not be discounted. The Mongols never won their battles by numerical superiority. They owed their impressive series of victories to the shrewdness with which Genghis Khan led his people and with which he discerned and exploited his enemy's weaknesses. The great Mongol systematically eliminated his opponents one by one. To do this he made clever use of the intelligence he received about the problems of his enemies. His conquests were the fruit of an extraordinary military genius. The running of the conquered countries was only partly ensured by troops. The elimination of any effective opposition to the occupier, played an important part in this. In China, where this technique could not be employed (the huge Chinese population could not be eliminated), the war dragged on for a long time and a contingent of troops had to be left behind. They were confronted with an almost superhuman task (see pages 72–3).

It is difficult to make an estimation of the strength of the Mongol army after the death of Genghis Khan. In the various khanates of his sons, armies came into existence in whose ranks there were only small numbers of Mongols. As time went on even this Mongol element dwindled in the armies in Persia and south Russia.

6

The rapacious barbarians at China's northern frontier

THE ART-LOVING SUNG BUY PEACE[1]

After the fall of the T'ang dynasty in 907 there was political chaos in China. Between 907 and 960 the country was ruled by a number of quickly succeeding dynasties; this was the so-called Period of the Five Dynasties. None of them, however, ever ruled the entire heritage of T'ang, but only north China. South China was in the hands of a number of families who are not regarded as legitimate dynasties.

A threat that contributed greatly to China's disintegration was the rise of the Khitan. Coming from south-east Mongolia (where they had driven the Kirghiz to the north-west) they had migrated eastwards in the beginning of the tenth century. As early as the closing years of the T'ang dynasty they began to cause trouble. After the fall of the dynasty they conquered what is now south Manchuria and then turned to the south, adding the northern part of Shansi and Hopeh to their empire. Peking, which was their capital, had not then acquired its later greatness, but from then on it became progressively more important. The Khitan maintained their position in north China for two centuries. Following Chinese custom they called their rulers after 937 the Liao dynasty. They quickly adopted the civilization of their highly cultivated neighbours, their former nomadic way of life giving place to a Chinese social structure. They even studied the Chinese language and literature. The consequences were inevitable: the adoption of Chinese culture had always been fatal for the nomads from the north.

In the rest of China a recovery became apparent about 950.

In 960 the popular general Chao K'uang-yin founded a new dynasty, which he named Sung. He united a large part of China under his sovereignty, although in south China a few states retained their independence. The Northern Sung dynasty, however, began with Chao K'uang-yin; the capital was K'ai-feng. Under the Sung China remained culturally dominating; the period of this dynasty developed into an era when Chinese culture reached previously unknown excellence. Politically, however, the Sung dynasty was timid and defensive. What the Han and T'ang emperors would have considered as a scandalous peace, was normal for the Sung. Good relations with foreign foes were often purchased at the cost of large indemnities, and in the Chinese empire regional rulers offering resistance were even persuaded to become incorporated into the great empire by a policy of reconciliation and clemency. The rivals in the southern states were mostly spared, which would have been unthinkable in the Han and T'ang dynasties. The Sung were too civilized for the world of the eleventh century. Their feeble attempts to drive the Khitan away ended when an additional threat appeared in the north-west.

The Tangut had been allowed by the T'ang to inhabit Ordos. The kingdom of this Buddhist tribe, called Hsi-Hsia in Chinese, grew rapidly more powerful as a result of enmity between the Sung and the Liao. In 1030 Hsi-Hsia conquered Kansu and Alashan, where a group of the Uighurs had established themselves. The Tangut dominated an important trade route by their possession of these regions, so that the Sung were denied their traditional overland link via east Turkestan (present-day Sinkiang) with South-west Asia. Fearing a conflict with their two neighbouring states, the Sung paid large sums of money to both the Khitan empire and Hsi-Hsia.

In the beginning of the twelfth century the Khitan, who had earlier been converted to Buddhism, were strongly influenced by Chinese culture. Their combative, energetic spirit had been modified by an appreciation of a more cultivated life-style. A Tungus tribe, the Jurchen, living in the Sungari Valley and subjects of the Khitan, began at about this time to rise in rebellion. The Sung adapted the old Chinese adage: 'Fight barbarians with barbarians'. They offered the Jurchen the lands of the Khitan, on the understanding that the territory of north

China should be returned to the Sung. The Jurchen were further offered the opportunity of taking over the large indemnities which were being paid to the Khitan. In the war that followed the Khitan were defeated and in 1125 their role was reversed: they became subjects instead of the masters of the Jurchen. A group of the Khitan, however, headed by a member of the Liao dynasty, rode off to the west and led a nomadic existence for a number of years. Then, strengthened by tribes with whom they had joined forces, they invaded the eastern part of Turkestan, where they founded the 'Western Liao' or as this kingdom is better known, the Qara-Khitai (see pages 78–9).

After their success against the Khitan, the Jurchen marched into the Sung empire. It was soon realized that they were a more dangerous enemy than the Khitan had ever been. With their cavalry they moved rapidly south and in 1126 captured the Sung capital K'ai-feng, where the emperor and his court were taken prisoner. In 1129 they even crossed the Yang-tze River but later evacuated a part of the conquered territory. A branch of the Sung dynasty fled southwards to form in 1127 the Southern Sung dynasty with Lin-an (present-day Hang-chou) as its capital. The whole region of the Yellow River and a great part of the country between this river and the Yang-tze remained in the hands of the Jurchen. In their turn they established an empire, and their ruling family also assumed a dynastic name in accordance with Chinese custom. They called themselves Chin (Gold). In 1153 the Chin emperor moved his capital to Peking, which was then named Chung-tu.

The struggle between the Sung and the Chin continued for some time, but in 1138 peace was made. Once again the Sung had to pay an indemnity. The Jurchen empire quickly became powerful, until in the beginning of the thirteenth century it was one of the most formidable empires in East Asia. Although the Chin tried to prevent themselves from undergoing the same rapid softening process that affected the Khitan, the Jurchen had exchanged their tough cavalry life for 'silken tranquility' by the time Genghis Khan approached their borders in 1211. A further anxiety for the Chin arose because the Jurchen demanded so many privileges for themselves that the whole population was deeply discontented.

A CAREFUL BEGINNING: THE ATTACK ON HSI-HSIA

After the unification of the Mongol-Turkish tribes, a nomadic empire once more came into existence on China's north-west frontier. The mighty country with its treasures had always been an attraction to the covetous nomads in the north, either as a rich source of plunder or as a profitable partner in trade agreements. Throughout the centuries the invading barbarians, who set up their own kingdoms in the conquered provinces, had been absorbed fairly quickly into Chinese society and Chinese culture. In the long history of China this phenomenon occurred constantly; only the details of each absorption varied.

Every nomad state that grew to any significance in Central Asia invaded China and enriched itself at the cost of the Celestial Empire, and Genghis Khan, now master of a united Mongolia, found himself contemplating a similar course. He too was attracted by the rich booty waiting to be gathered in the south-east.

Careful and systematic as always, he opened his invasion of Chinese territory with an attack on Hsi-Hsia. There were many reasons for starting with this kingdom. For the first time Genghis Khan was fighting a sedentary people. The problems which this might entail were unfamiliar to the Mongol leader. Hsi-Hsia, the weakest of the three states of China, was a good place to learn whatever lessons were necessary for this type of warfare. Moreover, he had received a great deal of intelligence about Hsi-Hsia from the Ongut, the Kereit, the Naiman and the Uighurs, all of whom had relations with that kingdom. Another important factor was that Genghis Khan saw his most dangerous enemy in the Chin empire and, while he was attacking it, he had to be sure that Hsi-Hsia could offer no threat to his rear.

Before Genghis Khan marched into Chinese territory he also wanted to make certain that the Ongut, who inhabited the country adjoining China, would not become disloyal to him. It was not inconceivable that both Hsi-Hsia and the Chin empire might buy over the Ongut to stab him in the back while he was engaged in China. Alaqush Tegin had been as Khan of the Ongut a loyal supporter of Genghis Khan; however, he had been murdered. To ensure the friendship of his successors,

Genghis Khan married off one of his daughters (Alaqa Beki), and later a granddaughter, to Alaqush Tegin's first and second successors. Alaqa Beki was an energetic woman and governed the Ongut herself for a time as regent. The bond with the khans of the Ongut was later further strengthened by several marriages with daughters of the Genghisids.[2]

The first cautious incursion into Hsi-Hsia (or Qashin as the Mongols called this kingdom)[3] took place in 1205[4] in the region of the Edsin.[5] The second, in the autumn of 1207, was directed against Ordos. Both raids yielded Genghis Khan not only prisoners and booty, but also information about the country.[6]

In 1209 the real attack against Hsi-Hsia was launched. King Li An-chüan (1206–11) sent an army under the command of the heir to the throne to meet the Mongols. The first encounter ended to the advantage of the Tangut, but they hesitated to exploit it, giving Genghis Khan time to regroup his army.[7] Both armies renewed the battle near the town of Wu-la-hai, and this time the Tangut suffered a decisive defeat. The town of Wu-la-hai and Yi-men fell into the hands of the Mongols and the inevitable looting followed.[8]

The Mongol army then moved over the Holan Shan towards the capital, the present day Ningsia which was then named Chung-hsing (or Eriqaya as the Mongols called it).[9] Outside the town the Mongols were awaited by the Hsi-Hsia army. The Tangut general, Wei-ming, carried out a heavy attack on his approaching enemy, but neither he nor Genghis Khan was able to win the day. Both armies then waited for some time, not far from each other; neither leader seemed to want to attack. A strategem was needed to provide a solution to this impasse. The Mongol army feigned a retreat, leaving behind a small detachment to entice Wei-ming to attack it. When he took the bait, the entire Mongol army seemed to him to have returned from nowhere. The Tangut were defeated and Wei-ming himself taken prisoner.[10] The road to Ningsia lay open and the siege of the capital began. Li An-chüan himself conducted the defence with great skill. The siege started in August, but by October the Mongols had made little progress. When the autumn rains came, Genghis Khan tried to flood the town by having a dam built in the Huang-ho. Although this plan certainly succeeded, it did not have the desired result. The

Mongols were themselves threatened by the rising water and were forced to seek the higher ground around Ningsia.[11]

When Li An-chüan's appeal to the Chin for help remained unanswered, the beleaguered town had no further chance of being relieved. On the other hand, Genghis Khan saw no way of taking Ningsia in the immediate future and therefore decided in January 1210 to negotiate with Li An-chüan. The latter agreed to this; Genghis Khan was given one of the daughters of the Tangut king as a wife.[12] Although he did not become wholly a vassal of Genghis Khan, Li An-chüan had to acknowledge his suzerainty to a certain extent. The war contribution that Hsi-Hsia had to make to the Mongols included large numbers of camels, which were of great value in the coming wars with the Chin empire and the Khwarazm sultanate.[13]

The conquest of Hsi-Hsia brought with it some important gains for Genghis Khan. The caravan route from China to Turkestan fell largely under the control of the Mongols. In an attack on the Chin empire, Genghis Khan had no need to fear any threat from the west. He could assume that Li An-chüan would ignore any appeal for help by the Chin. One weakness had become very obvious during the siege of Ningsia: that the Mongol army was ill equipped to besiege towns. For the time being Genghis Khan could find no solution to this problem, yet it was essential that he should do so, as was made clear in the coming conflict with the Chin.

THE WAR WITHOUT AN END

Although Genghis Khan was not a full vassal of the Chin emperor, in a certain sense a condition of vassalage had come into existence since 1198, when Genghis Khan with the Ong-Khan had defeated the Tatars at the request of the emperor. After the victory Genghis Khan (like Toghril of the Kereit) had been given a title by the Chin emperor (see page 18). It was indeed not a very exalted title (ja'utquri, meaning keeper of the frontier), but by accepting it Genghis Khan had to some extent become the emperor's subordinate, liable to pay an annual tribute to him.[14]

In 1207 Genghis Khan considered himself strong enough to end this submission. An embassy from Peking led by Yun-chi, the prince of Wei, who came to collect the tribute, was told that it would no longer be paid. Shortly afterwards the Chin emperor died. Yun-chi succeeded him under the name Wei Chao Wang (1208–13). Genghis Khan made use of this succession to announce the abandonment of his relationship with the Chin emperors. After the enthronement of Wei Chao Wang an ambassador from Peking came to demand his submission to the new emperor. In unambiguous terms Genghis Khan told him of his contempt for Wei Chao Wang. 'I thought', he said, 'that the emperor in Peking was appointed by Heaven. So how can it be that such a weak and stupid man as the prince of Wei has been appointed to this honourable position?' Then he mounted his horse and rode away.[15]

In March 1211 Genghis Khan held a quriltai on the banks of the Kerulen River to make plans for the war against the Chin empire.[16] His vassals, such as Barshuq, the idiqut of the Uighurs and Arslan the khan of the Qarluqs, were also present.[17] Genghis Khan, declaring that this war was to be waged against the hereditary enemy of the Mongols, described it as the first national war of his people; he reminded the quriltai of two things. First, he solemnly declared that the coming war against the Chin was to exact vengeance for the murder of two of his relatives: in the first half of the twelfth century they had been treacherously taken prisoner by the Tatars and delivered to the Chin emperor who had put them both to death. This was one argument to justify taking up arms. The second was significant for the conduct of the war. Genghis Khan presented himself as the avenger of the earlier masters of north China, the Khitan: they were of proto-Mongol origin and had been forced into submission by the Jurchen, a Tungus tribe. In this way he hoped that the Khitan would support him by revolting against the Chin emperor.

Before starting this ambitious war, Genghis Khan made a pilgrimage to the holy mountain Burqan Qaldun to pray for help from the Eternal Heaven. Just before leading his army into battle he went into seclusion for three days in his jurt; he wished to be alone with Tengri. On the fourth day he emerged, saying that Tengri had promised him victory.[18]

In addition to the information he received from the Ongut, Genghis Khan learned much about the Chin empire from

Muslim merchants, who monopolized trade between China and Central and South-west Asia. Most of these merchants were intelligent observers, able to provide Genghis Khan with data of many kinds. They had a good knowledge of China's geography and were familiar with the problems facing the three Chinese states.[19] Genghis Khan had already co-operated with the Muslim merchants for a number of years and realized that he could make use of them in many ways. He therefore gave them all he thought they should have. On their side the Muslims saw that Genghis Khan had brought order and security into Central Asia, which was to the good of their business. Trade had been stimulated, for the Mongols had to buy much that they themselves were unable to produce. This mutual interest and understanding for each other's position created a kind of alliance between the Mongols and Muslim merchants. The merchants were therefore loyal followers of Genghis Khan, a relationship which the great Mongol exploited fully and with great skill.[20]

While Genghis Khan was preparing for war, matters in the mighty Chin empire were anything but satisfactory. In 1194 the Yellow River had once again changed its course; north of Shantung it had found a new route to the sea that took it south of that peninsula. This change had been accompanied by the widespread floods which, together with the Chin's financial politics, led to a situation of extreme chaos. Conditions were not improved by the consequent famine, which caused great distress among the people.

The Chin army, which originally consisted of Jurchen cavalry, had been later extended to employ infantry and early in the thirteenth century was recruited multinationally; it included not only Jurchen but also Khitan, Chinese and members of other peoples.[21] The Chin were not in a position, however, to throw their whole army into the fray against Genghis Khan. They were still on hostile terms with the Sung, and in 1206 the Sung and the Chin had once more been at war with each other. The Sung would let 'barbarians fight against barbarians' if Genghis Khan attacked the Chin empire, hoping to profit from a defeat of the Chin. The Sung would probably have preferred to help Genghis Khan than the Chin, so troops had to remain in the south. Hsi-Hsia, obliged to acknowledge

that Genghis Khan was more or less its suzerain, had been left
in the lurch by the Chin during the siege of Ningsia. Finally the
unrest in the Chin empire meant that watchfulness throughout
the whole country was essential. The strength of the Chin lay in
the formidable fortifications in the north, which compelled the
Mongols to by-pass them. On the other hand the manning of
these border forts claimed many troops.

The strength of Genghis Khan's army is not known.
Auxiliary troops had been included in the Mongol army, but at
that time they could not have been many. Undoubtedly, units
stayed behind in Mongolia, for Küchlüg, who had fled to the
west, still presented a threat to the Mongol rear. It is probable
that Genghis Khan started his invasion of north China with
60–70,000 men (see pages 52–4).

The war that Genghis Khan began in 1211 against the Chin
lasted (though there were intermittent truces) until long after
his death. His son and successor Ögödei was not able to end the
struggle against the stubborn enemy until 1234. The protracted
nature of the war was due in great part to the Mongols' method
of fighting. They could find no way of taking strong fortifications with their mobile cavalry units. As was their custom in
the steppes, they conquered the countryside and plundered all
they could find. In this way they were able to take the less
strongly defended places in north China. A large part of the
population was slaughtered. Other inhabitants were taken
prisoner. After the Mongols had left a place, however, the
Chinese repopulated it. Sometimes it was necessary for the
Mongols to capture the same area two or three times. The
massacre of the people to eliminate the likelihood of risings
against them was not practicable in China: it was impossible to
exterminate the great mass of the Chinese population.

After the 1211 quriltai Genghis Khan marched against the
Chin. During the years 1211 and 1212 the struggle took place
mainly in north Shansi and north Hopeh, where the country
was scoured in all directions and systematically laid waste by
various units of the Mongol army.[22] However, only small, badly
defended towns fell into their hands; the frontier forts remained
secure. In 1211 near the Yeh-hu mountains (between Kalgan
and Hua-lai) the Mongols encountered a Chin army and
heavily defeated it. Nine years later this battlefield was seen by

the Taoist monk Ch'ang-ch'un on his way to Genghis Khan; it was still covered with human bones.[23] After the battle Jebe forced his way to the gates of Peking.[24]

In 1212 events occurred which had favourable results for Genghis Khan. In the Liao River region his call to avenge the Khitan, who had been conquered by the Jurchen, won success. A member of the deposed Liao dynasty, Yeh-lü Liu-ko, revolted against the Chin.[25] Genghis Khan, who had apparently anticipated this, sent Jebe with an army unit to Yeh-lü Liu-ko to offer support. The Mongol general had first to capture the town of Liao-yang, but saw no chance of doing so with his cavalry. He pretended to withdraw, leaving behind quantities of military stores which tempted the defenders to open their gates to take possession of them. Under cover of night Jebe returned, charged through the open gates and the town was his.[26] Yeh-lü Liu-ko proclaimed himself king of the Khitan,[27] recognizing Genghis Khan as his suzerain. Until his death in 1220 he remained a loyal vassal of the great Mongol.[28] The new Liao state was probably not a very powerful one, but at least it presented a threat to the Chin.

In the summer of 1213 the first fortification within the border area, Hsüan-hua, fell into the hands of the Mongols.[29] Shortly afterwards a Chin army was routed near Hua-lai.[30] It is likely that this action and the defeat in 1211 made the Chin more careful, for thereafter, during the period that Genghis Khan was himself present in north China, there were no more large-scale engagements. The Chin recognized that although the Mongol cavalry was a dangerous force in the open field, they could do little against fortified positions. The Chin army therefore withdrew for the most part within the walled towns and contented itself with carrying on the war from a position of comparative safety.

Genghis Khan obtained more and more help from the Khitan. A number of their captains went over to him. The important bastion in the north, Kupeik'ou, fell into the hands of the Mongols through the treachery of a Khitan commander.[31] Genghis Khan's army was meanwhile marching against the capital Peking. Jebe was ordered to take the fortress Chü-yung, as it commanded a pass whose access was difficult. The Chin had strengthened this bastion impressively; here the Mongols were briefly held up.[32] After an attack the energetic Jebe again staged a mock withdrawal. When the Chin troops pursued him, he turned to launch an attack in co-operation with the main army under Genghis Khan; this time the Chü-yung defence was destroyed, the pass could be entered and only 30 kilometres separated the Mongols from Peking. Genghis Khan realized that he would only be able to take the heavily defended capital after a very long siege. He therefore decided not to attack Peking for the time being, but left a screen of troops to observe the town.

In September 1213 an act of violence in the capital resulted in a change in the occupant of the throne.[33] General Hu Cha Hu, who for some unexplained reason had quitted his troops and gone to Peking, disapproved of Emperor Wei Chao Wang's half-hearted conduct of the war. He therefore murdered him and set another member of the Chin dynasty on the throne.[34] This measure did not improve matters much; the new Emperor Hsüan-tsung (1213–23) was apparently as insignificant as his predecessor. Genghis Khan, who had hoped that the Khitan would again play a dominant role following this revolt, found that they were not acceptable as an alternative to the Jurchen by the Chinese, who considered them to be equally foreign.

Handicapped though he was by lameness, Hu Cha Hu made a vigorous start as the new supreme commander of the Chin army. He even carried out a successful attack on the Mongols. However, the jealousy of another general, Kao-chi, proved fatal to him. Kao-chi took him prisoner, and Emperor Hsüan-tsung accepted the turn of events. Hu Cha Hu was beheaded and Kao-chi became the new supreme commander.[35]

Genghis Khan decided to cross the territory of the Chin with three columns. Accompanied by his youngest son Tolui, he himself took command of the main army. His three eldest sons, Jochi, Chaghatai and Ögödei, led the second column; the third was commanded by his brothers, Qasar and Temüge.[36] Before the end of December 1213 the three armies began their march from the area of Peking,[37] the troops under Genghis Khan and those of his sons moving in a southerly direction to the fertile region north of the Yellow River. Most of the land in this plain was under cultivation. The value of agriculture was almost unknown to the steppe nomads. Many fields of crops, harvests and farms were damaged or burned. A large number of small towns were plundered and then destroyed. The Peking government had given the farmers instruction to seek protection as far as possible within the walled towns. To storm a town, the Mongols made use of the method (which was later to cause so much misery in Khwarazm) of forcing prisoners to fight in the front ranks against their own compatriots. If the prisoners refused, merciless mass executions followed. The stronger forts were generally able to withstand this kind of attack, but the smaller towns often fell to such assaults or to stratagems.

With his troops Genghis Khan marched through the plain of Hopeh, where the town of Hochien was captured. Cheng-ting and Ta-ming, however, offered successful resistance; as at Peking, Genghis Khan made no effort to take these towns.[38] Tsinan, the capital of Shantung, was less fortunate. With its valuable art treasures it fell into the hands of the Mongols.[39] East of the holy T'ai mountains Genghis Khan proceeded towards the Huang-ho, called by the Mongols Qara Mören, the Black River. At this great water barrier the Mongol army marched east towards Shantung. Near Teng-chou, on the north coast of this peninsula, the Mongols saw the sea for the first time.[40] Genghis Khan reached the Dolon Nor area, carrying enormous loads of booty on captured horses and oxen. The Mongols had, moreover, taken with them large numbers of boys and girls from the areas through which they had marched.

The right wing, the army of Jochi, Chaghatai and Ögödei, went via Pao-ting towards the south. Near Lu-an they split their troops up so that they could better plunder the rich areas on the banks of the Huang-ho. Near Hua-ching they turned west, then moved north again through the valley of the Fen River. The towns of Ping-yang and Fen-chou were captured in the usual way; T'ai-yüan, the wealthy capital of the Shansi province, also fell. With large quantities of booty Jochi and his brothers marched via Tai-chou to Tat'ung. Leaving their plundered treasures behind for the time being in the region of the Ongut,[41] they rejoined their father's army near Peking.

The third column, under the command of Qasar and Temüge, had apparently been given a special task. Via Yung-ping on the Gulf of Chih-li and Cheng-te, north of Kupeik'ou, the two brothers first went to the area around the Liao River[42] and then to the Sungari and the Nen rivers. The apanages which Genghis Khan was later to present to Qasar and Temüge lay in this area. It is not impossible that they had been ordered to undertake this march for the express purpose of conquering their own inheritance. It is thought that Qasar died during this campaign.[43]

In April 1214 Genghis Khan reassembled his armies north of Peking.[44] They were much weakened when they met at the rendezvous. During their campaign in north China an epidemic of the plague had raged there and had not spared the Mongol armies. After two unsuccessful attacks on the strongly defended town, Genghis Khan realized that a third attack might also prove fruitless.[45] With his army of cavalry he could only hope to drive Peking to surrender by starving the inhabitants out; that might take a long time.

In the town a difference of opinion had arisen between general Kao-chi and some of the imperial advisers. The former wished to take advantage of the weakness of the men and horses of the Mongol army; a sortie with the maximum possible number of defenders might force a decision. The party advocating peace prevailed, however. Genghis Khan, well informed as always, came to hear of this and made use of the information to ask the Chin emperor what it was worth to him if the Mongols called off the siege of his capital.[46] Genghis Khan's generals, coveting the ample booty they knew to be available in the great city, were all in favour of attack.[47] Genghis Khan was shrewd enough not to conceal the wishes of his generals from the emperor, who finally acceded to the Mongol leader's proposal. The emperor offered as indemnity large quantities of silk and gold, 500 boys and girls, 3,000 horses, and one of his daughters as a bride for Genghis Khan.[48] Early in May the peace terms were settled;[49] the Chin acknowledged Genghis Khan's suzerainty over the state of Liao.

The Mongol army marched through the pass near Chü-yung north-west of Peking.[50] It must have been a heart-breaking spectacle for the native people to watch this shaggy army with its enormous trains of plunder leaving the mighty country of China. The hundreds of youthful prisoners forming part of the procession were a sad demonstration of the human misery caused by this war. Genghis Khan did not retire further than the Dolon Nor oasis, for he could not cross the Gobi Desert in the summer with an army so hampered by booty and prisoners. Perhaps also at that moment it was not in his mind to do so.

The peace purchased so dearly by the Chin turned out to be a truce. Now the riches of north China lay open for taking. For this reason the emperor felt himself to be threatened in Peking. In June or July he moved his capital to K'ai-feng,[51] south of the Huang-ho.[52] At that time K'ai-feng was called Nan-ching.[53] The supreme commander, General Kao-chi, went with him southwards. In the former capital, where the crown prince continued to live,[54] General Wan-yen Fu-hing was put in command.[55] He did his best to strengthen the defences of the northern part of the Chin empire. Liao-yang, the capital of the new Khitan state, was even conquered.

The news of the removal of the Chin capital was ill received by the Sung. They feared that the Chin would try to find compensation for their losses in the north by looking southwards. A Sung embassy did not get much satisfaction from Genghis Khan; the continued rivalry between the Sung and the Chin could only be to his advantage.

The emperor's move to a new capital was regarded by his subjects as desertion. While he was travelling south, a number of the Khitan troops accompanying him mutinied, returned to the north and offered their services to the Mongols.[56] Genghis Khan did not fail to make use of this opportunity. He sent two generals, Muqali and Samuqa, to north China. Muqali went to the Liao River region and Samuqa to Peking to give as much support as possible to the revolts which had broken out there.[57] Muqali succeeded in recapturing Liao-yang and the rest of the territories of Genghis Khan's vassal, Yeh-lü Liu-ko.

A year earlier Genghis Khan had decided against the capture of Peking, which had been then defended by a strong garrison. The revolts in the army, and the departure of the emperor with a part of the garrison, had considerably changed the situation. Genghis Khan always understood very well what he could do and what he could not do with his available resources. He undertook nothing that was beyond his ability. This time too he judged correctly.

An army sent by the Chin emperor to reinforce the defences at Peking was driven back north of Hochien.[58] As a result of this reverse the Peking generals, already demoralized by the departure of the emperor, became desperate. Wan-yen Fu-hing committed suicide by poisoning himself.[59] Before the Mongols entirely surrounded the town not only the crown prince,[60] but also a general with a number of troops managed to escape.[61] Although the position was hopeless, Peking at first resisted bravely. An attempt by Genghis Khan to compel the emperor in K'ai-feng once more to make peace failed.[62] In March 1215 Genghis Khan concentrated his army in front of the town. The trapped inhabitants were desperate because of the flight of their principal commanders and the serious shortage of food. It was only their fear of the terrible retribution awaiting them, that prevented them from surrendering to the Mongols. The famine even drove the terrified population to cannibalism.

Thanks to the support of Ming-Ngan, a Khitan general who had defected to the Mongols,[63] Peking fell in May 1215.[64] Genghis Khan, who had stayed only a short time with his besieging troops, had already returned before the fall of Peking to Dolon Nor. After the entry of his troops into the town, he did not return to enjoy his triumph. With Ming-Ngan a number of Chin troops had gone over to his side, bringing with them into Mongol hands not only siege machines, but also technical troops who could operate them.[65]

Peking, then one of the largest cities in Asia, contained a number of splendid palaces, temples, gates and parks. All these were laid waste by the Mongols. The sacking of the town lasted more than a month and was done on a vast scale.[66] There exists an eye witness account of Peking's fate. The Khwarazm shah had sent an embassy led by Baha al-Din Razi to Genghis Khan to obtain news of the neighbouring Mongol state, which was very rapidly growing in power (see page 84). What this ambassador saw and experienced in China, he told on his return to the Persian historian Juzjani, who recorded it in one of his chronicles. The embassy reached Genghis Khan soon after the fall of Peking. In the town they saw signs of terrible destruction. The bones of people who had been killed were piled in great heaps. Rotting corpses caused fevers from which some of the ambassadors died. Near one of the city gates lay an enormous pile of bones, said by Baha al-Din Razi to have been those of 60,000 girls who had hurled themselves from the walls to avoid falling prey to the Mongols.[67] In the early years of their rise to power under Genghis Khan, the Mongols had no idea of the social function of a town. All they knew was to plunder and destroy it and massacre its inhabitants.

Genghis Khan sent three trusty friends, Shigi Qutuqu, Arqai Qasar and Onggur, to Peking to take custody of the treasures the Chin emperor had left behind. These treasures were guarded by Qada, a Chin officer who had early co-operated with the Mongols. He offered the three Mongols a small part of the treasure for themselves. Shigi Qutuqu refused, considering that everything that formerly belonged to the Chin emperor now belonged to Genghis Khan. This incident came to the ears of Genghis Khan; he praised Shigi Qutuqu and voiced his disapproval of the behaviour of Arqai Qasar and Onggur, who had not been so scrupulous.[68] Week after week caravans set off to Dolon Nor loaded with goods from the imperial palaces. These caravans, guarded by troops, were accompanied by artisans, artists, scholars and officials, who had been taken prisoner.

The capture of Peking was an important event, marking the beginning of Mongol domination of China. It also announced the increasing might of the Mongols under the leadership of Genghis Khan, whose name began to arouse increasing awe and respect throughout Asia.

In the summer after the fall of Peking the Mongol army reduced its activities in China. North of the Huang-ho the Chin army was no longer of much significance. Genghis Khan returned late in 1215[69] (after an absence of four and a half years) to the Kerulen and the Onon. Large numbers of prisoners, who were of no further use to the Mongols, were killed before the departure from Dolon Nor. Genghis Khan sent an embassy to the Chin emperor with the proposal that he renounce his claim to the provinces of Hopeh and Shantung and to the imperial title; the emperor should be satisfied by calling himself king of Honan. In spite of the inauspicious situation in which Emperor Hsüan-tsung found himself, he rejected this insulting condition for peace.[70] Genghis Khan therefore decided to attack the Chin south of the Huang-ho.

He detailed Samuqa Baghatur, a native of the Saljut tribe, for this task.[71] The military strength of Samuqa, which had been reinforced by some Tangut cavalry, is not known. Probably there were two tümen.[72]

The exact course of Samuqa's campaign is difficult to follow. Probably he crossed the Huang-ho north-west of Tat'ung.[73] In the winter of 1216–17 he moved towards the Wei River via Ordos and Shensi. On the south bank of the Wei he plundered the old town Hsi-an, after which he attempted to take T'ung-kuan. This important fortified town proved too formidable for him, however. Samuqa now showed that he possessed great daring and perseverance. Turning his back on the fortifications of T'ung-kuan, with the strongly defended town of Lo-yang ahead of him, and far from his own main army, he moved in the winter through the mountainous territory south of the Huang-ho towards K'ai-feng. He avoided Lo-yang, turned south and took Yu-chou. It seems unlikely, in view of his circumstances, that he intended to cut K'ai-feng off and invest it. The Chin army's resistance increased so much that it began to form a threat to Samuqa. At the gates of K'ai-feng he suffered a defeat, which persuaded him to withdraw in a northerly direction. An early and rigorous winter enabled him to cross the frozen Yellow River.[74]

Samuqa's marches were presumably not only intended to put the Chin emperor under pressure. It is not unlikely that he had also been instructed to reconnoitre the region south of the Huang-ho. Although his operations were less spectacular than the raid undertaken some years later by Jebe and Sübedei in Iran, Caucasia and south Russia, Samuqa's achievements in his campaigns were such that he may be considered one of Genghis Khan's most skilful generals. Surprisingly, he disappears from the history of the Mongols after this campaign as suddenly as he entered it.

The fact that Samuqa was able to make such a daring raid so deep into Chin territory shows how quickly this empire had become enfeebled by the Mongol assaults. Its internal strength in 1211 was apparently such that it was one of the most powerful empires in east Asia only in name, and Genghis Khan probably knew this very well. At any rate, he paid little further attention to the struggle in north China after Samuqa's return. Content with the departure of the Chin to the region south of the Huang-ho, he made no more serious attempts to dislodge them from there either. He devoted his thoughts increasingly to his next enemies: Küchlüg and the Khwarazm shah. It was only in Peking that the Mongols maintained a garrison of troops. The rest of the conquered territory north of the Huang-ho was unoccupied; they did not know what to do with it, regarding it mainly as a sort of plunder zone.

Quickly perceiving this indifference, the Chin made use of the breathing space thus offered by the Mongols to reinforce the remnants of their army. Then they began to operate north of the Huang-ho to reconquer a part of their lost territory, and succeeded so well that soon large areas came again under their control.[75] Genghis Khan realized that if he ignored the Chin advances, which although initially hesitating became more and more obtrusive, he would eventually find himself in trouble. To keep the Chin in check he left a force (the 'left wing') in north China under the command of Muqali,[76] in whom he had the greatest confidence.

As after 1215 Genghis Khan devoted most of his attention to the west, the commander he appointed for north China had to be not only a capable general, but also loyal to Genghis Khan under all circumstances. With his infallible knowledge of human nature Genghis Khan chose Muqali as his lieutenant in that theatre of operation. Although Muqali was perhaps not as great a general on the field of battle as Jebe, he undoubtedly possessed remarkable qualities in other respects.

The task given to Muqali by Genghis Khan was almost certainly to drive the Chin forces behind the Huang-ho. Genghis Khan would not have concerned himself overmuch with the presence of those troops north of the Yellow River. That they were able to hold out there was the result of the Mongols' indifference. Moreover, the Chin were threatened from the south by the Sung, who were biding their time in the hope of regaining their lost territory. The limited extent of the task given to Muqali is clear from the fact that he had to ask Genghis Khan in 1221 whether he should continue the campaign or not.[77] The strength of his left wing had probably been determined by the task he had been given. The course of the seven-year war that Muqali waged in north China shows that the number of troops he had at his disposal was not large. I believe he started with one Mongol tümen, reinforced with

Tangut and Khitan contingents. Later, Chinese troops were also enlisted. Altogether they amounted to three or four tümen, which (as was customary at this time throughout the Mongol army) were certainly not up to full strength. Muqali's left wing will have consisted of about 25,000 to 30,000 men. Generally, however, historians give higher figures, varying between 40,000 and 70,000 men.[78]

At first Muqali continued the normal Mongol methods of warfare: conquering small towns and undefended regions. However, he soon came to see that other tactics would give better results. He therefore embodied, alongside his cavalry, infantry and engineers with siege machines.[79] He also changed the traditional Mongol treatment of defeated townspeople and soldiers; for endless massacres he substituted a more conciliatory attitude. In so doing he showed that he knew it was impossible to combat the enormous masses of the Chinese population. Nevertheless the Mongols had won such a reputation for themselves, that the Chinese people defended themselves to the last. In the thickly populated regions of north China, with their many natural impregnable defensive positions, Muqali was not able to avoid the long-drawn weariness of siege warfare.[80] Captured towns had even to be relinquished eventually.

In 1217 Muqali began his march against the province of Hopeh and the northern parts of Shantung and Shansi. The town Ta-ming was captured,[81] but fell again into the hands of the Chin. In that year the Sung resumed war against their northern neighbours. In the following year Muqali directed himself mainly against Shansi; the towns T'ai-yüan and Pingyang surrendered to the Mongols.[82] Although this important agricultural province was largely under their control in 1219, small enemy bands continued to cause trouble.

In 1220 it was the turn of Shantung, but this province took more time to subdue than Muqali had anticipated. It is true that he took the towns of Tsinan and Ta-ming,[83] but elsewhere the Chin resisted obstinately. It was only in May of the following year that Shantung came partly under control of the Mongols. In south-west Shensi the Chin also lost the towns of Pao-nan and Fu-chou, and indeed throughout that year they were hard-pressed. In addition to the Mongols and the Sung,

Hsi-Hsia now also joined forces with the enemies of the Jurchen empire. The emperor Hsüan-tsung begged Genghis Khan for peace, offering to accept the status of vassal if he could only retain his imperial title. Genghis Khan persisted in his earlier demands: surrender of all areas north of the Huang-ho and acceptance of the title of king of Honan. Hsüan-tsung refused to agree to the last condition.[84]

Muqali began his last campaign in the autumn of 1222. Taking approximately the same route that Samuqa followed in the winter of 1216–17, he passed through Ordos and Shensi to the river Wei.[85] South of this river he took the ancient town of Hsi-an, which had already been plundered by Samuqa. In the autumn the Chin emperor made another attempt to conclude peace. Genghis Khan, now master of the whole area north of the Huang-ho thanks to Muqali's campaigns, refused to make terms.[86] In the spring of 1223 during the siege of Fenghsiang, Muqali learned that the Chin had invaded the province of Shansi via the fort of T'ung-kuan. Hurriedly he went in pursuit; they did not wait for him, but retreated again. Muqali surrounded the town of Pu-chou. During this siege he became seriously ill and shortly afterwards, in April 1223, he died[87] at the age of 54. On his deathbed he declared proudly that he had never suffered defeat. He was succeeded by his son Bol, who also inherited his title of Gui-Ong.[88]

Muqali had more than carried out the task with which he had been entrusted. In the seven years that he represented Genghis Khan in north China, he had reduced the Chin empire to the province of Honan. He had worked untiringly for the Mongol cause, showing himself to be an excellent general and a loyal servant. The struggle was indeed to continue after his death, but there were no more military actions of any significance in this theatre of war. Not until the death of Genghis Khan did his two sons, Ögödei and Tolui, resume and end the war in north China.

VICTOR AND VANQUISHED

In his campaigns against the Chin, Genghis Khan gained an enormous amount of plunder, consisting of gold, silver, silk and beasts of burden, as well as numerous prisoners. The latter were doomed to become slaves; their lives had been spared on account of their knowledge or specialist skill. Most of them were craftsmen or artists, but there were also scholars and officials. Although the best and finest of this newly acquired wealth went to Genghis Khan, his higher commanders also had their share. After the return from north China the simple dwellings of the aristocracy of the steppes became more luxurious.[89] Their servants were mostly slaves who were specialists in their tasks. In spite of this prosperity, however, Genghis Khan demanded that the traditional customs, law and life-style of the nomads should be strictly maintained.[90]

The growth of his empire required a large number of officials for administrative posts, for which the uneducated Mongols were ill suited. Educated people from the subject tribes supplied this deficiency.[91] After the fall of Peking a descendant of the former Liao dynasty of the Khitan, Yeh-lü Ch'u-ts'ai (1189–1243) was brought to Genghis Khan as a prisoner. The young Khitan was a person of high intelligence who had entirely adopted the Chinese culture. As an astrologer he was one of the more educated prisoners. When Genghis Khan first saw him he was immediately impressed: his tall stature, his long beard and his sonorous voice pleased the Mongol conqueror greatly. Genghis Khan told the Khitan that his forefathers were avenged now that the Chin were defeated. Yeh-lü Ch'u-ts'ai said nothing to denigrate his former superiors. He replied: 'My father and grandfather have both served the Chin respectfully. How can I, as a subject and a son, be so insincere at heart as to consider my sovereign and my father as enemies?'[92] The loyalty of a captured servant for his defeated master was always highly appreciated by Genghis Khan. The Mongol conqueror felt that he had found in the young Khitan somebody very suitable to administer his ever-growing empire.

In making this choice Genghis Khan showed that his knowledge of human nature extended to those who were much more educated than he himself. The astrologer Yeh-lü Ch'u-ts'ai was to develop in a very short time into an eminent statesman. His Chinese upbringing gave him the right qualities to introduce gradual changes in the government of the Mongol Empire that would enable it to incorporate sedentary civilizations. The process, started under Genghis Khan, was continued by Yeh-lü Ch'u-ts'ai during the rule of Ögödei. He combined the office of scribe-secretary in charge of official documents in Chinese with that of court astrologer-astronomer.[93]

It was not the endless caravans bringing booty from China that were of most profit to the Mongols. It was the fact that Genghis Khan had the foresight to appoint educated men to govern his rapidly growing empire. Chinese governmental organization became the model for the administration of the Mongol Empire. Yeh-lü Ch'u-ts'ai took advantage of the opportunity presented to him to ensure that the administration was as efficient as possible. From the prisoners captured by the Mongols in north China, he selected those he thought could help him in his task. He also took the child prisoners under his wing. Among the booty brought from China by the Mongols there were books and medicines, of which Yeh-lü Ch'u-ts'ai made use. When an epidemic broke out in Mongolia, he succeeded in saving a great many lives with the aid of these medicines.[94]

The vast number of dead and the enormous destruction caused by the Mongol campaigns in north China were because the Mongols, in comparison with other tribes, had lagged far behind in cultural development. The Khitan in the tenth century and even the Jurchen in the twelfth century had reached a higher stage of civilization. Their successive conquests in north China caused less misery than did the Mongol invasion. No large-scale devastation followed their usurpation of power. The Khitan and the Jurchen considered that the country they conquered had now become their home.

For Genghis Khan and his Mongols human life had no value, and they did not understand the worth of a static civilization or of an agricultural population. They had no interest in anything that could not be adapted to their native steppes. Undoubtedly the Mongols did not kill, ravage and plunder out of sadism: they did not know any better. Their actions conformed with the practice of warfare current at that time. As shown earlier (see pages 48–9), any chance of an effective rising against the Mongols was quashed by killing all the able-bodied members of the population or by removing them as prisoners.

Some historians defend Genghis Khan against accusations of

cruelty and blood-lust by drawing attention to the fact that during the war in north China large numbers of Khitan and later even Chinese deserted voluntarily to the army of Genghis Khan, 'with whom they sought refuge'.[95] This is a risky argument to use to refute the charge of cruelty; not only Khitan and Chinese deserted but also Jurchen.[96] This occurred, however, when the Chin army units realized that the Mongol invasion was not merely an incidental raid by a nomadic tribe, but a conquest conducted by a man of powerful personality, against whom the half-hearted Chin resistance was of no avail. At that time it was common for troops of a defeated army to desert to the victor. And Genghis Khan's remarkable skill in swiftly forming disciplined units out of the deserters[97] naturally made a deep impression in the enemy camp.

7
The prelude

In 1125 the Khitan were defeated by the Jurchen in north China (see pages 56–7); however, the majority of the Khitan remained in north China.[1] Under the leadership of Yeh-lü Ta-shi, a relative of the last Liao emperor, a group of them, mostly belonging to the tribes living in south Mongolia, departed in a westerly direction.[2] The Khitan reached the Tarbagatai mountains and built the town Emil in the neighbourhood of the present-day Chuguchak.[3]

The Qara Khanids (a confederation of Turkish tribes) asked the Khitan for help against the incursions of the Turkish tribes from the north. The Khitan repelled the invaders, but decided not to move away themselves. They settled permanently in Semirechye and the kingdom they later established was called by the Muslims Qara Khitai (Black Khitai). In Chinese history they are called the 'Western Liao'.[4] Yeh-lü Ta-shi, who chose Balasaghun as his capital, took the Turkish title of Gur-Khan (see page 20). He conquered many regions from the Qara Khanids, gaining control consecutively in Kashgar, in the country south of Issyq Kul and in Khojend; Samarkand was also threatened. The Qara Khanids called on the Seljuqs for help. Sultan Sanjar (1097–1157), the most important Seljuq of his time, resolved to put a stop to the pretensions of the Qara Khitai and on 9 September 1141 a battle took place north of Samarkand on the Katvan Steppe which ended in a decisive defeat for the Seljuqs.

The victory of Yeh-lü Ta-shi over what was then the mightiest Muslim empire made a great impression. Via Syria the news reached the crusaders, who were at war with the Muslims in Palestine and Syria. However, the story that the crusaders heard had undergone a slight change. The victory on the Katvan Steppe had been won by a Christian prince, the legendary Prester John (see note on page 83), who had attacked the Muslims from the east and was advancing on Jerusalem. In 1145 there was even a rumour that Prester John had reached the Tigris.[5] The Qara Khitai, however, did not advance further west than the Amu Darya River. Samarkand and Bukhara fell into their hands.

The Qara Khitai kingdom differed considerably from the usual nomad kingdoms. Ruling princes were not driven away; the Qara Khitai demanded recognition of their suzerainty and were content with an annual tribute of money and goods.[6] The result of this policy was that the Qara Khanids were able to continue in Samarkand and Bukhara as vassals. In spite of their Islamic surroundings the Qara Khitai remained true to their Buddhism. Although they tolerated much religious freedom in their kingdom, they were considered as enemy heathens by the neighbouring Islamic tribes.[7]

At the end of the eleventh century a former slave, who had risen to the rank of general, was appointed Seljuq governor of Khwarazm. After his death his son was chosen for the same post and showed such loyalty in service that his own son, Atsiz, succeeded as governor in 1127. Atsiz is the real founder of the dynasty of the later Khwarazm shahs.[8] In the early years of his rule Atsiz showed himself to be, like his forefathers, a faithful subject of Sultan Sanjar. As time went by, however, he began to appreciate his subordinate role less and less, but Sanjar managed to keep his governor under his thumb.

The Qara Khitai kingdom in its final stages had become very large. It became a power to reckon with (particularly after the death of Sultan Sanjar in 1157 when the importance of the Seljuqs began to decline). In the east the Qara Khitai territory extended as far as Lop Nor and Khotan. In the south-west the towns of Tirmid and Balkh had been overcome, while in the west Transoxiana and Khwarazm were subdued. Atsiz was compelled to pay an annual tribute to the gur-khan.[9] After the death of Yeh-lü Ta-shi in 1142 the authority of the ruling dynasty weakened. The successor to the throne being too young to rule, Yeh-lü Ta-shi's widow became regent until 1150, the year in which her son became gur-khan. After his death in 1163 his sister conducted the regency. In 1178 Yeh-lü Tsi-lu-ku as gur-khan assumed control himself. During his rule Küchlüg, who had been defeated by Genghis Khan and who was the son of the last tayang of the Naiman, asked the Qara Khitai for protection in 1208. Küchlüg had first attempted to settle among the Uighurs, but the idiqut had driven him away.

When Atsiz and Sanjar died (in 1156 and 1157 respectively), Atsiz had still been a vassal of the Seljuqs. Atsiz bequeathed a powerful state to his son, Il Arslan. The old Iranian title Khwarazam shah came to be used more and more for the new dynasty.[10] After the death of Sanjar the might of the Seljuq sultans practically disappeared in the eastern part of Iran, while the importance of the Qara Khitai and especially of the Khwarazm shahs increased. Although he was still tributary to the Qara Khitai, Il Arslan was the most powerful prince in the eastern part of the Muslim world.[11] After his death his son Tekish ascended the throne.

In the growing strength of the Khwarazm shah the caliph of Baghdad saw an opportunity to rid himself of the Seljuq domination. Since the middle of the twelfth century the political and military influence of the Abbasid caliphate continued to grow as the power of the Seljuqs declined. After two centuries of submission the Abbasids had become only spiritual leaders of the Muslim world; they retained little real power.[12] An-Nasir li-Din-Allah, who became caliph in 1180, developed gradually into a central figure.[13] He asked Tekish to attack the Seljuq sultan.[14] Tekish complied, hoping to enlarge his own possessions at the cost of the remnants of the once so mighty Seljuq sultanate. In March 1194 the sultan was defeated near Rayy, taken prisoner and beheaded.[15]

An-Nasir, who had hoped to be able to restore the caliphate of the Abbasids, seemed to have misjudged matters. Apart from Iraq-Arabi, which fell to the caliph, Tekish added most of what was left of the Seljuq sultanate to his own realm. He even attempted to appropriate as his own the influence which the Seljuqs had exerted on the Muslims. He asked the caliph to have the khutba (the Friday prayer) read in his name in Baghdad, as had been done for the Seljuqs.[16] The refusal of the caliph to accede to this request was one of the reasons for the strained relationship that existed between the Khwarazm shah and the caliph, which gave rise to mutual suspicions that grew as time went on. This feud would lead eventually to the downfall of both dynasties.[17] It was characteristic that, during the attacks that the rivals made on each other's territory, the population was the victim of cruelties which were often worse than those that this same population had to endure later at the hands of the Mongols.[18]

When Tekish died in 1200 the power of the dynasty had reached its peak. Yet even then there were circumstances which were later to have disastrous consequences for his son and successor. The bitter enmity between the caliph of Baghdad and the Khwarazm shah meant that the latter could not expect any support from the Muslim leaders.[19] The other circumstance was that Tekish had formed a strong army in which the Turkish element predominated. These alien mercenaries, consisting partly of non-Muslims, often committed atrocities which gained for them among the people the reputation of being barbarians.[20]

The first appearance of Muhammad II, the new Khwarazm shah, resulted in the conquest of Afghanistan from the Ghurids. The Khwarazm shah received support from the Qara Khitai and from the khan of Samarkand. The defeat which the Qara Khitai troops particularly inflicted on the Ghurids was such that in 1206 the greater part of their kingdom had to recognize the suzerainty of Muhammad. In 1215 the shah completed his conquest of Afghanistan.[21]

Muhammad had his suzerain, the gur-khan, to thank for the defeat of the Ghurids. His gratitude was of short duration. After the defeat of the Ghurids he was the paramount prince in Islam, in which capacity he could not be the vassal of a heathen. The khan of Samarkand and Bukhara, who was also the subordinate of the gur-khan, was of the same opinion. In 1207 Muhammad exploited these views to lay siege to and to conquer Samarkand and Bukhara, after which the Qara Khanids became vassals of the Khwarazm shah. The Qara Khitai refused to acquiesce and in 1210 the gur-khan and Muhammad went to war against each other.

During the reign of Yeh-lü Tsi-lu-ku (1178–1211) the prestige of the gur-khan declined. In the east a number of vassals cast off his suzerainty to seek protection from the increasingly powerful Genghis Khan. The first to take this step, in 1209, was the idiqut of the Uighurs. In 1211 Arslan, the khan of the Qarluqs and Buzar, the chief of a Turkish tribe from the upper Ili River, followed his example.

Küchlüg, who had fled to the gur-khan in 1208, married a daughter of his protector. Küchlüg, however, had aspirations to seize power himself in the Qara Khitai kingdom. The gur-khan committed the folly of permitting him to organize the remnants of the Naiman tribe as a military unit. During the invasion of the Khwarazm shah in 1210 Küchlüg rebelled against his father-in-law. The gur-khan resisted this usurpation, but Muhammad supported Küchlüg, if only half-heartedly,[22] and this struggle broke the strength of the once so powerful Qara Khitai.

The army of the gur-khan, threatened from two sides, withdrew towards the capital Balasaghun. The Islamic population of this town, hoping to be freed from the 'heathen' Qara Khitai authority by the Khwarazm shah, shut the gates against the gur-khan. In 1210 the Khwarazm shah defeated the gur-khan on the Talas River or somewhere in Ferghana, but he was unable to exploit his success.[23]

Because of a defeat the gur-khan had inflicted on Küchlüg's army, Muhammad either could not or did not dare advance any further.[24] The people of Balasaghun felt themselves betrayed by the mightiest prince of Islam. The gur-khan recaptured his capital, after which the customary punishment was administered. In 1211 Küchlüg took the gur-khan prisoner. Although he allowed his father-in-law to continue in name as gur-khan, he assumed power for himself. Yeh-lü Tsi-lu-ku died two years after his disposition.

The continuous warfare brought a serious problem to light in Khwarazm. It became clear that Muhammad was in no position to keep his army under control. He could hardly protect his own population from the pillaging and atrocities of his army.[25] The soldiers were hated; in 1212 this led the khan of Samarkand and Buhkhara to throw in his lot again with the Qara Khitai. The Khwarazm troops were murdered. Muhammad allowed the revolt to be suppressed with great bloodshed and cruelty. The khan of Samarkand was executed, which meant the end of the dynasty of the Qara Khanids.[26]

After this victory Muhammad moved his capital in 1212 from Gurganj to Samarkand. He thought the moment had come to improve his position; he assumed the title of sultan and called himself Sultan Sanjar. Even after his death Sanjar, because of his long and impressive rule, was remembered as a prince worthy of respect. To suggest that he had ambitions to become a world ruler, Muhammad also called himself Iskender (Alexander the Great); in the seal of the new sultan appeared the words, 'Shadow of God on Earth'.[27] Muhammad's personal qualities, however, offered a glaring denial of the titles he bestowed upon himself.

After Küchlüg had emerged as the victor from the struggle for power in the Qara Khitai kingdom, there came a sudden end to the friendship with Sultan Muhammad II. Küchlüg ignored the wishes of his former ally, who wanted certain territories in payment for the help he had given. This situation marked the beginning of the enmity between the Khwarazm shah and the new Qara Khitai ruler. During the wars that they waged against each other, both leaders terrorized the population of the disputed regions. Muhammad could not succeed in gaining a decisive victory over his opponent.[28] The result was that the Syr Darya River (from Khojend to the Aral Sea) came to represent approximately the frontier between the two kingdoms.[29]

The wars that Küchlüg waged against Sultan Muhammad II led him to a pronounced hostility towards Islam;[30] as a Naiman he was a confirmed Nestorian and, under the influence of his Qara Khitai wife, tended more and more towards Buddhism.[31] Tales about the conflicts between the mighty sultan and Küchlüg now began to reach the crusaders in Palestine; one of the stories was again that of the legendary Prester John attacking the Muslims from the east. This time it was Küchlüg who filled the role of Prester John.*

---

* The origin of the story of Prester John is difficult to trace. In addition to Yeh-lü Ta-shi and Küchlüg, Toghril (the Ong-Khan of the Kereit) has also been considered as the personification of this legendary figure, presumably because Nestorianism had many supporters among the Kereit. During the Crusades (1217–21), Genghis Khan's campaign against the most powerful Islamic kingdom in Asia took place. The legend of Prester John revived among the crusaders, who hoped for help from the victorious armies of the east; but now it was Genghis Khan who was identified with that sacred hero. (Richard, 1957, pp. 225–42; Bezzola, 1974, pp. 20, 61, 128.)

Küchlüg, a native of a nomadic tribe, became in a short time the head of a state having a largely sedentary population; it is not surprising that he could muster little sympathy for such people. In the years 1211 to 1214 he terrorized various regions, particularly those in the east, without having any clear motive.[32] The Islamic people were often confronted with the choice to be either Buddhist or Nestorian; if they refused both, bloody retribution usually followed.[33] The Imam of Khotan, objecting to these cruel impositions, was nailed to the door of his *medrese* (a Muslim institution of higher education) by Küchlüg.[34] Kashgar and Khotan especially became the victims of Küchlüg's hostility towards Islam.

So there came into existence, on the borders of Küchlüg's territory and that of Genghis Khan (who saw in the former his personal foe), a zone of unrest which was hostile to the Qara Khitai ruler. The Islamic population there, which believed it could count on the support of Sultan Muhammad II, was bitterly disillusioned when the sultan left his fellow believers in Kashgar, Yarkand and Khotan to fend for themselves. The people of that border region would gratefully accept any ruler who would free them from the arbitrariness of Küchlüg.

CONTACTS BETWEEN THE RULER OF THE WEST AND THE RULER OF THE EAST

The accounts by various writers of the first connections between Genghis Khan and Sultan Muhammad II are difficult to reconcile,[35] because there are few points of contact in the stories. The dispatch of embassies to and fro does, however, indicate that both rulers were interested in each other.

After the fall of Peking the Khwarazm shah wished to learn more about the conqueror of this important city. This was the reason why he sent an embassy to Genghis Khan, with Baha al-Din Razi at its head[36] (see page 69). During the first meeting with Genghis Khan the son and a minister of the Chin emperor were led in, shackled;[37] this was done, of course, to make an impression. For the rest, Genghis Khan received Baha al-Din Razi courteously and asked him to inform Muhammad that he regarded the sultan as the ruler of the west and himself as the ruler of the east.[38] He urged that both rulers should conclude a treaty of peace and concord in the interest of commerce between the two empires.[39]

There was an embassy in the reverse direction in 1218[40] led by two Muslims: Mahmud of Bukhara and Yusuf Kanka of Otrar.[41] Mahmud was apparently Mahmud Yalavach, later to become one of Genghis Khan's advisers.[42] This embassy brought a number of expensive gifts for Sultan Muhammad, including a very large nugget of gold from China.[43] In the spring of 1218 the Khwarazm shah received both ambassadors in Transoxiana (presumably in Bukhara). They told Muhammad that Genghis Khan had heard of his power and his victories. The Mongol ruler offered the sultan not only a peace treaty, but also a position 'on a level with the dearest of his son'.[44] Muhammad, who wished to obtain intelligence of Genghis Khan, called Mahmud into his presence. He told the ambassador that for him, as Khwarazmian, the interests of his own country were paramount; Mahmud should therefore remain in the court of Genghis Khan as the Khwarazm shah's spy. Muhammad explained that he was very angry that an infidel had called him, the master of a Muslim empire, 'his son' (in other words 'vassal').[45] Mahmud assured the Khwarazm shah that Genghis Khan had no intention of attacking the ruler of the west. Moreover, the Mongol army was not to be compared in strength with that of the Khwarazm shah. Relieved at this news, Muhammad assented to the proposed treaty of peace and friendship.[46]

From contemporary accounts it cannot be concluded that Genghis Khan's intention was in fact to go to war with the Khwarazm shah.[47] His embassies certainly had the assignment of maintaining trade links between Central Asia and South-west Asia in view of the changed political situation.[48] Caravans going to and from Mongolia avoided as far as possible the territory of Küchlüg.[49] It is true that the Mongol embassies had also been told to gather intelligence;[50] the use of Muslims for this purpose showed some nerve.

It is known that the Muslim merchants played a significant part in the spread of Islam. That they were equally important as informers and intelligence agents cannot be too strongly emphasized. They were indispensable for espionage. Disguised as innocent merchants they succeeded, by their own observation and by keeping their ears open, in learning a great deal about a country, its people, towns, troop strengths, military equipment, public opinion and sometimes even secret plans.[51] It may be accepted that this state of affairs was known to Sultan Muhammad. Presumably his objection to free trade with Mongolia stemmed primarily from suspicion that it would be used for espionage on behalf of Genghis Khan.

Commerce with settled neighbouring tribes was of great importance to the nomads. Most of their clothing derived from this trade. After the military operations in north China (during which large areas of agricultural land were laid waste) grain had to be imported from other regions into Mongolia. In this trade also Muslims were the middlemen.[52] Genghis Khan's request for free trade between Central and South-west Asia therefore served a common interest – that of the Mongols and that of the merchants – which caused may Muslims to support Genghis Khan.[53] These Muslims were convinced, moreover, that the Mongol ruler, although he professed a different religion, was a tolerant and most powerful monarch.[54]

Sultan Muhammad II, on the other hand, took little account of the advantages that would accrue from this trade. Not only was he suspicious about it, but he could not see that trade with Russia and China would yield enormous profits.[55] The Khwarazm shah's difference of opinion offered many advantages to Genghis Khan; he exploited them to the full. The Muslim merchants who supported him brought him much intelligence about Muhammad's sultanate.[56]

After Mahmud's and Yusuf Kanka's embassy had left Khwarazm territory,[57] a richly laden caravan from Mongolia arrived in 1218 in the frontier town of Otrar. It consisted of about 450 men (mostly Muslims) and 500 camels.[58] Genghis Khan had sent an ambassador, Uqana,[59] with this caravan, who carried a message for the Khwarazm shah. The governor of Otrar was a relation of Sultan Muhammad's mother, named Inalchuq. He was authorized to bear the title Qayïr-Khan. All the members of the caravan were taken prisoner by Inalchuq, partly because one of the merchants (who had known Inalchuq earlier) addressed him without his title, and partly because the governor coveted their rich cargoes.[60]

Inalchuq sent a report to Muhammad in which he announced that his prisoners were spies for the Mongols.[61] He proposed to execute them all. It is not certain whether Muhammad believed in the story of the spies, although this is not improbable in view of his suspicion of Muslim merchants in the service of other rulers. Possibly he, like his governor, was motivated by greed for the caravan's valuable booty. In any event, he agreed to the execution of the men of the caravan (including Genghis Khan's ambassador Uqana). He ordered the stolen goods to be sold in Bukhara.[62] The responsibility for this murder, a wanton violation of a custom regarded by Genghis Khan as sacred, lay in any case with Sultan Muhammad:[63] by a timely intercession he could have prevented this crime.

One of the camel drivers succeeded in escaping the massacre; he fled to Genghis Khan. The Mongol was furious. He went to the top of a mountain (as was the custom of the shamans) and remained there three days and three nights. During his sojourn there he told Tengri: 'I was not the author of this trouble; grant me the strength to exact vengeance.'[64]

Nevertheless, Genghis Khan made a final attempt to avoid war. To demand satisfaction, he sent an embassy consisting of one Muslim and two Mongols to Sultan Muhammad. He not only protested against the behaviour of Inalchuq, but he also demanded the surrender of the governor of Otrar. Muhammad refused to grant this request. He ordered the execution of the Muslim (who was the leader of the embassy) and both Mongols had their beards shaved off.[65] Genghis Khan viewed this second murder of one of his ambassadors as a gross insult demanding vengeance.

Before he could take up arms against Sultan Muhammad there were two matters requiring his attention: the overthrow of the Qara Khitai kingdom and the settlement of the succession to the Mongol Empire, which was becoming more and more powerful.

THE 'LIBERATION' OF EAST TURKESTAN

Before Genghis Khan could take vengeance on the Khwarazm shah he had to conquer the Qara Khitai kingdom, located

between his own country and the sultan's. He had no need to
seek a *casus belli* or to bide his time. The fact that his great
enemy Küchlüg was the new monarch in the adjoining kingdom
was unacceptable to Genghis Khan. This Turkish Naiman
would have been, during a war between Genghis Khan and
Sultan Muhammad II, a continual threat to the unification of
the Turkish-Mongol tribes which had been so laboriously
achieved.

The last gur-khan of the Qara Khitai had to resign himself to
the fact that some of his vassals had renounced his sovereignty
and gone over to Genghis Khan. After Küchlüg had made
himself master in the Qara Khitai kingdom, he attempted to
win back control over these renegades. In 1211 Arslan (the
khan of the Qarluqs) and Sugnaq Tegin (the son of the
chieftain Buzar) had gone with the Mongol General Qubilai, to
inform Genghis Khan personally of their submission.[66] For this
the chieftain Buzar, now a vassal of Genghis Khan, was
murdered by Küchlüg who attempted to occupy Buzar's capital
Almaliq.[67] Buzar's widow refused to surrender the town.
Sugnaq Tegin therefore urged Genghis Khan with great
persistence to go to war with Küchlüg.[68] In view of his action
against the Qarluqs, it seemed that the Qara Khitai ruler did
not intend to tolerate Arslan's desertion.[69]

Küchlüg, who was encircled by two powers, both of which
were hostile towards him, was apparently over-confident about
his position. The manner in which he terrorized his own
country (especially the eastern part) and so drove the Islamic
population into the other camp, showed little foresight. Later he
would have to pay heavily for this.

The amicable relationship between Genghis Khan and the
Muslim merchants led to advantages to the Mongol ruler also.
These Muslims had every motive for wishing to see an end to
the oppression suffered by their fellow worshippers in Kashgar,
Yarkand and Khotan. It is likely that Genghis Khan was able
to get all the intelligence he needed for his struggle against
Küchlüg from these merchants.

Genghis Khan also wished to eliminate opposition by the
Merkit tribe before beginning his offensive against the
Khwarazm shah. The remnants of opposition were led by the
sons of Toqto'a Beki, the Merkit chief who had been defeated

and killed by Genghis Khan in 1208 (see page 30). After this defeat the Merkit had fled to the Uighurs. The idiqut, however, drove them away. Opinion is divided about the place where they settled subsequently. Most probably they went to the region north-west of Lake Balkash.[70] Although they did not present any great threat, Genghis Khan did not wish to run any risk: their hostility could have created difficulties for him during his campaign against Sultan Muhammad. The Mongol ruler sent one military force against Küchlüg and another against the Merkit almost simultaneously.[71] The troops attacking the Merkit were commanded by Sübedei and Genghis Khan's eldest son Jochi;[72] those against Küchlüg were commanded by Jebe.[73] Unfortunately there is little information available about the strength of these two Mongol detachments, which might have thrown some light, as will later appear, on the comparative strength of Sultan Muhammad II and Genghis Khan. It must be assumed that Sübedei's force was roughly equal to Jebe's, which consisted of two tümen.[74]

As it is fairly certain that Jebe's attack against Küchlüg took place in 1218, the course of events in that year (assuming simultaneous action by the two Mongol armies) must have been somewhat as follows. The route taken by Jebe is known.[75] It ran via the Altai and Tarbagatai mountains to Almaliq, the town which had been unsuccessfully besieged by Küchlüg for a long time. Little is known of the route followed by Sübedei. Presumably his line of advance was at first the same as that of Jebe: after passing the Tarbagatai mountains he proceeded through the territory of the friendly Qarluqs south of Lake Balkash. One of the principles of Genghis Khan's military practice was that a threatened flank should be protected at all times, a measure which often took the form of an offensive move in the direction of the force posing the threat. The Mongols had to take into account that were Küchlüg to be defeated, the Khwarazm shah might attempt to forestall any annexation of the Qara Khitai kingdom by Genghis Khan. Jebe's action against Küchlüg was undoubtedly the main attack, while Sübedei's operations were aimed at not only eliminating the Merkit but also preventing any attack by Muhammad on Jebe. It is therefore likely that Sübedei marched before Jebe; once he had reached the country of the Qarluqs he formed a danger to

Küchlüg who was in Semirechye. In this way Jebe and Sübedei supported each other's advance.

Where Sübedei and Jochi defeated the Merkit we do not know. There is, however, a point of contact to be found in another event. The Khwarazm shah had to protect his territory regularly against attacks from the north; in turn he made frequent raids into the regions north of the Syr Darya River. During one of these skirmishes he ran into the Mongol army of Sübedei and Jochi, which was in pursuit of the fleeing Merkit. Sultan Muhammad ordered an engagement with Sübedei's troops. Darkness put an end to an indecisive battle and under cover of night the Mongols withdrew. Their valour in battle made a deep impression on Muhammad.

Küchlüg's situation became increasingly hopeless as Jebe approached. Sübedei and Jochi were in the north and Sultan Muhammad in the west. In Semirechye Küchlüg made a vain attempt to restrain Jebe.[76] Balasaghun surrendered without battle to the Mongols.[77] Jebe carried out his task in characteristic manner: rapidly he thrust his way over large distances, offering his opponent no opportunity to recover. Küchlüg fled in the only direction still open to him: south. He went to Kashgar, where the Islamic population hated him on account of his anti-Muslim persecutions. The town accordingly gave Küchlüg no sanctuary and turned to help the approaching Jebe.

Genghis Khan, well informed by the Muslim merchants, skilfully used the intelligence he obtained. The Mongol troops, accustomed to strict obedience to orders, were told to leave the population undisturbed; there was no plundering and violence usually experienced by a defeated tribe. All were permitted to practise their religions in accordance with their convictions. Everywhere he went, Jebe made this clear.[78] After the cruel and arbitrary conduct of Küchlüg, the people of Kashgar, Yarkand and Khotan regarded the coming of the Mongols as 'one of the mercies of the Lord'.[79] The reaction of the people of Transoxiana and Khurasan two years later would be very different.

Küchlüg was not given any respite. Jebe's troops pursued him, 'and so they chased him like a mad dog'.[80] This pursuit, over a distance of about 500 kilometres, was a remarkable achievement. Küchlüg fled via the Muz Tagh Ata range and the Pamir to the border region of Badakhshan. This plateau, with heights of 3,000 to 5,000 metres, consisted of a desolate and arid landscape with bare peaks, deep ravines and huge glaciers. The place where Jebe's men finally caught up with Küchlüg cannot be determined with any certainty.[81] At the border of Badakhshan Küchlüg entered a valley where he was trapped between a group of hunters and the Mongols. The former delivered him, in return for a rich reward, to the Mongols who beheaded him.[82] Küchlüg's severed head was displayed everywhere in Kashgaria. Jebe's march back was a triumphal procession.

The news of these events received from Jebe, made Genghis Khan uneasy, however.[83] No one was more aware of Jebe's high ability as a general than the Mongol ruler; he feared that Jebe would himself assume the leadership of the Qara Khitai kingdom. He therefore sent him a warning not to become too proud of his success. As soon as his authority was at stake, Genghis Khan became highly distrustful. Jebe, however, was too intelligent to set himself up in a kingdom so enclosed (like that of Küchlüg) and surrounded by two hostile powers. The shrewd Jebe gave a clear sign of his loyalty: from the conquered territories he brought Genghis Khan 1,000 chestnut horses with white muzzles. These horses were similar in appearance to the horse that Jebe had shot from under Genghis Khan during the subjection to the Taijut (see page 21). Jebe knew that his sovereign had been most attached to that horse.[84] This gesture apparently succeeded in dispelling all suspicion about Jebe.

Jebe's victory and the manner in which it had been exploited made a great impression everywhere – all of which had unpleasant consequences for Sultan Muhammad II. Jebe's comparatively small army had defeated the great foe of Islam in a surprisingly short time. What the most powerful Muslim monarch had not been able to do, had been done by Jebe: giving the Islamic people of Semirechye, Kashgar, Yarkand and Khotan security and freedom in matters of religion. This, and his massacre of hundreds of Muslims in Otrar, later made it impossible for Sultan Muhammad to give his struggle with Genghis Khan the character of a holy war.[85] Nor could he expect any support from the caliph of Baghdad to this end: Muhammad had attempted to attack Baghdad in 1217. It is true that this act of aggression came to a stop in the Zagros mountains, foiled partly by the Kurds and partly by a snowstorm, but the attempt to take his capital had only strengthened the enmity of the caliph.[86]

Some historians tentatively record the possibility that the caliph asked Genghis Khan to attack Sultan Muhammad II.[87] Rumours to this effect appear to have circulated during the thirteenth century,[88] the consequence of the unfriendly relationship between the caliph and Muhammad. The former undoubtedly sought contact with the eastern neighbours of the Khwarazm shah, but it is nowhere confirmed that he sent an embassy to Genghis Khan.[89] If however caliph an-Nasir did indeed ask Genghis Khan for help, this leader of the Muslims can hardly have anticipated to what a dreadful disaster he was thus exposing Islam.[90] Whether such an embassy would have gained the result planned by the caliph remains an open question. It was not the custom of Genghis Khan to allow himself to be influenced by other potentates.

The conquest of the Qara Khitai kingdom had made Genghis Khan's empire an immediate neighbour of the Khwarazm sultanate. Although Muhammad had sealed the trade routes to the east,[91] he could do nothing to prevent Genghis Khan from gathering intelligence about Khwarazm much more directly. In this way the wealth of the towns, the strength of the army, Khwarazm's weak government and the serious dissension in the sultan's family, all became known to Genghis Khan. After his conquest of Qara Khitai (which would have taken place eventually even without the Otrar incident), the Mongol ruler had discovered without any shadow of doubt the fundamental weakness of the Khwarazm empire. In these circumstances an invasion would in any event have been launched, perhaps later.[92]

ÖGÖDEI, THE SUCCESSOR TO THE THRONE

The impending war against Khwarazm caused some anxiety among those close to Genghis Khan. In 1218 he was about 56; the coming campaign would take place against a distant and powerful empire. One of his wives, the Tatar beauty Yesüi, impressed upon Genghis Khan the importance of proclaiming his successor before he left.[93] A dominating ruler like Genghis Khan must have needed a great deal of self-control to comply with this reasonable suggestion. His successor had to be found among the four sons of his chief wife, Börte.

The eldest son, Jochi, could not be considered in view of the uncertainty that existed regarding his paternity. There is, however, no evidence that Genghis Khan did not consider Jochi worthy of merit; on the contrary he estimated him highly. Genghis Khan, a great judge of human character, entrusted his eldest son on various occasions with military commands. The second son, Chaghatai, as the guardian of the Yasa had shown himself to be a scrupulous and formidable upholder of justice. Although Chaghatai practised rigid self-discipline, Genghis Khan did not have a high opinion of this son. He described Chaghatai as obstinate and narrow-minded.[94] Moreover, Chaghatai was continually at odds with Jochi. Ögödei was the most intelligent of the four sons. Although he undoubtedly lacked his father's genius, he had a sound mind and a resolute character. Rather corpulent, he was not only good-natured and jovial but also unusually generous. One of his great defects was his enslavement to drink. He indulged himself in this way frequently and it was not at all unusual for him to be drunk. Genghis Khan had to reprimand him several times for drunken behaviour. The youngest son Tolui had great military gifts and was clearly an accomplished and courageous general. Unfortunately he was even more of a drunkard then Ögödei. Genghis Khan had some hesitation choosing between Ögödei and Tolui as the successor to the throne.[95] Although he must have seen in the youngest son the more gifted military leader, he considered him to be too hot-headed to take control of the Mongol Empire. He therefore chose Ögödei.[96] Genghis Khan discussed his choice with his four sons. They promised their father to respect his wishes and to carry them out.[97] Genghis Khan attached a condition to his choice, namely that if Ögödei's successors should appear to be unsuitable for the throne, it should fall to the descendants of another of his sons.[98]

8

The hurricane from the east

In 1218 the empire of Muhammad II consisted of Khwarazm, Transoxiana, Afghanistan, Sistan, Khurasan, Mazandaran and Iraq-Ajemi. He had been considering the conquest of China[1] when news reaching him in 1215 that Peking had been captured by Genghis Khan disappointed his hopes. He had done little to unite the countries of his empire which were so different from each other.

In the preceding two centuries there had been many changes of power in Central and South-west Asia, most of the rulers one after the other putting their own interests first. Often one country was played off against another, so that the whole could be better controlled. The mass of the people were regarded as workers and were obliged to show utter submission.[2] The primarily Islamic population of those regions were only aware of a tribal relationship: there was no notion of nationalism.

Other unfortunate circumstances attended the rule of Sultan Muhammad. The incessant warfare, which had prevailed during his father's rule and continued under his own, caused much suffering in most of the regions. In Transoxiana and Afghanistan the fighting had only recently stopped. The Khwarazm army, recruited mainly from foreign mercenaries of Turkish origin, terrorized the people with savage cruelty. This army of mercenaries was, however, the sole support of Muhammad's throne,[3] and in his own interest he was obliged to subordinate the protection of his peoples to the pleasure of the army. At all cost he had to avoid upsetting the military aristocracy which had developed among the leaders of the army.

The difficult position in which Muhammad found himself was not improved by the malevolent influence of his mother, Terken Khatun. This obstinate and dangerous woman was born in the foreign military caste and felt herself to be closely allied to this aristocracy. It was accordingly of great importance to Muhammad to consider his mother's wishes as much as possible. He had yielded to her views in the appointment of the royal successor: it was not the eldest son Jalal al-Din who became crown prince, but his youngest son (whose mother was related to Terken Khatun). The choice had unfortunate results for Muhammad. Jalal al-Din became governor of Afghanistan and the crown prince was awarded the central part of the empire. In this latter region, which incorporated the provinces Khwarazm, Khurasan and Mazandaran, the real authority was exercised by Terken Khatun.[4] In her wickedness she took not the slightest account of the interest of her son. Functionaries who had been dismissed by Muhammad were ostentatiously restored to their posts by Terken Khatun. It was impossible for friction between mother and son to be avoided; eventually it became so serious that Muhammad's authority in the regions governed by Terken Khatun, who had her own court,[5] was to all intents and purposes no longer recognized.[6] These conflicts created tension between the Khwarazm shah and his military leaders.

There was no question of any central administrative organization in the Khwarazm empire. Muhammad, after the conquest of the various regions, had either killed or dismissed their governors, and had not replaced them with anybody; he stood therefore alone.[7] Neither the population nor the Khwarazm shah could fall back on an adequate governmental organization under the very difficult circumstances which the invasion of Genghis Khan placed them.[8] Both the Muslim structure of the caliphate of the Abbasids and the political Seljuq structure had been destroyed. Muhammad was incapable of creating a system by means of which he could not only unify his empire, but also get rid of the disruptive influence of his mother. He did not have at his disposal any skilful minister who could do this for him.

In 1218 Sultan Muhammad II was the prince of a large but divided empire. Although he was, in comparison with Genghis

Khan, highly educated, he was so obsessed with illusions of grandeur that he imagined the mere size of his empire was sufficient to ensure his fame. He failed to appreciate that he could have better employed the resources of his largely sedentary people if his authority had been more acceptable to them, and that the constant brutality of his army alienated him from his subjects.

After the blood-bath of Otrar, Muhammad prepared for an attack by Genghis Khan. Even before the approach of the Mongol army, the Khwarazm shah called a council of his military advisers to discuss measures to be taken against the anticipated invasion.[9] His son Jalal al-Din (or perhaps another council member) thought that the Khwarazm army should be concentrated on the Syr Darya to attack the Mongols as soon as they appeared there. The opportunity to rest after their long approach march would thus be denied them. Jalal al-Din offered to assume command of the Khwarazm army on the Syr Darya, if the sultan did not dare to do so himself. Most of the military advisers, judging by their proposal to withdraw behind the Amu Darya River, and then in the direction of Ghazna or of Iraq,[10] did not appear to view the coming battle with much confidence.

Muhammad decided not to engage the Mongols east of the Amu Darya. He realized, however, that he could not leave Transoxiana to the Mongols without a battle. In a number of towns he left strong troop concentrations behind. The citizens of his capital, Samarkand, were ordered to build a wall round the town; to pay for it they had to pay three years' tax in advance.[11] Many historians criticize the Khwarazm shah for not concentrating his forces to meet the Mongol attack; however, he did not have much opportunity to do so, for Muhammad had manoeuvred himself into a difficult position.

To cope with the increasing tension on his eastern frontier, he had to reinforce his army. To do this high taxes had to be imposed,[12] a measure strongly resisted in his newly formed empire. Here and there the people rose in rebellion. He could not therefore concentrate his army in one place; in order to keep the peace the Khwarazm shah was obliged to post numbers of his troops all over his territories,[13] a dislocation of the Kwarazm army which Genghis Khan swiftly and expertly exploited.

Muhammad was, however, not free to dispose of his army as he wished for other reasons: it consisted of members of various tribes who were often mutually hostile. In the garrisons a balance had to be maintained between troop units who hated each other.[14]

The Mongol army had made a great impression on Muhammad after the battle against Sübedei and Jochi in 1218 (see page 90). This battle was the reason why the Khwarazm shah subsequently avoided engaging in combat with the Mongols.[15] In deciding on his timorous and half-hearted plans of operation, the intelligence he received from his envoy Baha al-Din Razi from China played an important part. In north China the Mongols seemed to be invincible on the field of battle, but to be confronted with many difficulties when it came to capturing fortified towns. The Mongols had not gone further than the Huang-ho in north China.

In spite of his own high opinion of his grandeur, Muhammad was undoubtedly afraid of the Mongol conqueror who had succeeded in 20 years in subduing not only Central Asia, but also the mighty Chin empire. In so doing Genghis Khan had not suffered a single defeat. Muhammad did not dare to face such a brilliant general, who compelled universal respect. The giant with feet of clay began to collapse even before he had been touched.

His decision to retire behind the Amu Darya and to strengthen the garrisons in Transoxiana was probably taken in the hope that the fortified towns would present the Mongols with insuperable problems and that Genghis Khan would not march further than the Amu Darya. Muhammad did not know that Genghis Khan employed Chinese engineers to build and man siege engines such as battering rams, catapults and fire-floats. That the Khwarazm shah later did not even wish to use the Amu Darya as a line of defence caused him to be strongly criticized by his contemporaries.[16]

There are few reliable facts about the strength of the Khwarazm shah's army. In all probability it was considerably stronger than Genghis Khan's.[17] The numbers detached to garrison the various towns make it difficult to estimate the total strength of Muhammad's army. The contemporary sources contradict one another and give the impression that they are exaggerated.[18] The conclusion can indeed be drawn that Sultan Muhammad left a strong garrison in his capital Samarkand; but this was probably the largest body of troops in Transoxiana, which was abandoned to its fate.

TRANSOXIANA OVERRUN

On the basis of reports received from his Muslim advisers, Genghis Khan had been able to form an idea of the strength of the 'ruler of the west'. He certainly did not underestimate his prospective opponent. The war against the Khwarazm empire was carefully prepared.

In the summer of 1219 Genghis Khan gathered his army together on the Kara Irtish River. He took his young Merkit wife Qulan[19] and his minister Yeh-lü Chu'u-ts'ai[20] with him on this campaign. His youngest brother Temüge-otchigin remained behind in Mongolia as 'the guardian of hearth and home'.[21] In the autumn he moved forward over the Altai and Tarbagatai mountains to Qayaliq (the present-day Taldy Kurgan southeast of Lake Balkash), where Arslan, the khan of the Qarluqs, Barshuq, the idiqut of the Iughurs, and Sugnaq Tegin of Almaliq joined him.[22] It is known that Arslan brought 6,000 men with him and the Idiqut a tümen.[23]

The strength of Genghis Khan's army can only be guessed. The Russian orientalist Barthold writes: 'Our information on the distribution of the Mongol forces compels us to assume that Genghis Khan's army numbered scarcely less than 150,000 men in all and hardly more than 200,000 men.'[24] In chapter 5 it has been argued that this estimate by Barthold is too high. The manpower resources of the Turkish and Mongol tribes could not have yielded so many fighting forces. During the war in north China the Mongol army, in spite of its conquests, had suffered considerable losses. Many Mongols probably also died from epidemics. Bearing in mind the estimate given in chapter 5, and remembering the numbers of Muqali's army in north China, I cannot see that Genghis Khan took the field against the Khwarazm empire with an army of more than 90,000 men. That the Mongol army was able to fight an army stronger than itself was proved in north China.

We do not know what Genghis Khan's plan of campaign was. The possibility that he had only a limited objective in mind (to reach no further than the Amu Darya) cannot be ruled out. However, almost as soon as the Mongols had passed the Syr Darya any show of organized resistance was abandoned by the Khwarazm army. Such a skilled strategist as Genghis Khan perceived very quickly the shortcomings of his enemy. Armed with the intelligence he had received from his Muslim advisers, he turned the situation to his advantage.

The rule of terror which Muhammad had in the past often applied to quell subversive attempts now began to operate against him. As the Mongols drew near, many of his subjects went over to Genghis Khan. From them the Mongol conqueror obtained exact information about the political situation in Khwarazm and particularly about the quarrels between Sultan Muhammad on the one hand and Terken Khatun and the generals on the other. The success of his often daring operations indicates that Genghis Khan was well aware of all relevant political, military and geographical factors. During the campaign both he and his sons had the support of friendly Muslims who were familiar with local conditions and able to act as intermediaries with the population.[25]

In Genghis Khan's army there were many Turkish units. At first sight it appears strange that the Mongols in 1220 made no attempt to win the Turkish troops of the Khwarazm shah over to their side. These troops were apparently often ready to enter the Mongol service during parleys about a town's capitulation if they could thus save their lives. The unscrupulous Mongols accepted this offer to hasten the town's surrender, but soon afterwards the fate many others had received was meted out to the renegades – execution.[26] The fact that the Turkish troops could disown their sultan when driven into a tight corner showed how unreliable they were. Nor had Genghis Khan any guarantee that the deserters would always remain loyal to him. The numerical inferiority with which he marched into Khwarazm demanded (at least as long as the enemy's army was still unbroken) absolutely loyal troops. In 1221, when he no longer had much to fear from the enemy and it was necessary to replace his losses, Turkish troops were indeed accepted from the Khwarazm army, and even in fairly large numbers.

Coming from Qayaliq, Genghis Khan moved with his army through Semirechye, passing the Chu and the Talas rivers to Otrar, which lay on the eastern bank of the Syr Darya. He realized that the march to Khwarazm would make heavy demands on the horses; in order to spare them as much as possible he gave express orders that no one should go off hunting on his own accord. Hunts were only to be organized for the purpose of replenishing supplies.[27] Chaghatai had prepared the route followed by the Mongol army; in the section between Sairam Nor and Almaliq alone 48 bridges had been built, all of them suitable for carrying the heavy transport wagons.[28]

In the late autumn of 1219 Genghis Khan reached the border town of Otrar. Here he divided his army into four groups. Chaghatai and Ögödei were given command of the troops investing Otrar; among them were the Uighurs under Barshuq's command. Jochi marched off with a unit along the eastern bank of the Syr Darya to the towns of Signak and Jand. A detachment of about 5,000 men went upstream long the Syr Darya to Banakat.[29]

Genghis Khan, accompanied by his youngest son Tolui, moved with the main force in a south-westerly direction. The Mongols had no difficulty in crossing the Syr Darya: the rivers were probably frozen over.[30] The first place that Genghis Khan besieged was the fortress of Zarnuq; it surrendered without offering resistance. Instead of doing the obvious thing, namely marching on the capital Samarkand, Genghis Khan, led by some Turcoman guides, went along a little-used road to Nur. This town also surrendered without resistance to the troops under Sübedei's command.[31] Nur was one of the few towns in which the Mongols did not play havoc; they merely demanded a comparatively low tribute.[32]

In February 1220 Genghis Khan reached Bukhara.[33] After three days of siege the enemy garrison attempted to fight their way through the Mongol lines. Only a few of them managed to reach the Amu Darya and safety; the rest were slaughtered by the pursuing Mongols.[34] Abandoned by the troops, the demoralized town gave itself up. The citadel outside the town continued to fight, its garrison of 400 cavalry resisting courageously for twelve more days. The population of Bukhara had to give the Mongols every support in compelling the citadel to capitulate. After the surrender the surviving defenders without exception were put to death.[35]

Next it was the turn of Bukhara itself. The merchants who had bought up articles from the Mongol caravan (which had been massacred and robbed in Otrar) had to return these articles to Genghis Khan.[36] All the inhabitants were ordered to leave the town and were only permitted to take the clothes they were wearing with them. Everyone who hid in the town was mercilessly killed. The empty town offered much to the plundering Mongols. The people were divided into various groups. The artisans went as slaves to Mongolia; the strong young men had to follow the army to provide an expendable vanguard at the next storming of a town. Families were separated for ever. Women were also shown no mercy and there were heart-breaking scenes. The Mongols raped the women under the eyes of their fellow victims, who could only weep in their helplessness. Many chose death in the face of such terrible things.[37] The imam, his son and other Muslim leaders could not endure all this misery; knowing that it would mean their death they protested to the ruthless conquerors. As a final disaster a great fire broke out in the town. Most of the buildings were made of wood and the town was almost entirely destroyed.[38]

In March Genghis Khan left the stricken people and the burnt ruins of Bukhara. His next goal was Samarkand, the capital of Sultan Muhammad. The governor was Turghay Khan, a brother of Terken Khatun. Although little had been done about the wall around the town which the Khwarazm shah had given instructions to be built, the fortifications of Samarkand had been much strengthened. Genghis Khan was informed about this situation and about the numbers of the defending troops when he approached Otrar. This was the reason why he had first taken Bukhara, which lay further west.[39] The fall of Bukhara would undermine the morale of the inhabitants of the capital; moreover, the large numbers of prisoners taken at Bukhara could be used for the storming of the stronger Samarkand. Many of these doomed captives were in fact then driven forward before the Mongol army.

Genghis Khan approached Samarkand along both sides of the Zerafsan River.[40] After surrounding the town, he first occupied himself in inspecting the fortifications and the adjacent terrain.[41] To leave the defenders in uncertainty about the strength of his army, he had the prisoners also drawn up in battle order. As Chaghatai and Ögödei had joined their father when the siege began, bringing with them their own troops and large numbers of prisoners, the troops in the town got the impression that they were enclosed by a vast army.[42] Genghis Khan apparently wished to take no risk at Samarkand. During the siege he also added to his main force the unit that had reduced Banakat. Apart from the strong defences of the town, there was the possibility, which Genghis Khan did not ignore, that the Khwarazm shah might attempt to come to the rescue of his capital. Sultan Muhammad, although not risking a meeting with the Mongols himself, did in fact make two such attempts, sending first 10,000 cavalry and later a further 20,000. Before these troops reached Samarkand, they were forced to withdraw.[43]

To aggravate the Khwarazm shah's mistrust of his generals, Genghis Khan caused false letters to reach the sultan's hands. Among these letters, addressed to Genghis Khan, were the names of generals belonging to Terken Khatun's party.[44] This series of set-backs was apparently too much for Sultan Muhammad. In his despair he fled to the western part of his empire. During the siege of Samarkand Genghis Khan learned that the Khwarazm shah had passed the Amu Darya River near Tirmid in a state of fear and perplexity; only a few faithful followers accompanied him on his flight.[45] Little danger now threatening from outside Samarkand, Genghis Khan sent out some detachments while the siege was still going on.

On the third day of the siege the defenders made a sortie. The Mongols followed their usual tactics; slowly retreating until they were some distance from the town, they prepared an ambush from which they launched a counter-attack. About 50,000 of the Samarkand troops lost their lives in this battle. During the various assaults on the beleaguered town the Mongols as usual drove their prisoners in front of them as cannon-fodder. On the fifth day the garrison and citizens decided to surrender, although one unit of about 2,000 men declined to do so and shut themselves up in the citadel. The Turkish part of the garrison, under the leadership of the governor Turghay Khan, offered to go over to the Mongol service. The Mongols accepted this proposal only to speed up the surrender, as appeared later. The citadel defenders made one sortie and 1,000 men succeeded in breaking through the Mongol lines. The rest died in the fighting.

The Turkish deserters did not escape their fate. After the fall of the citadel the Mongols settled accounts with them. The whole contingent, numbering 30,000 men and including Turghay Khan, was put to death.[46] In Samarkand the population was also divided into different groups: artisans were sent to Mongolia; the young men reserved for the next siege; and the women forced to submit to the outrages of the victors. Everybody had to leave the town to allow the Mongols to plunder undisturbed. The Muslim priests were spared as they had not attempted resistance. The conquest of Samarkand ended in utter disaster for the townspeople. When the Chinese Taoist Ch'ang-ch'un stayed in Samarkand in 1221 and 1222, the great city had only a quarter of the original number of its inhabitants. Before the Mongol invasion Samarkand had housed 100,000 families.[47]

The siege of Otrar lasted longer than that of the other towns in Transoxiana. Governor Inalchuq had every reason to fight to the last. Here also the Turkish soldiers deserted, but Chaghatai and Ögödei wasted no time, merely ordering the traitors to be executed. After the surrender of the town the same procedure as in Bukhara and Samarkand was followed. The citadel, in which Inalchuq carried on the fight, lasted out for a month. Genghis Khan had given orders to take the governor alive. Inalchuq fought on until there was nobody else to help him in his resistance. He was taken prisoner and led to Genghis Khan, who made him pay cruelly for his behaviour in 1218.[48]

Jochi's march on Signak and Jand was carried out successfully. Jochi had been assigned this sector and any territory he conquered would become a part of his apanage.[49] He sent a Muslim to Signak to propose to the inhabitants that they should surrender without fighting. The envoy was murdered and a furious Jochi ordered the town to be stormed. After seven days of ceaseless fighting the Mongols forced their way into the town. Nearly all the inhabitants were killed. After a short period of rest Jochi moved on to Jand. The garrison had left the town when Jochi reached it on about 20 April 1220. The town opened its gates without resistance and as a reward Jochi spared the people. They were obliged, nevertheless, to leave the town for seven days to allow the Mongols to plunder in peace. A detachment sent out by Jochi also won the town of Yanikant.[50]

The troops which Genghis Khan had sent to Banakat were commanded by Alaq Noyan. Banakat resisted for three days. On the fourth day the Turkish units of the defending army surrendered, asking to enter the service of Genghis Khan. Alaq granted the request, but after the fall of the town they were put to death. There is some evidence that after the town was taken, Alaq joined Genghis Khan at the time of the siege of Samarkand.[51]

During the siege of Samarkand, when Genghis Khan had heard that Sultan Muhammad had fled, he dispatched three units on various tasks. He commissioned two of his best generals, Jebe and Sübedei, to pursue the Khwarazm shah.[52] Their campaign, which turned out to be one of the most daring raids in all military history, will be dealt with later. Alaq was ordered to take Kulab and Talikan consecutively.

The third detachment, presumably consisting of the troops which had taken Otrar under Chaghatai and Ögödei, went to Khojend, the capital of Ferghana.[53] The garrison there was not strong. The governor, Temur Melik, escaped with about 1,000 men to an island in the Syr Darya lying at a great distance from both shores. There he was fairly safe, but eventually had to leave as he was running short of food and arms. In the night he and his men left in a number of boats, intending to sail down the Syr Darya. The Mongols pursued him on both banks. Near Banakat they had stretched a chain across the river, but Temur Melik managed to cut it. Approaching Jand he found that his pursuers had made better preparations; they had built a pontoon bridge and erected catapults on the banks. The brave Temur Melik put his troops ashore on the west bank, left all his baggage, and escaped in the direction of Gurganj. He reached this town accompanied by only a few of his comrades.[54]

After the subjection of Transoxiana, Genghis Khan marched to the mountainous country south of Samarkand to rest his men and horses until the autumn of 1220.[55] From his residence, in the neighbourhood of the present Karshi, he dictated measures to re-establish normal life in Transoxiana.[56]

THE PURSUIT OF SULTAN MUHAMMAD II

While Genghis Khan and his main force withdrew for their summer rest, a Mongol army corps pursued the fleeing Khwarazm shah. This corps consisted at first of three tümen, which were under the command of Jebe Noyan, Sübedei Baghatur and Toquchar Baghatur.[57] Genghis Khan had given orders to follow Muhammad and to liquidate him before he had a chance to assemble fresh troops.[58] As speed was crucial, sieges and plundering had to be avoided as far as possible. Genghis Khan appointed Jebe supreme commander of the units which were assigned to the pursuit; Sübedei was his deputy.[59]

The fact that the Mongol conqueror detached such a force from his own army and ventured it deep into the Khwarazm empire shows that even at that early stage he did not anticipate much more opposition. When he sent out the three tümen, he had received reliable information from deserters about the weakness of the sultan's army.[60]

The facts reported about the flight of Sultan Muhammad and about the pursuing Mongols do not always agree. Between the middle of April and the middle of May 1220 the Khwarazm shah crossed the Amu Darya and went via Balkh towards Nishapur.[61] His pursuers adopted normal Mongol tactics in such operations: they moved forward as rapidly as possible, only engaging in combat when it became inevitable. Their first objective was Balkh, where they met no opposition. In Nishapur, Muhammad showed more interest in urban pleasures than in warfare. It was only when he heard that the Mongols were drawing near that he fled with his son Jalal al-Din in a north-westerly direction through Isfarayin to Rayy. He managed to conceal his tracks from the Mongols.[62]

At Zava (present-day Turbat-i-Haidari) the pursuers found the gates shut, and the citizens refused to give them food. In order to lose no time the Mongols were about to leave, but the people lined the walls and began to jeer at them, so they stormed the town and many of the inhabitants were punished by death.[63] The next town, Nishapur, presented no difficulties. Jebe gave orders that in future food had to be given to each Mongol unit.[64] Jebe and Sübedei lost the sultan's trail near Nishapur and went off in various directions seeking clues.

Sübedei went south-east to Jam, and then north-west. Travelling via Tus, Isfarayin and Damghan (none of which he spared) he went to Rayy. Jebe's route was from Nishapur to Mazandaran, where he caused much destruction in the region of Amol.[65] He left some troops behind along the Caspian coast. Later they took Terken Khatun and her followers prisoner in one of the castles there. The two Mongol generals met again at Rayy. Meanwhile Sultan Muhammad had fled from Rayy in the direction of Qazvin, where his son Rukn al-Din lay with an army of 30,000 men. The Khwarazm shah now had the opportunity to strike the scattered advancing tümen of Jebe and Sübedei one at a time, but he failed to do so. He sent his wives, who were accompanying him, to the fort of Qarun, west of Hamadan. He sought advice from the amirs of Iraq-Ajemi about the best place in the Zagros mountains to offer resistance to the approaching Mongols. His increasing suspicions, which had become obsessional, prevented him from being able to decide which advice to follow. The news that the arrival of the Mongols was imminent sent him off despairingly in the direction of his great enemy the caliph of Baghdad; half way there he changed his mind and returned to the fort of Qarun.

Jebe and Sübedei had been told in Rayy that the sultan was going to Hamadan. During Muhammad's journey from Qazvin to Qarun the Mongols actually caught up with him but did not recognize him. The sultan succeeded in reaching the fort of Qarun, but when the Mongols surrounded the place he had once more disappeared.[66] In the vicinity of Hamadan, Sultan Muhammad engaged in combat for the first and last time with his pursuers. He had with him an army of 20,000 men which encountered the tümen of Jebe. The desperate Muhammad had only one idea in his mind, however: to save himself. He left the army to fend for itself, and Jebe defeated it. With his sons Muhammad fled via the Elburz mountains to the Caspian coast, and now began the last stage of his journey. He sailed out to an island in the entrance of the bay of Astrabad (probably the present-day Ashurada Peninsula). He was a sick man, suffering from pneumonia. Soon after reaching the island he died in December 1220 (or January 1221).[67]

It is not clear what the Mongols did after the Khwarazm shah had fled to the Caspian coast. The fact that he was on the island was probably unknown to Jebe and Sübedei until later.[68] When they heard of his death they reported it to Genghis Khan. Jebe asked for permission to continue his conquests for a year or two and then to return to Mongolia via the Caucasus.[69] Eventually permission was granted; the resulting campaign, which lasted until 1223 and no longer had anything to do with the pursuit of Muhammad, developed into one of the most remarkable military operations in the history of the world (see chapter 9).

The role of Toquchar's tümen in the pursuit is difficult to determine. According to one of the sources Toquchar disobeyed Genghis Khan's orders to avoid the destruction and plundering of enemy property, and so fell into disgrace with the Mongol conqueror.[70] This story, however, is improbable, for the tümen of Jebe and Sübedei also plundered various towns during the pursuit.[71]

Genghis Khan apparently gave Toquchar different orders from those of Jebe and Sübedei. Toquchar's tümen had to remain in Khurasan to prevent (as will become apparent later) an escape southwards of the enemy troops in Gurganj, among whom were the sons of the dead Sultan Muhammad. During these operations Toquchar conquered Nasa and then made an unsuccessful attempt to take Nishapur, and may have been killed during the siege. His successor, Börkei Noyan, abandoned the attempt to take the town and went to Sabzavar, which he captured in three days. The citizens of this town also had to pay heavily for the resistance they had offered.[72]

THE DESTRUCTION OF THE WORK OF CENTURIES

After the flight of Sultan Muhammad his empire quickly disintegrated. In Khurasan and Ghazna, and later also in the original Khwarazm, power fell into the hands of the local governors or adventurers ambitious to carve out a princedom for themselves.[73] In Gurganj, Terken Khatun governed the central part of the sultanate. The province of Khwarazm, which since 1214 had been undisturbed by the invasions of enemy armies or tribes, had grown into one of the most prosperous parts of the empire;[74] its capital Gurganj, an important trade

centre and junction of caravan routes, lay near the marshy delta
of the Amu Darya. This estuary formed an oasis in the middle
of the Kara Kum and the Kizil Kum deserts. By means of a
system of canals the water was used for irrigation, while dikes
protected the town against flooding.[75]

Terken Khatun, who was highly respected by the army, was
in Gurganj at the time of the Mongol invasion. Genghis Khan
knew very well that there was a powerful army in this part of
Khwarazm, and that it formed a threat. Certainly Jochi's units
on the lower Syr Darya were in a dangerous position. Genghis
Khan therefore decided to win Terken Khatun over. He sent an
envoy to Muhammad's mother to tell her that the Mongols
were waging war only against her son and not against her. At
the moment when this envoy arrived in Gurganj, Terken
Khatun received news that the sultan had fled westwards. She
concluded that she had better follow his example. Before
departing she ordered about twenty princes, captured from the
territories subjected by the Khwarazm shah and held prisoner
in Gurganj, to be drowned in the Amu Darya. With her family
she fled to Mazandaran, to seek refuge in a fort; but it was later
taken by Jebe's troops. The whole family was sent to Genghis
Khan, at that moment in Talaqan. He immediately had all the
male members executed and divided the women among his sons
and sub-commanders. Terken Khatun was sent as a prisoner to
Mongolia. When she and the other women members of her
family were to leave on their journey, they were sadistically
instructed by the Mongols to show their grief by screaming at
the tops of their voices.[76]

It was only after Temur Melik reached Gurganj that the
troops there went into action. In the summer of 1220 the former
governor of Khojend attacked Jochi's positions, and even
recaptured Yanikant from the Mongols. Differences of opinion
in the military command at Gurganj was the reason why the
brave Temur Melik, the man who managed to imperil Jochi's
forces, took no further action.[77]

After the death of Sultan Muhammad three of his sons,
including Jalal al-Din and the crown prince Uzlagh Shah,
crossed the Caspian Sea with some followers to the Mangishlak
Peninsula, from where they travelled to Gurganj, arriving there
in the winter of 1220–1.[78] The crown prince, who had been

selected by Terken Khatun, relinquished his rights to the throne in favour of Jalal al-Din. Even the hopeless situation of the sultanate could not bring the Turkish amirs to form a front against the Mongol invaders. A plot to assassinate Sultan Jalal al-Din, in which Uzlagh Shah was probably involved, was betrayed.[79] The new sultan, accompanied by Temur Melik and an escort of 300 cavalry, left Gurganj. The two brothers of Jalal al-Din did not wait for the Mongols, who were advancing on Gurganj, but also escaped in a southerly direction.[80]

Genghis Khan, probably anticipating escape attempts from Gurganj, had ordered the tümen of Toquchar to lay a cordon in the north of Khurasan. Jalal al-Din wanted to go via the Kara Kum Desert to Ghazna in east Afghanistan, the region which he administered as governor before the Mongol invasion. The Mongol detachment of 700 men near Nasa was unexpectedly attacked by Jalal al-Din and his cavalry who managed to pass the Mongol lines and reach Nishapur. Jalal al-Din's brothers were less fortunate: they were killed either during some fighting or after being taken prisoner. Jala al-Din continued his flight and was immediately chased by the Mongols. By forced marches he managed to escape and reached Ghazna.[81] Although it is possible that Toquchar had incurred Genghis Khan's displeasure because his tümen had plundered against his orders, it is more probable that the Mongol conqueror, after learning that Jalal al-Din had escaped, was indignant that Toquchar had not succeeded in carrying out his instructions to prevent attempts at flight from Gurganj.

In the autumn of 1220 Genghis Khan went to Tirmid. The Mongols demanded surrender without battle, but were refused. The town fell after eleven days of siege, after which the usual treatment was given to the town: partial massacre of the population, plundering and destruction. From Tirmid the Mongol conqueror went with his army to a place north-east of this town, where he spent the winter on the banks of the Vakhsh River. When the winter was over he marched with his army across the Amu Darya. Balkh surrendered without a struggle; nevertheless many citizens were put to death.[82] After the occupation of Balkh, Genghis Khan left the conquest of the other regions to his sons. Chaghatai and Ögödei went to Gurganj to take the town, together with Jochi. Tolui was charged with the capture of Khurasan. Genghis Khan himself stayed between Balkh and Talaqan to await news from his sons.

The flight of Sultan Muhammad's family and the prospect of being trapped by the Mongols at last succeeded in creating a unanimous military leadership in Gurganj. One of the generals, Khumar Tegin, assumed the title of sultan now that the real sultan had left the scene. In order to engage the great and strongly defended town, Genghis Khan could not rely only on Jochi's troops. He therefore ordered the units of Chaghatai and Ögödei to join forces with Jochi to conquer Gurganj.[83] The siege of the town, which was partly surrounded by marshes, was not easy. As there were no large stones anywhere near, trees were cut into pieces to use as projectiles in the catapults.[84] The new leader of the Gurganj government, Khumar Tegin, was so impressed by the strength of the besieging army that he went to the Mongols to give himself up.[85]

After a few days the Mongols succeeded in entering the town, but the inhabitants defended themselves bravely. Heavy losses were suffered on both sides. The slow progress of the Mongols was attributed to Jochi's desire to take this large and important town undamaged, for it was intended that it should belong to his apanage. Jochi demanded several times that the people should quickly surrender and so avoid the destruction of their town. Chaghatai was very annoyed at Jochi's continual parleys. This led to a serious quarrel between the two brothers which did not pass unnoticed by the Mongol troops.[86] When Genghis Khan was informed of what was going on, he intervened and appointed Ögödei as supreme commander.[87] Ögödei forthwith resumed the siege vigorously. The desperate inhabitants carried on the unequal struggle bravely, the women, children and old people doing what they could to help. The Mongols had to fight district after district. When the situation had become hopeless and the town had caught fire, the exhausted defenders offered to surrender and asked for mercy. However, it was too late for Jochi to carry out his promises. The town fell in April 1221.

The misery which had been inflicted on the towns in Transoxiana was now the lot of Gurganj. A large number of artisans were sent off to Mongolia. Children and young women were taken prisoner; the rest were massacred. The fate of the town, already ravaged by fire and plundering, was however worse than that of most other towns. Either by coincidence or by the intent of the Mongols, the dike along the Amu Darya broke. A large part of the town was flooded and many of those who had survived the massacre were drowned.[88]

After the fall of Gurganj Jochi remained in the region of the Aral Sea. Chaghatai and Ögödei returned to Genghis Khan. In February 1221 the conqueror had sent Tolui to Khurasan with orders to subdue it. Tolui did this so thoroughly that the province never again recovered.[89] It is of interest to note that Genghis Khan's youngest son left with only a small contingent of the original Mongol army. He reinforced his fighting strength during the campaign with Turkish troops from the enemy's army – their desertion took place voluntarily or under duress.[90] The losses among the Mongols were presumably of such proportions that such reinforcement was necessary. Eventually Tolui led an army consisting largely of former Khwarazm troops.[91] As the wars dragged on this became common throughout the Mongol army, and more and more Turkish troops from Khwarazm went over to Genghis Khan.[92]

Tolui went first westwards, crossed the Murgab River, took the towns of Maruchak and Sarakhs and then made for Merv.[93] This was a considerable centre with an extensive cotton and silk industry. It was the town of the *Thousand and One Nights* and the former capital of the Seljuqs. On 25 February Tolui stood before the gates. For six days he made his preparations and on the seventh day gave the order to storm its walls. Although the people offered resistance they realized that they were in a hopeless situation. The governor offered surrender on condition that human lives were spared, an offer which Tolui accepted to hasten the capitulation. However, after the handing over of the town he broke his promise. The inhabitants were driven out through the gates and each soldier was given 300 or 400 victims to behead. The Turkish troops who had deserted to Tolui were also given a share in the work of the executioners.[94] Only 400 artisans were spared for transportation to Mongolia as slaves. The mausoleum of Sultan Sanjar was set on fire and his tomb plundered.[95] The irrigation works in the vicinity of Merv were heavily damaged.[96] This was not the end of the disaster for Merv. Those who had somehow managed to escape the mass beheading re-entered the town after the departure of the Mongols, but a detachment of the Mongol rearguard returned unexpectedly, enticed the survivors outside the walls with false promises and made sure that they did not again escape their grisly fate. Merv, once one of the greatest cities of Islam, had lost the majority of its inhabitants.[97]

The next large town to be approached by the Mongols was Nishapur. In the summer of 1220 it had offered no resistance to Jebe and Sübedei, but later it adopted a more hostile attitude. In November 1220 an assault by Toquchar's tümen was repulsed, and Toquchar was killed. When they saw Tolui's great army the inhabitants wished to parley about surrender, but Tolui refused to have anything to do with their spokesmen. The assault began on 7 April 1221. After three days the Mongols forced their way in.[98] As in Merv, the townspeople were driven out to be massacred. To avenge the death of his brother-in-law Toquchar, Tolui gave orders to raze the town to the ground so thoroughly that the land on which it stood could be ploughed. Even the cats and dogs were killed. Toquchar's widow demanded a share in the massacre of the townspeople. Pyramids were made of the heads which had been cut off. The heads of the men, women and children were kept in separate rows.[99]

After this treatment of Nishapur, where nothing and nobody was spared, Tolui went to Herat. He sent a small detachment to Tus, where it destroyed and robbed the mausoleum of the caliph Harun al-Rashid.[100] The garrison at Herat wanted to fight, but the people took no risk and opened the gates. This time Tolui spared the civilians but a number of the garrison troops were put to death. He made a Mongol and a Muslim responsible for the government of the town, after which he returned to his father, who was at Talaqan. Genghis Khan's youngest son had carried out his task of subjecting the most important towns in Khurasan in less than three months.[101] During Tolui's campaign much that had been created to the glory of the Islamic civilization had been irreparably destroyed.

Until the return of Tolui, Genghis Khan had remained in the neighbourhood of Talaqan, a fort situated at the junction of roads to Khurasan, Sistan and Ghazna. The fort had a strong and valiant garrison and had been earlier besieged without success. Genghis Khan decided to command the siege himself. Presumably he had too few troops to compel the fort to surrender, but in the summer of 1221, shortly after the arrival of Tolui, the town fell into the hands of the Mongols.[102]

Sultan Jalal al-Din Mangubirdi took steps to gather round him in Ghazna a number of local rulers, and with their help he assembled a reasonably well-equipped army of about 60–70,000 men, although there was little coherence among the widely different tribal units.[103] During the winter of 1220 to 1221 Jalal al-Din remained in Ghazna, but in the early spring of 1221 he moved northwards. Near the Ghori River he fell on a small Mongol detachment, inflicting on them heavy losses and compelling them to retreat. Genghis Khan reacted immediately: he sent Shigi Qutuqu with an army to punish the sultan. Jalal al-Din, who had gone to Parwan, marched to meet Shigi Qutuqu. Just outside Parwan they engaged battle. Jalal al-Din's troops, who were dismounted, fought with great courage. The action was broken off when darkness fell. Next day Shigi Qutuqu tried to alarm his enemy by using dummies to give the impression that he had received reinforcements. Jalal al-Din, however, made no attempt to avoid battle and his troops again fought as infantry. When the sultan judged the moment had come, he commanded his cavalry to mount and charge. The Mongols were badly defeated and Shigi Qutuqu was obliged to flee with what was left of his army to Genghis Khan.[104]

This victory roused some hope in the deeply humiliated survivors in Transoxiana and Khurasan. Yet it became the occasion for a renewal of the apparently intractable discord among the members of the dying Khwarazm empire, when Jalal al-Din's allies quarrelled over the booty. Tempers became so hot that a part of the sultan's army quitted his service,[105] so that his numerical strength dwindled considerably.

During the siege of Talaqan it was not only Tolui who had joined forces with Genghis Khan. After the fall of Gurganj, Chaghatai and Ögödei had also returned to their father. The news of Jalal al-Din's first victory near the Ghori River had led Genghis Khan to march in a south-easterly direction. His route passed through Bamian, which refused to give itself up to the Mongol army when it approached. The siege that then became necessary caused Genghis Khan much delay,[106] and during the fighting one of his favourite grandsons, Mö'etüken, a son of Chaghatai, was killed.[107] When the town fell, Genghis Khan ordered no prisoners to be taken: to avenge his grandson's death every living person in Bamian was executed. Even unborn children in their mother's wombs were run through with the sword.[108] The place where Bamian had stood was given the name of 'Accursed Town' and nobody was permitted to live there ever again. This prohibition was strictly followed: seven centuries later the ruins of Bamian still have a sinister look.

Near Bamian Genghis Khan was told of Shigi Qutuqu's defeat. He took the news calmly,[109] but he knew what these two successive reverses meant. To prevent the overthrown countries from plucking up their courage as a result of these victories and perhaps rising in rebellion, he went with all speed, marching day and night, to Parwan.[110] There he inspected the battlefield. He criticized the dispositions chosen by Shigi Qutuqu, and felt that this was enough of a punishment for his Tatar stepson.

Near Ghazna Genghis Khan received intelligence that Jalal al-Din had marched off in the direction of the Indus with his depleted army. He therefore left Ghazna undisturbed for the time being.[111] Somewhere near Dinkot (in the neighbourhood of present-day Kalabagh) at the end of 1221 he met Jalal al-Din on the west bank of the Indus. The sultan was busy collecting boats to cross the river. With the courage of desperation his forces took up their arms. For some time the issue was in doubt, but finally Genghis Khan's guards mounted an attack to bring the battle to a speedy conclusion.[112] When the battle was ending Jalal al-Din, who had led his troops with great courage, leaped on his horse into the Indus and swam across the river under a hail of arrows. Genghis Khan, who had ordered him to be taken prisoner, followed the brave conduct of his enemy with admiration.[113]

After the battle about 4,000 men managed to reach safety on the east bank of the Indus. Later they were joined by 300 cavalry who had crossed further to the south.[114] Jalal al-Din tried without much success to get help from the sultan of Delhi. Not until 1222 did Genghis Khan send one or two tümen to the east bank of the Indus, but the high temperature hindered the Mongols from achieving any victories. They did reach Multan, but were in no condition to take the town.[115]

Jalal al-Din's victory at Parwan had given hope to the people of Khurasan and some towns even rebelled against the Mongol occupation. Genghis Khan left no one in any doubt what would happen to such uprisings. Herat, which Tolui had spared in the spring, was one of these towns. The Mongol General Elchidei was ordered to take it and punish the citizens. They put up a long and brave fight and it was not until June 1222 that Herat capitulated. Elchidei carried out his instructions to the letter: without exception the townspeople were beheaded – a labour that lasted seven days. And as they had done previously, when they had finished their work and departed, they sent a detachment back to surprise and finish off any people who had escaped. Meanwhile some families who had started the resettlement of Merv committed the folly of murdering the Muslim governor appointed by Tolui. Shigi Qutuqu was told to deal with these people. In spite of his defeat near Parwan Genghis Khan had not disgraced his Tatar stepson. A unit of his army commanded by Törbei took the town.[116] The executions were carried out with great precision and here too, when they were over and the Mongols had gone, a detachment returned to trap and kill any survivors. In addition to Herat and Merv there were probably other towns which rebelled. The people of Balkh had saved their lives in the spring of 1221 by offering no resistance when Genghis Khan appeared; in the autumn, however, they decided to revolt, and the whole population was massacred.

After the defeat of Jalal al-Din, Genghis Khan went north along the Indus River to begin a remarkable campaign. His objective was a region south of the Hindu Kush, where he established his winter quarters. In this rough mountainous country, concealing a large number of still unreduced forts, he was confronted with a terrain that made invasion a precarious undertaking. It is indicative of the world conqueror's brilliant gifts as a general that his army never once got into difficulties.[117]

In the spring of 1222 Ögödei was ordered to overthrow Ghazna and take strong measures against it, so that it could not again be used as a base from which Jalal al-Din might make a sally. Most of the people were massacred and the town was methodically destroyed.[118]

9
The great raid

While waiting for Genghis Khan's reply to his request to withdraw via the Caucasus (see page 107), Jebe, together with Sübedei, laid a trail of destruction through Iraq-Ajemi and Azerbaijan.[1]

Rayy was the first to suffer: the town was mercilessly ravaged and the population partly massacred. Spurred on by the Sunnis they then wrought great damage in Qum, the chief town of the Shi'is.[2] The Sunnis' pleasure in this deed was short-lived, for they themselves were the next victims of the Mongols. Hamadan surrendered without a struggle, but was only able to stop any plundering by paying the Mongols an indemnity. Next it was the turns of Zanjan and then Qazvin. Both towns were sacked and partly destroyed, while the townsfolk suffered heavy losses from many acts of brutality. Özbeg, the atabeg of Azerbaijan, who lived in Tabriz, purchased immunity for his town by handing over a considerable sum of money and providing the raiders with clothing and large numbers of horses.[3] The Mongols took full advantage of this arrangement, returning several times to Tabriz for more supplies.[4]

From Tabriz, Jebe and Sübedei rode north, setting up their winter quarters in the Mugan Steppe. In this region the month of January is unusually mild.[5] While they were there Kurd and Turcoman nomads came down from the surrounding hill country to offer their services. They were really no more than freebooters and thought they could not do better than enter the service of the triumphant Mongol armies. In the Mugan Steppe the attention of Jebe and Sübedei was diverted elsewhere. In

January and February 1221 they made a reconnaissance towards the kingdom of Georgia, and entered it via the Kura River.[6] Their intention was not so much to attack the country as to plunder it. The Kurds and Turcoman who had joined them were sent off in the vanguard.[7] In defence of his country king Giorgi III Lacha (1212–23) advanced to meet them with an army of about 10,000 men. The two armies met south of Tiflis (Tbilisi), where the Mongols were driven back.[8] Jebe and Sübedei then withdrew, but began a campaign of attrition by constant counter-raids on the Georgian army.[9] Finally the Mongols went over to the attack and inflicted a shattering defeat on their exhausted enemy.

In March 1221 the two Mongol generals returned to Azerbaijan. In their usual way they besieged Maragheh by driving prisoners in front of them as cannon-fodder. At the end of the month they entered the town and large numbers of the inhabitants were put to death. Jebe and Sübedei planned to go to Baghdad to hold to ransom the caliphate of the Abbasids, which would have had disastrous results for the caliph. His small army was in the northern part of Iraq-Arabi and in any event could not possibly have resisted the Mongols. The crusaders, who had just taken Damietta, would undoubtedly have exploited to the full any defeat of the caliph. Jebe and Sübedei, however, turned against Hamadan, which did not surrender this time without resistance. The people fought to the bitter end and inflicted such heavy losses on the Mongols that they began to doubt whether they could continue the siege.[10] When at last the town fell, a terrible fate awaited the population: most of them were killed and what was left of the town was burned.[11]

Via Ardabil, where they made further havoc, the Mongols went again in the autumn of 1221 to Georgia. When they arrived there Jebe and Sübedei saw that a strong Georgian army had been formed in the neighbourhood of Tiflis; nevertheless, in November 1221[12] they again entered the little Christian kingdom along the Kura River. The brave Georgian cavalry rode out to meet them, but Sübedei, turning tail, enticed them into an ambush prepared by Jebe.[13] Once again the Georgians suffered a heavy defeat. The fugitives from the scattered army sought protection in Tiflis. The Mongols did not bother to take this town, but plundered the southern part of Georgia,[14] after which they went to the Islamic Shirvan. Here they occupied and ravaged the town of Chamaka, then moved northwards through the narrow pass of Derbent.

After getting permission from Genghis Khan, they left the country south of the Caucasus. There was no fear that it presented any threat to them, after they had destroyed and plundered Iraq-Ajemi, Azerbaijan and Georgia, and massacred so many of the inhabitants. With typical ingenuity and boldness Jebe and Sübedei forced their way along the difficult passes through the Caucasus. When Derbent refused to surrender, they promised to leave the town alone if they were given the services of ten guides to lead the way through the mountains. With typical brutality the Mongols warned the guides not to play any tricks; they beheaded one of them to show what fate awaited the rest if they did not point out the right way. North of the Caucasus the Mongols set foot for the first time on European soil. Russia was the first European country to make acquaintance of this until then unknown people.

In general, estimates agree about the strength of the combined armies of Jebe and Sübedei. Each of the two generals had one tümen under his command when they left a position near Samarkand in 1220. By the autumn of 1221 the composition of these armies had naturally changed because of losses and reinforcements; nevertheless it is unlikely that their maximum numbers ever exceeded 20,000. A larger force would not have been able to carry out the long marches and rapid movements which the Mongols made in the Caucasus, where the deep valleys, bad roads and narrow passes were unsuitable for the manoeuvring of larger units.[15] As it was, Jebe and Sübedei were able to mount unexpected operations in the mountainous terrain. Their troops often moved without full marching kit, and as they penetrated deeper into enemy territory they discarded more and more unnecessary baggage.[16]

THE FIRST MONGOL INVASION OF RUSSIA

In the beginning of the seventh century a Turkish tribe, the Khazar, settled in the south Russian steppes. The empire they founded there was a considerable one, but in the ninth century its significance began to decline. The Khazars were able to hold on until the beginning of the tenth century, when they were driven out by the Turkish Pechenegs. These Pechenegs, who in their turn were dislodged from the steppes between the Emba and the Ural rivers by the Oghuz, finally took possession of the region stretching from the Don to Moldavia. The Khazars were left with only the country lying between the Don, Volga and the Caucasus. By about 1030 the Khazar Empire, after the combined assaults of Byzantium and the prince of Kiev, had lost all its former might. In 1036 Kiev also inflicted a heavy defeat on the Pechenegs, who then claimed compensation from Byzantium for the territories they had lost to Kiev. The subsequent wars lasted for a long time. In them Byzantium was aided by newcomers in the shape of a Turkish tribe called Qipchaq or Cuman. Towards the end of the eleventh century the Cumans drove the Pechenegs towards the Danube. A combined attack by Byzantium and the Cumans in 1091 reduced the Pechenegs to a tribe from which nothing more was to be feared. The Cumans were now the unchallenged masters in south Russia.

These Cumans or Qipchaqs are known to history under various names. The Russians called them Polovtsy, while in Byzantium they were called Ko(u)manoi, from which the name Cuman was derived. The name Qipchaq was also kept after they had been defeated by the Mongols. The later Mongol khanate was given the name khanate Qipchaq (Dasht-i-Qipchaq).

After Jebe and Sübedei had ridden through the pass of Derbent, the Alans, the Cherkesses and Lezgians (tribes living in the north of the Caucasus) united against the unknown invaders. The Cumans also joined the alliance. The first battle of the Mongols against this league remained indecisive,[17] but Jebe and Sübedei had no intention of leaving matters like that. By subtle diplomacy they succeeded in persuading the Cumans to remain neutral; they reminded them of the Turkish-Mongol fellowship and promised them a share of the booty if the Caucasian tribes were defeated. When this arrangement had been satisfactorily settled, Jebe and Sübedei attacked the Alans and their allies with such violence that resistance was soon broken. Then the Mongols turned against the Cumans, who were also defeated. Without overdue haste the Mongols pursued the fleeing Cumans in a north-westerly direction.

Early in 1222 a Mongol detachment went to the Crimea, where there were some Genetian and Genoese trading stations. The Mongols subjected the biggest port, the Genoese Soldaia, to heavy plundering.[18] The defeated Cumans had withdrawn in the direction of Galich and Kiev, where they appealed for help from the Russian princes. Russia at that time was divided into a large number of princedoms; it did not extend further south than a line running east–west just south of Kiev (see page 164). The Russian princes were by no means allies of the Cumans; they regarded them as representatives of the plunderers who made perpetual inroads on their south flank. It is not impossible that if the Russian princes had ignored the problems of the Cumans, Jebe and Sübedei would have left the Russians in peace.

The khan of the Cumans, Kotian, was however the father-in-law of one of the powerful Russian noblemen, Prince Mstislav of Galich,[19] who proceeded to unite a number of princedoms, including the mighty Kiev, against the Mongols. The prince of Suzdal-Vladimir also promised support, but as he had no real interest in helping his rivals to solve their problems, he took his time about it.[20] The princes joined forces against the Mongols mainly because nobody in Russia had any idea where this unknown people came from, who they were, what language they spoke or what religion they followed.[21]

When the Mongols learned that the Russian princes had offered to help the Cumans, they sent ten spokesmen to assure the Russians that they had no hostile intentions against them. They were at war only with the Cumans who, they said, had also caused much harassment to the Russians. The Mongol truce bearers were all put to death.[22] Four years earlier the Khwarazm shah had brought disaster on his own head by such treatment.

A Russian army reinforced by the Cumans and totalling, it is said, 30,000 men[23] concentrated on the Dnieper. Yet the Russians could only oppose the iron discipline and great battle experience of the Mongol troops with their numerical superiority; this was a situation to which the Mongols were accustomed. From the beginning there was dissension between the most eminent Russian princes about the way the Mongols should be engaged. This quarrel between Prince Mstislav of Galich and Prince Mstislav of Kiev led to a lack of co-ordination in the Russian strategy.[24]

Jebe and Sübedei quickly learned that they were out-numbered. They therefore decided to retreat. A rearguard kept an eye on the Russian movements. The Mongols were able to sustain such a retreat for a considerable time, with their experienced and well-disciplined units. For nine days the two Mongol generals evaded the Russians,[25] who gradually found themselves further and further from their own borders. Once again the Mongols sent envoys to the Russians, this time to protest against the murder of their ten peace makers. They also reproached the Russians for wishing to attack them without reason. On this occasion the envoys returned. They bore a message that the Russians would not be content until the Mongol army had returned the way it had come, for they feared that after conquering the country of the Cumans, it would invade their own princedoms.

The first engagement resulted in favour of the Russians. The prince of Galich, accompanied by the prince of Volynia, defeated the Mongol rearguard east of the bend in the Dnieper. Prince Mstislav of Galich, wishing to claim the glory of the victory for himself, took his army, the Volynians and the Cumans across the little Kalka River, which flows into the Sea of Azov.[26] He did this without informing the other princes. He had become over-confident, and after making his river crossing he neglected to take sufficient security precautions. The prince of Kiev, with the rest of the Russian army, was still some distance from the Kalka River. Jebe and Sübedei took advantage of this situation, which had been created by their method of retreating; at the end of May 1222[27] they turned to attack.* They threw themselves against both the Russian front

---

* It is generally accepted that this battle took place on 16 June 1223 (Grekov and Iakoubovski, 1939, p. 193, and Spuler, 1965, p. 13). However, it is unlikely that it happened in June of that year. After crossing the Caucasus Jebe and Sübedei would have been in south Russia for nearly one and a half years. This period seems far too long for what had taken place before the battle at the Kalka River. The two Mongol generals returned to Genghis Khan while he stayed on the right bank of the Syr Darya River. The world conqueror arrived there in January 1223 and began his march back to Mongolia in the autumn of the same year (see page 128).

and flanks. In the marshy terrain the prince of Galich had little chance to manoeuvre and, in any case, the ferocity with which the Mongols fought was too much for their opponents. The Cumans fled, causing confusion among the Russian ranks. The prince of Galich, seeing that his position was hopeless, decided to retreat. He managed to escape with his life and a small number of his troops. Among the Cumans also only a minority survived.

Prince Mstislav of Kiev, watching from the western bank of the Kalka could, or would, do nothing to help his namesake. After the prince of Galich's defeat the prince of Kiev realized that a retreat would be fatal before an enemy who reacted so quickly. He therefore entrenched himself on a dominating hilltop, but before he could complete his defences Jebe and Sübedei attacked. After trying to repulse them for three days, the besieged prince offered his army's surrender on condition that he should be allowed to return to Kiev with his forces. As usual the Mongols accepted this proposal in order to hasten the surrender. As soon as the Russians were disarmed, however, they were slaughtered. The execution of Prince Mstislav of Kiev and his fellow princes took place in the manner the Mongols used for royal personages: without bloodshed. The Mongols buried them under a floor of planks on which they celebrated their victory with a feast.[28]

The prince of Galich was able to reach safety behind the Dnieper with the remnants of his army. In order to hinder the Mongols' crossing of this broad river, he destroyed as many ships as he could find. The troops of the slow-moving prince of Suzdal-Vladimir had advanced no further at that moment in the battle of the Kalka than Chernigov. But what the Russians feared did not happen: Jebe and Sübedei did indeed pursue the prince of Galich, but after plundering some towns in the south they turned around. Near Tsaritsin (Stalingrad, since 1961 Volgograd) they crossed the Volga. Then at the end of 1222 they moved in a north-easterly direction towards the Bulgars of the Volga-Kama.

The Mongols were defeated in an ambush prepared by this Turkish tribe.[29] Subsequently Jebe and Sübedei returned to Genghis Khan northwards along the Caspian and the Aral seas. In 1223 the two tümen, who were probably exhausted by then, rejoined the main Mongol army,[30] which was situated in the steppes east of the Syr Darya River.[31] Genghis Khan showed great appreciation of the deeds of his two generals. Jebe, whom he had charged with the supreme command of the expedition, was particularly praised, but Sübedei also received his share of honour.[32] Jebe did not survive this campaign long.[33] The man who was probably the greatest cavalry general in the history of the world disappeared from the story of the Mongol Empire, and we may assume that he died in 1223 or shortly after. The somewhat younger Sübedei was destined to place his great abilities in the service of the expansionist Mongol Empire for another quarter of a century.

The pursuit of Sultan Muhammad II and the follow-up via the Caucasus to south Russia was a unique achievement, a masterpiece of courage, persistence and self-confidence. Never before had such a small force dared to penetrate so deeply into unknown and hostile country for several years. This fantastic raid contributed largely to the legend that the Mongol cavalry was invincible and able to be in several places at once.

In Caucasia and Russia the Mongol invasion was regarded as the kind of episode these countries had experienced before. The depredations of the nomadic tribes, however, had not had any lasting influence until then on the political structure of East Europe.[34] It is significant that the Russian princes did not seem to be able to draw any lessons from the débâcle they had suffered at the hands of the Mongols. Their constant and violent internecine quarrels enfeebled any chance they may have had to fend off invading tribes. The mutual envy and hostility of these princes was to benefit the Mongols as much as it damaged the Russian people.

10
After the storm

After the completion of the conquest of Transoxiana in 1220 one has the impression that Genghis Khan began to live a more quiet life. He left the subjection of the rest of the Khwarazm empire to his sons and generals. It was only the campaign to avenge the defeats suffered by his sub-commanders at the hands of Jalal al-Din that he led himself. In 1220 Genghis Khan was 58, which at that time was a respectable age. Before taking his action against Khwarazm, he began to make preparations to settle the question of his succession.

During the wars in north China Genghis Khan had his attention drawn to a Taoist scholar, the monk Ch'ang-ch'un, who was highly regarded in the imperial courts of the Chin and the Sung.[1] Taoism had developed in China from the old scholars of the magicians; although it was later developed into a lofty system of metaphysics, it had succeeded in liberating itself from its mysterious origins. Taoist alchemy sought for the elixir of life, which would confer immortality; it was an alchemy that exerted great fascination. Ch'ang-ch'un, however, was a philosopher and poet who had nothing of the vulgar magician about him; the intellectual asceticism of the Taoist won for him widespread and deep regard.

The illiterate Mongol world conqueror, who was interested in 'the philosopher's stone' with its secret of immortality, wished to employ the magic powers of the famous monk – in whom he presumably saw a worker of miracles – for his own purposes. He wanted to know if Ch'ang-ch'un really possessed the medicine of immortality, and if so he intended to compel the heavenly forces, who had the power of life and death, to do his bidding.

At the moment in 1219 when Genghis Khan was preparing his army on the Kara Irtish River for the assault on Khwarazm, he asked Ch'ang-ch'un, who was then living in the province of Shantung, to come and visit him. The 71-year-old Taoist, realizing that to refuse was not possible, resolved to go to the world conqueror.[2] Genghis Khan had a special escort of 20 men sent to accompany Ch'ang-ch'un from Shantung.[3] Chinqai, one of the Mongol conqueror's advisers, was appointed to fetch the monk and to look after him during the journey. On the day of his departure the aged Taoist told his disciples that he would be away for three years.[4]

During their campaign the Mongol army regularly chose concubines from the defeated nations for Genghis Khan and his generals.[5] The learned ascetic was highly indignant when he discovered that he would have to travel in the company of a number of 'harem girls'.[6] His protests were successful and the concubines had to stay behind.

In Peking the monk was told that Genghis Khan had in the meantime departed for Khwarazm. In March 1221 Ch'ang-ch'un began his difficult journey across Asia to his new destination. One of his companions, Li Chih-ch'ang, kept a detailed diary, which became an important historical source. It did not, however, contain only historical facts. The information it gives about the geography, ethnography, climatology, and about the flora and fauna of Central Asia is of great value. Via Dolon Nor the company travelled to the camp of Genghis Khan's youngest brother, Temüge-otchigin, which lay on the River Kalka. On 30 April Ch'ang-ch'un was received by Temüge. They journeyed through the Kerulen Valley to the upper Orkhon, where, in spite of the summer season, it was very cold. Even the strongest members of the party suffered acutely from the climate.[7] The journey continued via the Altai mountains, north along the Tien Shan mountains, Sairam Nor and Almaliq to Samarkand, where the travellers arrived on 3 December 1221.[8]

Because of the wintry weather Ch'ang-ch'un remained for some months in Samarkand. In the middle of April 1222 he received a request from Genghis Khan to call upon him, and on

26 April the Taoist master set off with an escort from
Samarkand. He went via Balkh to Genghis Khan's camp, which
lay south of the Hindu Kush. The aged Chinese scholar arrived
on 15 May. He was most warmly received by the world
conqueror and thanked for the fact that, in order to make this
visit, he had travelled a distance of 10,000 li (one li being 573
metres). Ch'ang-ch'un replied that Genghis Khan's command
had been the will of heaven and that as a 'mountain savage' he
had no choice but to obey. (As a token of his hermit's humility
the monk had given himself the name mountain savage.)
Genghis Khan invited the Taoist to sit down, and came straight
to the point by asking the old monk if he really possessed the
medicine of immortality. Ch'ang-ch'un answered that there
were many ways of prolonging life, but that no medicine of
immortality existed. Genghis Khan was undoubtedly deeply
disappointed; he had hoped to be able to conquer death itself.
However, he gave no sign of his feelings, but congratulated the
monk for his honest answer. The world conqueror ordered that
two tents should be erected east of his own headquarters for the
master and his companions.

It was the intention that Ch'ang-ch'un should also give an
account of the Taoist philosophy, but enemy activity in
Afghanistan demanded all Genghis Khan's attention. At his
own request Ch'ang-ch'un therefore returned to Samarkand,
arriving there in mid-June 1222.[9] When Genghis Khan invited
the monk to call on him for the second time in September 1222,
his camp had meanwhile moved to a place south-east of Balkh.
Ch'ang-ch'un arrived there on 28 September, almost immediately moving north with the imperial household. It was not
until October that Genghis Khan was able to hear the master
give his exposition of Taoism. In an impressive pavilion
specially erected for the purpose, Ch'ang-ch'un was once again
received by Genghis Khan with great courtesy.[10] The conqueror
listened with close attention to Ch'ang-ch'un's words, which
were translated by an interpreter. This interpreter was Yeh-lü
A-hai, a member of the family of Genghis Khan's Khitan
minister, Yeh-lü Ch'u-ts'ai. The old monk returned after this
to Samarkand, but subsequently accompanied Genghis Khan
for a time on his moves. The Mongol conqueror wanted
Ch'ang-ch'un to travel back with him on the return journey to

Mongolia, but the master asked permission to leave earlier; he had promised his friends in China to be back after three years.[11]

Before the journey to China began, the monk found an opportunity to warn Genghis Khan to look after himself more carefully. In March 1223, during a hunt Genghis Khan shot a boar, but at the same moment his horse stumbled and the world conqueror fell. The boar, which had been wounded, stood still and did not attack, so that the attendants were able to rescue their prostrate sovereign. The master took advantage of this incident to point out to Genghis Khan that life was precious and to suggest that in view of his age he should not hunt so much. Genghis Khan could not agree to abandon his Mongol way of life. He admitted that the monk was right, but added that the Mongols learned to ride and to use the bow and arrow as children – it was difficult to give up these habits. He promised Ch'ang-ch'un, however, that he would bear his advice in mind.[12]

In April 1223 Ch'ang-ch'un at last obtained permission to leave. The return journey followed more or less the same route as the journey out. In January 1224 the company reached Peking.[13] Five months later the master received a message from Genghis Khan saying that the sender had not forgotten his old friend; the world conqueror hoped that he would also be remembered by the monk.[14] Ch'ang-ch'un died in 1227, the same year that Genghis Khan died.

A BROKEN WORLD LEFT BEHIND

When his army was again up to full strength[15] Genghis Khan decided in February 1222 to leave the region between the Hindu Kush and the Indus River, where he had spent the winter.[16] His first plan was to return to Mongolia through India, the Himalayas and Tibet.[17] For this purpose he sent an embassy to the sultan of Delhi.[18] It soon became apparent to him however that he would have to pass high mountains and dense forests on his way; moreover, the climate in India was not suitable to the Mongols.[19] Genghis Khan therefore decided to return along the route by which he had come. The fact that the king of Hsi-Hsia had in 1220 refused to send troop reinforcements must have confirmed him in this decision. He had to bring his army back to Mongolia in good condition, in order to be able to punish the Tangut king.

By way of Kabul and Bamian he went to Baghlan, where a large amount of his baggage was left behind.[20] After the battle on the Indus, Genghis Khan took no further direct part in military operations. The task he gave his generals was the destruction of the remaining mountain fortifications in Afghanistan, the maintenance of communications, and the protection of the baggage train. This assignment was carried out successfully in the difficult mountain country. The baggage train particularly, richly loaded as it was with enormous amounts of war booty and accompanied by large numbers of prisoners, was regularly the target of enemy attacks.[21]

In October 1222 Genghis Khan passed the Amu Darya River.[22] During the winter he stayed in the neighbourhood of Samarkand. At the end of January 1223 the world conqueror was already on the right bank of the Syr Darya.[23] Here in the spring he held a quriltai, at which not only Tolui, who had remained with him, but also Chaghatai and Ögödei were present – they had been hunting birds in the Zerafsan Valley during the winter. It was during the stay east of the Syr Darya that Genghis Khan fell from his horse during a hunt, and Ch'ang-ch'un advised him to be more careful in future.

Genghis Khan spent the summer of 1223 with his main army in the region of the Qulan Bashi Pass, which lay between Otrar and the Talas River.[24] At this place he had his first meeting for a long time with his eldest son Jochi. During his stay on the plains near the Qulan Bashi Pass a number of large battues were organized. Jochi had driven herds of wild donkeys from the steppes north and west of the Aral Sea in the direction of the Qulan Bashi.[25] He also brought 20,000 horses for his father.[26]

In the autumn of 1223 Genghis Khan left the Qulan Bashi Pass. Chaghatai, Ögödei and Tolui went back with their father. Jochi remained behind in the plains awarded to him along the Aral and the Caspian Sea. There he remained until his death, detached from events in Mongolia; he had little further contact with his father. Possibly Ögödei's election as successor to the throne had disappointed him. This aloofness gave rise to the rumour that he wished to revolt against his father.

In the summer of 1224 Genghis Khan reached the Kara Irtish River with his army, arriving in Mongolia in the spring of 1225;[27] his return caused no great problems. It is unfortunately not possible to ascertain Genghis Khan's thoughts at that time. He was now an older man, no longer capable of enduring the hard life of the Mongol cavalry. This is shown to some extent by his slow progress during the return to Mongolia. In the preceding quarter of a century he had developed from a simple tribal chief to the ruler of a great part of the world. The meeting with Ch'ang-ch'un had made it clear to him that death was unconquerable. Various comrades of his early days were already dead. Shortly before his return to Mongolia he had lost the most capable of them, Muqali and Jebe. Genghis Khan must have been aware that he was coming to the end of his life.

Genghis Khan left the conquered regions before the former Khwarazm empire was completely subdued. In Transoxiana and Khwarazm itself nobody doubted any longer the Mongol supremacy,[28] but this was not so in Khurasan, Afghanistan and Iraq-Ajemi. In these countries Jalal al-Din later attempted to restore his father's sultanate (see pages 154–5). As a result of this situation, the towns in Transoxiana and Khwarazm recovered more rapidly from the violence of war than the towns in Khurasan and Iraq-Ajemi.[29] The province of Khwarazm, where there had been heavy destruction, quickly returned to normal under Jochi's government. In a short time a new town rose on the right bank of the Amu Darya near the place where Gurganj had been virtually razed to the ground. The Mongols changed the name Gurganj to Urgench.[30] The town became one of the most important trade centres on the road between Europe and Asia.[31]

Little is known about Genghis Khan's own part in the organization of the government of the conquered territories. It was the Uighur Ta-ta-T'ong-a who taught him the first principles of governmental organization and demonstrated the importance of putting the imperial seal on written acts to confirm their authenticity. Equally helpful as an adviser in administrative matters was Chinqai, a Kereit who was already in the service of Genghis Khan during the retreat to the Baljuna Lake at the time of the struggle for supremacy in Mongolia.

Chinqai accompanied Ch'ang-ch'un during the Taoist monk's journey from China to Afghanistan, and was referred to by him as a *chärbi* (a chamberlain).[32]

After the conquest of Gurganj, Genghis Khan sought the advice of two Muslims, Mahmud Yalavach and his son Masud, on the significance and value of towns. It is probable that both Yalavachs, like Yeh-lü Ch'u-ts'ai before them, attempted to convince Genghis Khan of the value of urban cultures. The acceptance of these counsels and the inauguration of an administration, which was not only applicable to nomadic life, marks a new era in the history of the Mongol world empire. The highest authorities realized that the enormous expansion of the Mongol-controlled territories brought great responsibilities with it.

In the Mongol Empire two governmental bodies came into existence: the Uighur chancellery, led by Ta-ta-T'ong-a and Chinqai, and the Chinese chancellery of Yeh-lü Ch'u-ts'ai. The Yalavachs were entrusted with the administration of Transoxiana, Khotan and Kashgar.[33] Mahmud later had an administrative post in Peking.[34] Samarkand and Bukhara came directly under the central chancellery in Mongolia. The governor of Samarkand was a Khitan, Yeh-lü A-hai, who had acted as interpreter for Ch'ang-ch'un. His younger brother Yeh-lü T'u-hua had been one of Muqali's commanders in China.[35] In the newly won regions the Uighurs particularly played an important role in setting up a government system. The Mongols were ill equipped for this task. As leading officials (*darughachi*) many Uighurs, as well as Muslims, received appointments. There were therefore two government languages: that of the local population, and Uighur.

The ease with which the Khwarazm sultanate was defeated by the Mongols must be ascribed partly to its internal weakness and partly to the superior organization of the Mongol army. The highly disciplined Mongol warriors were not eager for personal fame; they merely carried out their orders to the letter. The Mongol commanders were skilful and obedient instruments of Genghis Khan's wishes. If the situation required it, military units could fight as detached groups or join into one force to deal with rapidly changing circumstances. On the other hand there were commanders in the Khwarazm army, such as Jalal al-Din and Temur Melik, who often performed remarkable exploits through their personal bravery. However, they seemed to be incapable of managing large forces or of rousing in their multinational army a national resistance to the Mongol invader.[36]

It is noteworthy that the Mongols had less difficulty in taking towns in Transoxiana and Khurasan than in north China. In addition to the use of siege engines in the Khwarazm empire, terrorist techniques had great success there. Terror had less effect on the Chinese, because in the course of the centuries they had become accustomed to the methods of the barbarians. The Mongols undoubtedly quickly observed this difference in enemy reactions. When laying siege to Khwarazm towns they therefore used prisoners as cannon-fodder to a greater extent than they had done in China. It was a military expedient that enabled the comparatively small Mongol forces to compel even large towns to capitulate.

The removal from a town of men of military age was a system in the Mongol method of warfare that was rigorously applied. The method was a double-edged sword: that part of a town's population capable of resistance was removed, to be employed as a terror weapon against the next town. If enough cannon-fodder for a besieged town could not be found by this means, it was supplemented by men from the surrounding countryside. This absolute form of terror sometimes resulted in crushing all will to resist.[37]

In the various sources mention is usually made of the slaughter of the population in China and Iran. The unification of Mongolia took place (as always in Central Asia) only after long and bloody wars. During the struggle for supremacy Genghis Khan massacred whole tribes if he judged it necessary. It is therefore difficult to determine whether his army put relatively more men to death in China or in Iran than in the steppes of Central Asia.[38]

East Iran never recovered entirely from the Mongol hurricane. Some towns still show signs of the Mongol destruction; they were unable to regain their former position as centres of Islamic civilization.[39] Even the Timuridic renaissance in the fifteenth century, which reached its golden age in East Iran, could not entirely restore this broken world. In these places

Genghis Khan is viewed as the greatest enemy of Arabic-Persian civilization. Muslim writers brand him as 'The Accursed'.[40]

The invasion of Genghis Khan was not followed however by the settlement of Mongols in the conquered regions, as it had been, for example, some centuries earlier with the Seljuqs. Most of the Mongol soldiers, like Genghis Khan himself, returned to Mongolia.[41]

11
The last campaign

Before he rode off in 1219 to attack the Khwarazm sultanate, Genghis Khan ordered his vassals to have troops ready for him. The Mongol envoy carrying this order to Ningsia was told that if Genghis Khan was not strong enough to undertake the struggle against Khwarazm he should not aspire to the role of emperor.[1] Although Hsi-Hsia was not entirely a vassal state, the Tangut king had promised after his defeat in 1210 to be Genghis Khan's 'right hand', which implied that he was prepared to acknowledge his subordinate position. At that moment Genghis Khan could do little about Hsi-Hsia; the imminent war with Khwarazm required all his attention and forces. It was not until 1225, when he had returned to Mongolia, that he prepared for vengeance.

The refusal to deliver troops was not the only reason why Hsi-Hsia was invaded. In the autumn of 1225 the Tangut had formed an alliance with the Chin emperor. To prevent Hsi-Hsia and the Chin from co-ordinating their forces, Genghis Khan resolved to act quickly. After eliminating the Tangut kingdom it would be the turn of the Chin empire, but in order to carry out the second part of the plan the Mongols would have to have full control of Ordos, Shensi and Kansu. Before he went off to battle Genghis Khan sent another envoy to the Tangut king demanding that he surrender one of his sons as a hostage. The king refused this too.[2]

During this campaign Genghis Khan took his Tatar wife Yesüi with him. He was also accompanied by his sons Ögödei and Tolui, his chancellor Yeh-lü Ch'u-ts'ai, his old and faithful companion Bogorju, and the most able of his surviving generals, Sübedei. Chaghatai stayed behind in Mongolia.[3] Genghis Khan attached great importance to the action against the Tangut. In spite of his advanced years he decided to lead his army personally; this shows that Genghis Khan retained his physical and mental powers until the end of his life.[4] Probably he decided to assume the leadership because he thought that in the densely populated country of China, where the people had shown that they could endure much punishment, difficult situations might arise. The war against the Chin was still being fought, and it was possible that the Sung were waiting for their chance. He did not entrust any of his sons or generals with the command of this campaign. Whether he would have given this task to Muqali or Jebe had they been alive is a matter for speculation.

It is not certain exactly when the march began in 1226: in the autumn[5] or in the spring;[6] the latter is more likely. Genghis Khan made for the oases of the Edsin River, north of Qara Khoto.[7] Along this river the Mongols forced their way into Hsi-Hsia. In May 1226 they were approaching the first towns of any importance: Su-chou and Kan-chou. As had happened in the Chin empire and the Khwarazm sultanate, the Tangut army fell back on the defended towns. The Mongols could therefore decide for themselves where to concentrate their forces. Moreover, they had a large number of siege machines, which made their task easier. Nevertheless siege operations usually cost them much time. Su-chou was entered after five weeks, while Kan-chou took five months to subdue.[8] As the weather was very hot, Genghis Khan continued his march along the northern spurs of the Nan Shan.[9] These mountains with peaks of about 5,000 to 6,000 metres (the 'Snow Mountains')[10] made further progress to the south impossible. During the war in Hsi-Hsia the Mongols once again mercilessly applied their terror. Although the Tangut generally offered stubborn resistance,[11] the cruel methods of their enemies succeeded. Many hid in vain in mountains and caves; after the Mongols had passed the fields were littered with corpses.[12]

In the autumn the Mongol army moved east to Liang-chou, which they besieged and stormed. Then they rode through the Alashan Desert to Ling-chou, the royal residence,[13] which lay on the east bank of the Yellow River. The king of Hsi-Hsia planned to relieve this town with a strong army, but Genghis

Khan, anticipating him, gave orders to cross the Huang River and attack the army advancing from Ningsia. The Tangut suffered a heavy defeat.[14]

As the winter was approaching, Genghis Khan set up his quarters in the Liup'an Shan. In February 1227 the war was resumed with the investment of Ningsia, where a large part of the Tangut army was concentrated. The Mongol conqueror felt himself so strong at that moment that he detached some of his troops to carry out other tasks. Sübedei conquered the T'ao Valley and the region of Lan-chou; Ögödei and Chaghan (a Tangut general in the Mongol service) thrust into the territory of the Chin along the Wei River and south Shensi.[15] They even sent some units over the Ch'in Ling mountains, thus threatening the Chin capital K'ai-feng. This action led the Chin emperor to make a further peace offer.[16]

During a battue Genghis Khan's horse was startled and reared unexpectedly; the old world conqueror fell and was injured. His condition worsened so much during the night that Yesüi thought it necessary to call Tolui and the generals to tell them that Genghis Khan had a heavy fever. One of the generals suggested they return to Mongolia to wait until their leader was better; the Tangut were a sedentary people and their punishment could always be carried out later. The other members of the council agreed with this proposal, but Genghis Khan refused to give his permission. He thought that if the Mongols withdrew the Tangut would think they were cowards and react accordingly. He ordered another envoy to be sent to Ningsia to demand satisfaction. When this envoy returned without success, the sick world conqueror gave the word to continue the campaign.[17]

During the siege of Ningsia Genghis Khan remained in the region of Lungte in the Liup'an Shan.[18] The Tangut king (who is called Li Hsien in Chinese history) refused at first to talk about capitulation. When, however, in July–August 1227 food supplies ran out in the beleaguered town he had no choice but to surrender. Feeling that he could expect no mercy,[19] he asked Genghis Khan for a month's respite to prepare gifts for his conqueror.

After Yeh-lü Liu-ko – who had been installed by Genghis Khan in 1212 – had died in Liao-yang (the hereditary country of the former Khitan dynasty) in 1220, his widow had governed the territory. His son and successor had ridden with Genghis Khan to the wars against Khwarazm and Hsi-Hsia. During the investment of Ningsia he was the commander of one of the besieging units. His mother asked Genghis Khan to allow him to take over the government of the Liao's country, and after the fall of Ningsia Yeh-lü Liu-ko's son was given permission to assume his father's position.

During the siege of Ningsia Genghis Khan learned that his eldest son Jochi had died in February 1227. There are a number of conflicting stories about difficulties which arose between Genghis Khan and Jochi after they had seen each other for the last time at the Qulan Bashi. It was said that Jochi intended to dissociate himself entirely from the Mongol Empire, and he refused to listen to his father's request to visit him. Some sources doubted the truth of the report that Jochi did not come to his father because he was ill.[20] That he died shortly afterwards may show that the illness was not simulated and that there were people close to Genghis Khan who wished to put Jochi in a bad light.

It is remarkable how curtly the contemporary Mongol and Chinese sources referred to the death of Genghis Khan. One of them simply stated: 'In the year of the Pig Genghis Khan ascended to Heaven'.[21] Presumably this event was a taboo to the Mongols.[22] However, much has been subsequently written about the possible cause of death. There is an inclination to assume that internal injury caused by the fall from his horse (an assumption supported by the resulting high temperature he had) hastened the end of the world conqueror.[23] It is almost certain that Genghis Khan died south of the Liup'an Shan.[24] Three dates have been given for the date of his death in 1227: 18 August, 25 August and 28 August.[25] It is difficult to say with certainty which date is correct.[26] If his year of birth was 1162, Genghis Khan was 66 when he died.[27]

Genghis Khan apparently knew that his death was approaching. On his deathbed he told Tolui (the only son who was near him during his last days) how to attack the Chin empire.[28] He declared that the Chin's best troops were in the strongly fortified T'ung-kuan. This stronghold dominated the western entrance of the province Honan, which was protected in the north by the Huang-ho and in the south by the Ch'in Ling mountains. The attack against the Chin should be launched from the south-west along the T'ang River in the direction of K'ai-feng;[29] to execute this operation violation of the Sung territory was unavoidable.

Before his death Genghis Khan ordered the Tangut king to be executed.[30] In the Mongol chronicle, the Secret History of the Mongols (see note on page 32), King Li Hsien has another name, Iluqu Burqan, meaning 'Exalted Buddha'.[31] In Buddhist Hsi-Hsia, kings were also priests of the state. In order to prevent the impression that by executing the Tangut king the Mongols had turned against Buddhism (the elimination of an 'Exalted Buddha' might give that idea), Genghis Khan changed the name Iluqu Burqan into Shidurqu,[32] meaning 'Loyal Follower'. In this way his subservient position was stressed: a Buddha could not be killed, but a vassal could.[33]

Genghis Khan wished his death to be kept secret if he should die before the surrender of Ningsia.[34] After the month's respite granted to the Tangut king, the latter delivered himself up in September in the Mongol camp. There he was told that the world conqueror was ill and he must therefore pay homage outside the imperial tent. With him the king had brought many gifts of gold and silver, as well as boys and girls. King Li Hsien had to make his obeisance in front of the entrance to the tent where lay the mortal remains of Genghis Khan. Three days later he and his family were put to death.

Ningsia was mercilessly plundered and largely destroyed: it meant the end of the Tangut kingdom of Hsi-Hsia which had existed since 1030. Genghis Khan seems to have intended to exterminate the entire Tangut people after the defeat of Hsi-Hsia,[35] but Yeh-lü Ch'u-ts'ai dissuaded him from this terrible project. The Khitan explained to the world conqueror that a subjected people would be of more use to the Mongols when they left the country, than a land in which the whole population had been massacred.[36]

The body of Genghis Khan was carried to Mongolia. During the journey the Mongols killed everybody they met.[37] The Mongol conqueror was buried on the sacred mountain Burqan Qaldun, a place he had chosen himself for his tomb, as was the custom among the Mongols.[38] The site of the grave is unknown;[39] it is possible that it lies on the upper reaches of the Onon.[40]

That the location of the world conqueror's tomb cannot be found is perhaps the result of the method by which the Mongols buried their illustrious dead. After filling in such a grave they drove large numbers of horses over it, and soon the place was once again covered with the local natural vegetation (see page 8). In a short time even family members did not know where the grave was. By the beginning of the fourteenth century it was no longer known where Genghis Khan's last resting place was. The area was so densely overgrown that it was impossible to cut a way through.[41]

After Ögödei was installed as Great Khan in 1229, he commanded forty beautiful girls to be chosen from the most distinguished families. Dressed in splendid robes and adorned with jewels, they were sacrificed on the grave of the world conqueror to wait on his soul in the hereafter. A number of selected horses were also sacrificed.[42] At Genghis Khan's burial place – 'the great forbidden precinct'[43] – several Genghisids were also buried later. It is accepted as certain that Tolui, his wife Sorqaqtani and both their sons Möngke and Ariq Böke also lie in the most holy place of the Burqan Qaldun.[44]

12

The world conqueror and his empire

THE WORLD CONQUEROR

There are only sporadic references to be found to Genghis Khan's personal appearance. The most detailed information on this subject was obtained from people who saw Genghis Khan during the war in Khwarazm. The world conqueror was then about sixty. He was remarkable for his distinguished figure and his strong constitution. He had cat's eyes and his hair was only partially grey.[1]

A judgment about Genghis Khan can only be made if he is seen in the context of his times and surroundings. In the twelfth and thirteenth centuries the Mongols were far more barbarous than their neighbouring tribes. For this reason Genghis Khan, as the cultivated Chinese put it, was nothing more nor less than a barbarian. However, this barbarian possessed a number of qualities that enabled him to become one of the greatest conquerors in the history of the world.

His unusual self-control and his ability to keep his temper were striking.[2] Although he never permitted himself to behave treacherously in his private life and in his personal relationships, he was certainly cunning and calculating. In his conduct of warfare he was even deceitful. He hated traitors: servants of opponents who betrayed their masters to win his favour were immediately ordered to be executed. We may assume that this attitude was adopted only partly for reasons of idealism. In those times it was not unusual to desert to the strongest. Genghis Khan must have believed that such opportunists would abandon him also if fortune turned. To make clear what a traitor in his army might expect if he were to fall again into his hands, he showed no mercy to deserters from the enemy. Supporters who remained loyal to him in difficult circumstances were richly rewarded; while those who served their leaders faithfully to the last in a defeated army he often spared, even giving them the opportunity of entering his service.

Another characteristic was his suspicious nature. This is clearly seen in the arrest of his brother Qasar after the prediction by the shaman Kököchü, and his reproof of Jebe after this general's swift and brilliant triumphal march against Küchlüg. This suspicion resulted in Genghis Khan's refusal to allow anyone but himself to wield any authority. As his power increased, he became more and more anxious to protect his own position.[3]

As was the case with all his contemporaries, Genghis Khan worked exclusively for himself, his descendants and his closest companions. There is no evidence that he entertained any ideas about the welfare of the whole nation,[4] not even in the form that such ideas were expressed in the Yasa. Nor did Genghis Khan see himself as the head of a people: he was the head of the Mongol aristocracy, to which he had given first unity and then power and wealth. It is characteristic of Genghis Khan that, although he won submission from a great part of the world and in other countries aroused fear and alarm, his giddy success never went to his head. Even such a cultured people as the Chinese were astonished at the noble bearing of this so-called barbarian.[5]

Like his fellow countrymen, Genghis Khan was fond of a drink; and hunting was his favourite sport. Although this world conqueror was undoubtedly drunk at certain times, he was not guilty of excessive use of alcohol. Ögödei and Tolui, who were both the slaves of drink, had to be regularly rebuked for their weakness.[6] Drunkenness was regarded by the Mongols as a manly virtue (see page 10). It was therefore difficult to prohibit this widespread vice in the Yasa.

Women played a great part in his private life. The four most important wives of Genghis Khan were Börte, Qulan, Yesüi and Yesügen. He kept an ordu for each of them. In addition to these women there were a few others, such as the daughter of the Chin emperor, the daughter of the king of Hsi-Hsia, and Gübersü, the former wife of the conquered tayang of the

Naiman. He also had a number of concubines. Whenever he rested, Genghis Khan loved to have attractive women around him and always liked to see girls who were busy at all kinds of work. During long campaigns he took one of his chief wives with him. He enjoyed being entertained by an orchestra consisting of 17 or 18 beautiful girl performers.[7]

Although Genghis Khan in his youth showed that he possessed courage and daring and often took risks, he never distinguished himself later as a military commander by personal bravery. In his eyes the leader of the battle was always more important than the fighter; all forms of romantic heroism were foreign to his nature.[8] In this respect he differs greatly from the later Asiatic conqueror Timur Lenk (Tamerlan). Genghis Khan directed military operations personally; but he did not think fighting in the front ranks of the cavalry was the job of the supreme commander.

In his later years, however, he cannot be accused of any lack of daring. From the way in which he progressed from a simple tribal chief to one of the mightiest overlords in world history, he did indeed show a great measure of personal courage. He never forced a decision but bided his time, realizing that he ran the danger of losing the opportunities among his supporters. Although he always approached a task with great circumspection, Genghis Khan took great risks when he and his small army attacked the powerful Chin empire and afterwards the vast Khwarazm sultanate. His successful conduct of these wars clearly reveals his military genius.

Genghis Khan did not use any original techniques of warfare. He simply perfected the methods of his predecessors in the steppes. Discipline guaranteed that his orders were strictly carried out. Not even the basic organization of the Mongol army was originated by the world conqueror. There is no doubt, however, that he played a unique role in making this organization faultless.

His profound knowledge of men enabled Genghis Khan to select efficient subordinate commanders. Usually origin and age played no part in his choice. The generals he picked were often given tasks they had to carry out independently, far removed from the Mongol main forces. Not one of the generals, entrusted with the confidence of the world conqueror, ever let him down.

This was the result of his absolute authority and the respect that he inspired everywhere. His choice of civil advisers also shows his gifts for shrewd assessment of human character. They were, without exception, able intelligent and loyal servants. He had, moreover, the good sense to listen carefully to what these ministers had to say. In this connection it is typical that, although he was illiterate and could only speak the Mongol language,[9] he recognized the need for and value of introducing the Uighur script as the official alphabet of the Mongols, who themselves had no alphabet.

Before the rule of Genghis Khan, Mongol society was dominated by complete licence. To obtain law and order in his state, rules of conduct were necessary. By his compilation of the Yasa and his demand for unquestioning obedience, Genghis Khan exerted a tremendous influence upon the morals of the Mongol people, who hitherto had lived in utter anarchy. It is significant that the Franciscan monk John of Plano Carpini, who visited Mongolia 19 years after the death of Genghis Khan, noticed that the Mongols followed the Yasa much more closely than European priests observed their regimen.

Naturally, the genius of Genghis Khan had limitations. The attempt to reconcile two opposing cultures – nomad and urban – was the weakest link in his system, and later it was one of the chief causes of the disintegration of the Mongol Empire.[10] But the organization he imposed upon his dominions was such that it remained in operation for 40 years after his death. This is a remarkable achievement; the more so because not one of his sons or grandsons inherited his genius.[11] That the Genghisids were able to maintain their rule over the member states after the partition of the Mongol Empire derived partly from Genghis Khan's enormous authority, which remained operative long after his death. During his lifetime this indisputable authority was the force that bound together the various camps in his world empire. The religious basis, which was the fundamental strength of his authority, was an important factor particularly in Central Asia.

Only the four sons of his first wife Börte were eligible to succeed their father. He was not misled by Tolui's military talents or the inflexible severity with which Chaghatai enforced the principles of his father's system. Genghis Khan looked to

Ögödei, who attracted many by his high-minded and affable character. As the father's strength of will was not inherited by any of the sons, it was inevitable that a coalition rule by all the members of the Genghisids should be instituted. The solidarity of the empire had to be maintained by somebody who could unite all members. For these reasons his eldest son Jochi, in view of the uncertainty about his paternity, could not be considered for the succession. If rule could not be enforced by strength of will and intellect, then it had to be done by somebody with an attractive character. During his reign Ögödei managed to bring a large measure of unanimity, thus proving that his brilliant father's hope had not been placed in him without justification.[12]

Genghis Khan has often been portrayed as a monster whose progress was marked by bloody deeds; in the places through which he passed, it is said, rose piles of corpses of murdered peace-loving people and the ruins of towns which, before his arrival, had been prosperous and busy centres. In Islam especially, he was thought to be an odious killer, spreading the silence of the grave over half the world.[13]

It is true that various sources speak of bloodthirsty deeds committed by the Mongol conqueror. The present-day impartial investigator, however, must reach the conclusion that neither as Temüjin, nor later as khan of the Mongols, did he exceed his contemporaries in cruelty or destructiveness.[14] However considerable his genius may have been, Genghis Khan was a child of his times and his country. The outrages must be viewed in the context of the times and the prevailing social conditions; it would be unfair to judge such events by different criteria. That the names of many other rulers, whose brutality was not much less than that of Genghis Khan, are hardly known, is because they are of no historical significance. During the Mongol conquest inconceivable numbers of people died and destruction was enormous, but this was the consequence of the extent of Genghis Khan's campaigns which covered vast areas of Eurasia. Numerically Genghis Khan's army was always smaller than those of his opponents. As all tribes had done in the steppes, the Mongols controlled subjected countries not with occupation troops but by terror. Genghis Khan's Mongols had hardly outgrown their primitive origins and this affected their methods of warfare. These nomads and forest-hunters had no idea how a sedentary people functioned. Nor did they recognize the importance of agriculture.

Genghis Khan was never guilty, during his great campaigns, of barbarities over and above those which were accepted in his day as normal features of war.[15] But like conquerors of any period, Genghis Khan was able (if it was necessary to reach his goal) coldly to do whatever was necessary, to sacrifice countless human lives and to order widespread devastation.

THE EMPIRE

The Mongol conquests were not only the most far-reaching in world history; they also had the most radical consequences. At Genghis Khan's death the Mongol Empire embraced approximately half of the then known world.[16] The slaughter of people and the destruction of towns were not, however, the only features of Genghis Khan's operations. In the huge areas that he united under his rule, close contacts occurred between countries that had hitherto hardly known of each other's existence, on account of their geographical situation and the unsafe conditions that had formerly prevailed. The empire included two old cultural centres, China and Persia, which now associated more intensively as member states. The whole of Asia was opened up; trade in particular benefited from the new order. This was possible because after the conquests the disciplines embodied in the Yasa were introduced in the subjected countries. These rules were undoubtedly harsh, but they brought about a large measure of security and peace, named the *Pax Mongolica*. A contemporary Persian historian wrote that in the region between Persia and Turfan public safety was so widespread that a traveller could journey without interference from the Levant to Central Asia with a gold plate on his head.[17]

The commander of a large military unit was also responsible for the protection of the mounted courier service (Yam). This benefited not only efficient military and governmental communications,[18] trade also profited with the Yam. Along the protected routes flowed an exchange of products, information, discoveries and ideas. After the violence and their defeat, came the activity of travellers dedicated to the spirit of enterprises or to peaceful undertakings. Multicoloured throngs of messengers, merchants and missionaries during the coming years would move along the opened communication routes between South-west Asia and China.[19] Thanks to the *Pax Mongolica*, commerce especially was able to develop vigorously.

Although the Mongol conqueror was well aware of the value of this international trade, the Mongols themselves did not participate in it. For centuries their activities had been limited to barter with China; in exchange for furs and skins they obtained clothing, food and metal goods from the vast neighbouring country. There was particularly busy commerce between the mediterranean countries and China. The profits from this trade remained long one of the chief financial pillars of the Mongol Empire.

The opinion that the Mongols wished to convert all con-quered territories into steppes is not borne out by the facts. The account of the travels of the Chinese philosopher Ch'ang-ch'un relates that the Mongols strove to restore the prosperity of the defeated countries very soon after the battles were over. Influenced by his advisers Ta-ta-T'ong-a, Yeh-lü Ch'u-tsai and the two Yalavachs, Genghis Khan was convinced that he could obtain more income from a prosperous country, run on a municipal and agricultural basis, than from nomads.[20] In order to govern his enormous empire, with its various nationalities and religions, Genghis Khan relied upon the knowledge and experience of the more sophisticated countries. The Mongols had the upper hand, but they were not really the ruling class. For most of their administrative work they had to rely on foreign co-operators recruited from the conquered popula-tions.[21] As nomads they were not well adapted to regular work. The number of Mongols engaged in the higher governmental departments, was therefore very small. For such functions it was usually the Uighurs, the Khitans, the Chinese and Persians who were appointed.

Until the end of his life Genghis Khan remained convinced that the Uighur civilization was the one that was best suited to his empire. Nor was this conviction shaken after the world conqueror had gained some experience of the Chinese and

Persian cultures. Even his close association with Yeh-lü Ch'u-ts'ai failed to change his ideas. The Chinese and Persian civilizations naturally exerted an influence upon Mongol society, but Genghis Khan wanted the ruling Genghisids to adhere to their nomad life and the teachings of the Yasa, even after his death. For this purpose the Uighur culture was the most acceptable.[22] Genghis Khan, who assumed that his clan would remain overlords for ever, demanded that his descendants and the Mongol aristocracy should not abandon the life of the steppes. It was a simple life and was not restricted by a fixed location. The Yasa, which he thought should be followed for all eternity, was attuned to this way of life. By so doing, the imperial clan could continue to dominate the settled peoples.

Even after gaining control of the territories of the more developed countries, Genghis Khan applied the policies used when uniting all tribes of Central Asia. Whatever the real social and economic causes of the Mongol conquests were, Genghis Khan himself motivated his wars of conquest in terms of an order received from Tengri (Eternal Heaven). His successors followed his example and further elaborated on this scheme. In their eyes the Mongol Empire was not merely a state among states but a 'world empire in the making'. The building of it was the will of Tengri. According to this conception, the right to rule over the world was conferred by the Eternal Heaven on Genghis Khan and his successors. Orders of submission were therefore sent out to inform other states that they had to conform with the orders of the representative of the god of the Mongols. Refusal to surrender was regarded as rebellion.[23]

Genghis Khan regarded the state as a possession belonging to his clan. His empire's constitution was formulated in such a way that he, his family and his loyal associates could derive from it as large an income as possible, with a view to guaranteeing for themselves, a grand life-style. In Genghis Khan's time no moral justification of rule seems to have been current. To rule over others was a pleasure and therefore the Genghisids called the throne the seat of joy.[24] Dwellers in the civilized countries were to Genghis Khan the permanent slaves of his empire, whose job it was to see to it that their nomad masters lived an agreeable life.[25]

It was only the descendants of Genghis Khan who had the

right to rule. The principle of the common overlordship of the Golden Clan did not conflict with the personal power of whoever stood at the head of the empire. The empire had to remain an entity, with a khan as its leader. This khan was at the same time the head of the imperial clan. 'My dignity', said Genghis Khan, 'can only be inherited by one son. My words are irrevocable; I will not permit them to be infringed.'[26]

The common ownership of the imperium is seen in the allocation of regions and tribes (*ulus*) to members of Genghis Khan's family. The extent of these apanages varied: they were larger or smaller according to the age of the family member. There was an agreed scale by which each member of the Golden Clan was given a number of army units, artisans and artists. A ulus extended only over regions where nomadic people dwelt. Countries such as China and Persia were not represented in the uluses of the Genghisids. The revenues from China and Persia were, however, divided between the Great Khan and all members of the family.[27] Countries like China and Persia were governed by officials (darughachi), who were responsible to the central chancellery in Mongolia. Neither in financial nor in governmental matters could the other members of the Golden Clan interfere. The Great Khan, who had his own ulus, artisans and artists was, however, the only one who had authority over the guard.

The principle of possessions shared by the Genghisids is revealed in the quriltai (the assembly of the imperial clan and the military Mongol aristocracy). Here also Genghis Khan pursued his policy of keeping the quriltai subservient to whoever stood at the head of the empire and who reigned in the name of the 'Eternal Heaven'.

The control of various branches into which the Golden Clan was divided remained intact for a number of generations. But as the uluses began to go their own way and were no longer dependent upon each other, the cohesion of the enormous empire began to weaken. Various branches of the Genghisids came into being which made assassination attempts upon each other. In all these independent apanages, however, the organization laid down by Genghis Khan was successfully adhered to for a considerable time. This is further proof of the Mongol conqueror's enormous gift for organization.

Genghis Khan's wishes were eventually forgotten. His empire collapsed and the Mongols, who had been compelled by the military and administrative genius of their greatest son to enter the world arena, were unable to maintain their position. They were absorbed or driven back by the countless educated peoples among whom they lived. Later, many of them relapsed into the circumstances in which they had lived at the time of the birth of their brilliant leader.[28] The hope that his clan would remain intact and would for ever continue to rule his empire proved vain. The Yasa, which was to exert the rule of law for all time, was not influential enough to preserve the solidarity of the Genghisids.[29]

13
In the footsteps of the father

THE INHERITANCE

After Genghis Khan's death the regency, as was the Mongol custom, fell to his youngest son Tolui. In his capacity as otchigin (guardian of hearth and home) he was given the original territory of the Mongols (which lay between the Onon and Kerulen) as apanage. It was therefore Tolui who called the quriltai which in the spring of 1229 appointed the successor of the deceased world conqueror. As otchigin, Tolui controlled the imperial residences of Genghis Khan's household[1] and 101,000 troops of the Mongol army, during the period of his regency.

There is no doubt that Genghis Khan owed his conquests west of Mongolia to his three eldest sons. During their father's lifetime Jochi, Chaghatai and Ögödei already enjoyed their rights in the apanages they had been allotted. It is not clear, however, where the boundaries of these apanages lay. Nor is it certain what rights the sons had in comparison with those of Genghis Khan.[2]

Jochi was given the area between the Ural and the Irtish rivers. In the south his ulus (apanage) extended to the west coast of the Aral Sea, the Syr Darya (as far as Signak) and Lake Balkash; it included part of the east coast of the Aral Sea.[3] At the moment of Genghis Khan's death Jochi's ulus had already been divided among his sons. Orda, the eldest,[4] was given possession of the right bank of the Syr Darya and the districts around the Sari Su.[5] Batu, Jochi's second and most able son,[6] received in 1227 the north coast of the Caspian Sea as far as the Ural River. His possessions were considerably extended after the conquest of south Russia. The ulus of Jochi's fifth son,

Shiban,[7] was situated north of those of Batu and Orda, and comprised the region from the upper reaches of the Ural River to the Irtish; the area enclosed the courses of the Tourgai and the Irgiz rivers.[8]

Genghis Khan's second son, Chaghatai, received the territory of the former Qara-Khitai kingdom, namely the districts of the Talas, the Chu and the Ili rivers, and Issyq Kul,[9] but excluding the towns of Samarkand and Bukhara. Transoxiana was administered by the central government in Mongolia. Ögödei, destined to succeed his father, received as his own ulus the lands of Ala Kul, the Tarbagatai mountains, the Kara Irtish River, and the region extending from the Altai mountains to Lake Baikal.[10] His residence was near the former town of Emil, in the neighbourhood of Ala Kul.[11]

Each of Genghis Khan's brothers also received an apanage. Qasar's descendants gained possession of an ulus near the Argun and the Kailaer rivers.[12] An apanage south-east of Buyr Nor, which presumably included Korea,[13] went to Temüge. The apanages of the members of Genghis Khan's family sometimes comprised the feudal lands of vassals. One of Genghis Khan's remarks reveals that the feudal lands of the Liaos (Liao-yang) were to be found in Belgütei's ulus.[14] In addition to their own apanages Genghis Khan's sons and brothers owned so-called hereditary feudal estates from which they derived revenues, although they did not govern them.[15] These feudal estates were later to be the cause of many quarrels.

THE NEW RULER

Tolui, after governing as regent,[16] called a quriltai in 1228 to choose his father's successor. The quriltai took place near Köde'ü aral, a plain on the left bank of the upper reaches of the Kerulen River.[17] This assembly of the empire's notabilities had only one purpose, namely to follow Genghis Khan's wishes by installing Ögödei as ruler of the Mongol Empire. Those present were Chaghatai, Ögödei, Temüge and Belgütei, each with their sons, and the sons of Jochi and Qachi'un.[18]

The quriltai proposed Ögödei, 'in accordance with the

command of Genghis Khan,' as his father's successor.[19] Ögödei objected and suggested that Tolui, who had always attended Genghis Khan, should be given this honour. The meeting, however, had no wish to go against the wishes of the late world conqueror, and in the autumn of 1229 Ögödei was called upon to become the ruler of the Mongol Empire. While the members of the quriltai took their hats off and threw their belts over their shoulders, Chaghatai and Temüge stood one on each side of the new khan and escorted him to the throne of his father. Tolui held a beaker aloft, all those present knelt three times and chanted in chorus: 'May the realm be blessed by his being khan'.[20] It is not known when Ögödei was given, or assumed, the title of Great Khan.[21]

Nothing definite is known about the dates of birth of Genghis Khan's sons; it is assumed that Ögödei was born in 1186.[22] He was called at first by some other name, but as this did not please him, he was given a new name, Ögödei, meaning 'upward' (uphill).[23] Like his father, Ögödei had a liking for women.[24] The new khan had two chief wives, Boraqchin and Töregene. Although not his first wife, Töregene was certainly the more imposing of the two. There is rather a pungent comment about her: 'Töregene was of no great beauty but of a very masterful nature.'[25] The new ruler had inherited none of his father's brilliant talents, but he was undoubtedly the most intelligent of Genghis Khan's sons. He was a calm, conscientious and shrewd ruler, although his qualities of leadership and initiative were not the highest. The Mongol Empire continued to function thanks to the Yasa and the capable ministers of Genghis Khan. Ögödei, who co-operated well with Tolui,[26] was tolerant and noble-minded[27] but, of all the Mongol rulers of the later Yüan dynasty in China, he was the greatest drinker.[28]

For the government of his empire Ögödei relied largely on Yeh-lü Ch'u-ts'ai and Chinqai. Yeh-lü Ch'u-ts'ai exercised a powerful influence on the constitution and functioning of the administration, which was formed on Chinese models. His renown rests chiefly on the administrative improvements that were carried out under his direction during the reign of Ögödei and his constant endeavour to mitigate the merciless Mongol rule in north China. The task he had set himself was fraught with immense difficulties. No real transformation could in fact be achieved without first educating the Great Khan and bringing him to an understanding of the social situation he had to deal with in his newly conquered empire. The Mongols were not interested in the customs of the conquered countries but merely in the exploitation of these territories and their resources.[29]

The Khitan chancellor staffed his offices with Chinese, Tangut and Uighur officials. For a long time the Uighurs predominated, but gradually Chinese influence became stronger. In addition to Yeh-lü Ch'u-ts'ai, the Kereit Chinqai (one of Genghis Khan's chief advisers) played an important role in the central government. Not a single ordinance could be passed in north China unless Chinqai had approved it in Uighur writing.[30] Probably urged to do so by his ministers, Ögödei promulgated a number of laws during a quriltai held in 1235.[31] Yeh-lü Ch'u-ts'ai wished to introduce a budget in the Mongol Empire, and had therefore to standardize the taxes, which were paid by the various peoples in kind. A settled population had to pay 10% of its income or harvest, while the nomads had to surrender one animal out of every hundred as tax. The Khitan minister wished to forbid the officials of the Mongol Empire from accepting gifts from the people. According to tradition Ögödei could not understand what was wrong with this: 'As long as the official does not extort gifts, why should he not accept them?' he said.[32]

Although it is known that the mounted courier service (Yam, see pages 40–1) was organized on Genghis Khan's orders,[33] Ögödei introduced a number of measures to improve it shortly after becoming the new khan.[34] At the time of the quriltai of 1235 the service was greatly extended, and this year is sometimes given as the date of the official opening of the Yam.[35] Chaghatai played an active role in its development.[36] Throughout the whole empire staging posts were established, each run by a number of officials, and each having its own horses, cattle and food.[37] In Central Asia wells were dug along the routes. The most important links in the empire ran between the residences of Ögödei, Changhatai and Batu.[38] Yeh-lü Ch'u-ts'ai and his staff made provision in the staging posts for storage of grain.[39] The improvement and expansion of the mounted courier service and the digging of wells were regarded by

Ögödei as his greatest achievements in government.[40]

By 1219 Genghis Khan had already fixed on a more or less permanent location for his most important residence. It lay on the upper reaches of the Orkhon River, near the place where the Uighurs had established their Ordu Baliq (Qara Balghasun) in the eighth and ninth centuries. It is noteworthy that this seat did not lie between the Onon and the Kerulen rivers, but in the border regions of the later apanages of Ögödei and Tolui. We may assume that from 1220 it was the central point of the whole Mongol Empire. Ögödei had this surrounded in 1235 by a wall; he is generally considered to be the founder of the Mongol capital.[41] He sent for craftsmen from China to embellish Qaraqorum, as the capital was called.[42] Qaraqorum never grew into a large town. The Franciscan monk William of Rubrouck, who visited the Mongol capital in 1254, characterized it as follows: 'As for the city of Qaraqorum I can tell you that, not counting the Khan's palace, it is not as large as the village of Saint Denis, and the monastery of Saint Denis is worth ten times more than that palace.'[43] After Qubilai had moved his seat in 1260 to Peking, Qaraqorum rapidly fell into decay. In 1585 the Buddhist monastery Erdeni-ju was built on or near the ruins of what had once been the centre of a mighty empire.[44]

The establishment of a permanent seat for the government aided the efforts of Yeh-lü Ch'u-ts'ai in making the central authority more powerful.[45] Even after founding the capital Ögödei, as a real Mongol (like his successors Güyük and Möngke), could not be bound to one place. In the spring Ögödei stayed in Qaraqorum until about 21 April. He then went to the lakes and marshes of the Orkhon River, just north of the capital. At the end of May or early June he returned to Qaraqorum, but shortly afterwards he moved into the mountains south-east of Qaraqorum. At the end of August he went to the Ongiin River in the south, where he had his hunting grounds and winter residence. In February he returned once more to Qaraqorum.[46]

THE RECONQUEST OF PERSIA AND CAUCASIA

When Genghis Khan marched home to Mongolia after the destruction of the Khwarazm empire, he left behind him a

Khurasan, an Afghanistan and a central and western Persia that were totally ruined and largely depopulated. Anarchy prevailed there, particularly in the regions ravaged by Jebe and Sübedei, who had taken little account of the chaos their operations caused.[47] There was no longer any central government to restore order to these provinces; reconstruction of the administration could therefore only be undertaken locally. In particular the inhabitants of the town against which the Mongol terror had been chiefly directed were again the victims of this confused situation.

The apparent indifference of the Mongols created a vacuum which Jalal al-Din Mangubirdi, who had fled to Delhi in 1221, made use of to win back Fars and Kirman in 1224. His younger brother, Giyath al-Din, had meanwhile settled in Isfahan, which Jalal al-Din also added to his sultanate. Özbeg, the atabeg of Azerbaijan, who had been able to buy immunity from plundering at the cost of high indemnities during the raid of Jebe and Sübedei, had to recognize in 1225 the suzerainty of the new ruler of those regions.[48] In order to ensure his authority in Azerbaijan, Jalal al-Din carried out successful attacks on the Christian kingdom of Georgia between 1225 and 1228. In 1227 Tiflis (Tbilisi) fell into his hands.[49] King Giorgi III Lacha, who died in 1223, was succeeded by his sister Rusudan.

Jalal al-Din managed to some extent to restore his empire, which had been destroyed by Genghis Khan. In 1230 it included the provinces of Fars, Kirman, Iraq-Ajemi, Azerbaijan and Mazandaran; the capitals were Isfahan and Tabriz.[50] During his struggle for power the new sultan had no hesitation in perpetrating atrocities no less terrible than those of the Mongols; the common people, already stricken by the Mongols, now had to suffer heavily again at the hands of the sultan's undisciplined troops. In order to maintain his position Jalal al-Din ordered the assassination of his brother Giyath al-Din, whom he regarded as his rival.[51] The son of Sultan Muhammad II was undoubtedly a brave military commander, but as a statesman he had as little foresight as his father. Instead of thoroughly organizing his Persian kingdom in order to be prepared for a possible return of the Mongols, he caused difficulties with the caliph of Baghdad, who had already been watching the restoration of the Khwarazm sultanate with deep suspicion. In addition there were confrontations with the sultan of the Rum-Seljuqs and the Ayyubids in Syria.[52]

Meanwhile a serious threat to Jalal al-Din materialized in the east. In 1230 Ögödei sent an army of 30,000 men commanded by Chormaghun Noyan to put an end to the unexpected restoration of the former Khwarazm sultanate. Chormaghun's army moved with remarkable rapidity via Khurasan and Rayy to Azerbaijan, its vanguard reaching the neighbourhood of Tabriz and finding the defenders totally unprepared.[53] Jalal al-Din was sensible enough to conclude a treaty as quickly as possible with the Rum-Seljuqs and the Ayyubids.[54] It is noteworthy that this prince, who did not lack courage, decided to evade the Mongols. He fled to the plains of Mugan and Arran, then to Diyar Bakr. The Mongol cavalry followed his trail as they had ten years previously pursued his father. During his flight Jalal al-Din lost more and more supporters.[55] How the sultan met his end is not known, but he was probably murdered by Kurds in 1231, when he had been abandoned almost entirely. The way that he met his inglorious death resulted, for several years, in a number of adventurers posing as Jalal al-Din in order to claim his rights.[56]

Chormaghun remained as military governor in the part of Persia he had conquered. He established his residence in the plains of Mugan and Arran, which were very suitable as the winter quarters of a cavalry army.[57] In Khurasan and Mazandaran Chin Temür, who was a Qara Khitai, became governor; he filled this function until his death in 1235. In 1239 Körgüz was entrusted with the administration of Khurasan and Mazandaran; this Uighur, a Nestorian Christian and a great friend of Chinqai,[58] developed into an able governor.[59] During the ten years (1231–41) of Chormaghun's leadership he subdued the surrounding countries, following the familiar Mongol custom. His progress, however, was slow, partly because a large number of states in the Caucasus lay in particularly difficult terrain. Moreover, the opposition he had to overcome, especially from the Georgians, was not inconsiderable.[60] Diyar Bakr and its environs, against which he was operating in 1233, had as much to suffer as the towns in Transoxiana and Khurasan in 1220 and 1221.[61] Chormaghun next turned his attention to Caucasia, destroying Ganja, and then entering the kingdom of Georgia in 1236. Queen Rusudan fled from Tiflis to Kutaisi and Georgia was added to the Mongol Empire as a vassal state. One of Chormaghun's last deeds was the occupation of the towns of Kars and Ani.[62]

Chormaghun granted freedom of worship to both Christians and Muslims. In 1241 he suddenly lost the power of speech; his governorship had to be assumed by his wife until the arrival of the new commander, Baiju Noyan. Baiju, who like his predecessor was to remain as governor in Persia and Caucasia for a long time (until 1256), was less tolerant than Chormaghun towards the Christians.[63] The most important result of Baiju's measures was the eventual fall of the lordship of the Rum-Seljuqs in Anatolia.

The Konya sultanate, which seceded about 1075 from the Seljuq empire, had in the course of time become so influenced by the Greek empire that its Muslim fanaticism had practically disappeared; the entire country had in fact adapted itself to Christian civilization.[64] After a period of prosperity (1200–37) it quickly lost its influence during the rule of Sultan Kay Khusraw II, who came to power in 1237 and soon revealed himself to be a person of weak character.[65] In 1242 the Mongols entered the Konya sultanate. The town of Erzerum was surrounded, but offered strong resistance.[66] It fell at the end of 1242 and after being heavily plundered was destroyed by fire. As the winter was approaching the Mongols returned to the Mugan Plain.[67] The Rum-Seljuqs could expect little support from the caliph of Baghdad and the Ayyubids in Syria and Egypt; these had troubles of their own to face.

In the early summer of 1243 Baiju went with an army of 30,000 men back to Anatolia to subdue the Rum-Seljuqs completely. Sultan Kay Khusraw II marched to meet the Mongols with an army of 80,000 men, which included reinforcements from his vassal states. On 26 June 1243 the two armies met near the Kösedagh mountain, north-east of Sivas.[68] The Seljuq vanguard was defeated; when he heard the news, Kay Khusraw fled westwards with his main force.[69] Baiju's troops continued their advance and took Sivas and Kayseri. The sultan sent an embassy to Baiju, who had meanwhile returned to the Mugan Plain, promising to pay the Great Khan an annual tribute, which was tantamount to recognition of the Mongol's suzerainty by the Rum-Seljuqs.[70]

In the south-east of Anatolia was the small Armenian Christian kingdom of Cilicia. Its ruler, King Hethun I (1226–69), was a skilful and astute monarch. As the vassal of the sultan of Konya he was attracted to the rising power of the Mongols and therefore made a spontaneous offer of submission to the Mongol suzerainty. In this way he escaped invasion by Baiju's army. His example was followed by the atabeg of Mosul.[71]

THE WAR IN CHINA CONTINUES

After the death of Muqali in 1223 the Chins had taken advantage of Genghis Khan's absence to reconquer a great deal of territory from the Mongols, particularly in the Wei Valley and in Shensi. In Shensi the town of Pu-chou fell into their hands. Genghis Khan had always been aware that the Chin empire was an opponent which had to be taken seriously,[72] as the advice he gave his sons on his deathbed shows.[73] He warned them that the Chin's best troops were those of T'ung-kuan, a fortified town lying between the Huang-ho and the Ch'in Ling mountains which dominated the approaches to Honan. Genghis Khan therefore advised his sons to exploit the hundred-year-old enmity between the Sung and the Chin. Through the territory of Sung they could reach K'ai-feng. Twelve years before his death Genghis Khan himself negotiated with the Sung on this matter;[74] the Chin had learned of this and had taken steps to concentrate their defences in Honan.

In 1230 the Mongol offensive began. The Chin resistance took the Mongols by surprise. The old Jurchen fighting spirit had returned. The Chin General Wan-yen Yi repulsed the attackers first in the eastern part of Kansu and then in the Wei Valley. In the spring of 1231 the Mongols, now commanded by Sübedei, made a fresh attempt. Fenghsiang fell into their hands, but south-east of Hsi-an they were again pushed back by Wan-yen Yi.[75]

Ögödei now decided to follow his father's advice. He sent an ambassador to the Sung, but on his arrival in the Sung territory this ambassador was killed. After much difficulty a second mediator succeeded in making an agreement.[76] Ögödei set off with the main body of his army and all his siege material for Shansi. After taking the militarily important town of Pu-chou,[77] Ögödei marched in an easterly direction on the north side of the Huang-ho. Tolui carried out a wide flanking movement with his army of 30,000 cavalry, deliberately violating the Sung's frontiers.[78] During his march his troops suffered much distress from food shortage and adverse weather conditions.[79] Tolui crossed first the Wei, then the Han River, conquered the town of Hang-chung on the Sung territory and then moved south via the Chia-ling River. In Szechwan he turned again towards the north-east, passing the Han River at the end of January 1232 and appearing suddenly in Chin territory.[80]

By February 1232 Ögödei had crossed the Huang-ho between T'ung-kuan and Lo-yang and had taken possession of Lo-yang. Near Yüshien the two Mongol armies joined forces and almost immediately came into contact with a Chin army of 15,000 men under the command of the capable Wan-yen Yi. After a hard-fought battle during which the outcome remained in doubt for a considerable time, the Jurchen were defeated. Wan-yen Yi was captured by the Mongols. Tolui, who knew at first hand the qualities of this general, attempted to persuade him to enter the service of the Mongols. The proud Jurchen refused, even when Tolui tried to force him to consent by means of torture. Wan-yen Yi chose a martyr's death rather than service with the enemy.[81] After this lost battle the Chin withdrew all their troops to K'ai-feng and its environs, abandoning to the victor the rest of their territory. Ögödei surrounded the capital; he asked the Emperor Ngai-tsung to surrender his imperial title and as governor of Honan to recognize Mongol suzerainty. The Chin sovereign, feeling that he could not honourably accept this proposal, rejected it.

Ögödei and Tolui left the siege of K'ai-feng to Sübedei. The two brothers went off to the mountains in the north to pass the hot summer.[82] The investment of K'ai-feng presented many problems to the Mongols. Not only did the Chin capital offer an obstinate defence, the inhabitants also made use of a kind of power that they were able to make explode: 'The Chin had great mortars which roared like the thunder in heaven.'[83] The losses of the Mongols began to assume such proportions that

Sübedei tried to reach some sort of agreement with the Emperor Ngai-tsung. Probably his losses were not Sübedei's only worry. Ögödei, who was with Tolui north of Ling-hu-t'ai, became seriously ill. What happened exactly to the two brothers while they were there is not known. After some time Ögödei recovered, but Tolui died shortly after, probably as a result of excessive drinking.[84] When Tolui's descendants became the rulers of the empire it was necessary to idealize his manner of dying, so a legend was created claiming that Tolui had sacrificed himself for Ögödei. According to this legend the condition of the seriously ill Ögödei caused great concern. Shamans were summoned to drive his illness away by means of spells and charms. When this failed, Tengri was asked whether a member of the family might die in place of Ögödei. A favourable reply was received upon which Tolui decided to sacrifice himself for his brother. After he had entrusted his wife and children to the care of Ögödei, Tolui drank a magic draught and died.[85] Ögödei recovered after a short time. When Tolui died on 9 October 1232, he was about 39 years of age.[86] Important to later developments was that Ögödei regularly asked Tolui's widow, Sorqaqtani, for advice.[87] The shrewd Sorqaqtani was thus able to continue to exert some influence.

During the time when the two supreme commanders were out of action, it was Sübedei who had to take responsibility for decision making. The Emperor Ngai-tsung had rejected his offer of reconciliation. In order to make an end quickly and finally to the Chin empire, Sübedei decided to renew contact with the Sung in Hang-chou. The Sung were ready to help the Mongols if they were given Honan and K'ai-feng. Soon after this was agreed, an army of 20,000 men under the command of General Meng-Hung arrived at K'ai-feng.[88] A hundred years earlier the Sung had made the same mistake: they had then helped the Jurchen during the subjection of the Khitan; the Jurchen appeared later to be much more aggressive than their Khitan predecessors. Now that the Jurchen overlordship was coming to an end, the Chinese supported the new barbarians from the north. What disaster this was to be for them would become apparent thirty years later.

In K'ai-feng the situation became steadily more hopeless. In

1233 the Emperor Ngai-tsung managed to escape from his beleaguered capital to a town in the east surrounded by water. There he tried without success to urge the Sung to change their plans.[89] In the spring of 1233 K'ai-feng surrendered to Sübedei,[90] a step hastened by the treachery of Ts'ui-li, a Chin general. Sübedei executed all the male members of the Chin dynasty, as well as the entire family of Wan-yen Yi. The women of the imperial dynasty he sent to Qaraqorum. Sübedei also proposed to wipe out the whole of the population in the capital, but thanks to the energetic intervention of Yeh-lü Ch'u-ts'ai, this massacre was not carried out. Plundering, robbery, violence and arson could not be avoided after such a long siege, however. The Sung troops also joined in these activities.[91]

As long as the emperor remained alive, it could not be said that his rule was over. The Mongols and the Sung set off in pursuit of Ngai-tsung, who had fled south. He committed suicide in the spring of 1234. The last resistance of the Chin was swept away in the same year near Junan.[92] The end of the hated enemy was enthusiastically celebrated in Hang-chou. The Sung were rewarded for their help by being granted the southeast part of Honan and north-western Anhwei. K'ai-feng was not included in this gift. The Mongols, who were now the undisputed rulers in north China, kept the former capital for themselves. After Ögödei had appointed the deserter Ts'ui-li as governor of K'ai-feng, a part of the Mongol forces retired northwards. Before and during this departure the Chin population suffered much hardship, but Yeh-lü Ch'u-ts'ai was also able to put an end to this.

The presence of the aggressive Mongols on their northern frontier was a serious threat to the Sung, but the Chinese were presumably not sufficiently aware of it. The Sung Emperor Li-tsung (1225–64), influenced by a few over-zealous advisers, committed the folly of occupying the whole of Honan. In July and August of 1234 Lo-yang and K'ai-feng fell without much resistance into the hands of the Sung.[93] In the former Chin capital the people murdered Ögödei's governor, Ts'ui-li. Ögödei, who had called a quriltai in Qaraqorum, decided in 1235 to punish the Sung. Three Mongol armies invaded the Chinese empire. The first army, commanded by Ögödei's second son Köten, entered Szechwan. The second army, commanded by another son of Ögödei, Köchü, captured Siang-yang on the Han River in March 1236.[94] The Tangut General Chaghan, with the third army, reached the Yang-tze near Han-k'ou,[95] then advanced against eastern Hupeh and western Anhwei. The Sung had a very skilful general in Meng-Hung; he was able to put up a good opposition to the Mongols. In 1236 he gave them a thorough defeat near Chiang-ling in Hupeh and freed 20,000 prisoners. In 1239 Siang-yang itself fell again into the hands of the Sung.[96]

All these Chinese successes did not prevent the Mongols from undertaking plundering raids as far as the Yang-tze. They were indeed uncoordinated actions, during which the Mongols even took temporary possession of Ch'eng-tu in Szechwan in 1241.[97] But this gradual pressure of the Mongols towards the south was merely a foretaste of what was to come for the Sung.

THE MARTYRDOM OF THE KOREAN PEOPLE

Korea (Kao-li), together with the Koryo dynasty, which had come to power in 918, formed an independent kingdom. Since 1170 the Koryo kings were heads of the state only in name; the real power was in the hands of military governors.[98]

The first encounters between Mongols and Koreans took place in the years 1216–18. The Mongols were pursuing on the Liao-tung Peninsula rebellious Khitan forces who had sought shelter behind the Yalu River, where they occupied a number of towns. The Mongols asked the Koryo to help them to punish the Khitan,[99] and, making use of the fact that they had invaded Korea, the Mongols compelled the Koryo to pay a tribute that became increasingly heavy.[100] The death of Muqali in 1223 and the absence of Genghis Khan was an opportunity not only for the Chin, but also for the Koryo, to make an attempt to cast off the Mongol yoke. In 1225 the situation became serious when a Mongol envoy, who had made all kinds of demands, was murdered on his return journey. The Mongols were, however, at that moment too committed elsewhere for a punitive expedition: this had to be postponed for some years.

After his elevation to the rank of Great Khan, Ögödei decided to march against Korea, which the Mongols regarded as a part of Temüge's apanage.[101] At the end of August 1231 a strong Mongol army under the command of Sartaq crossed the Yalu River, initiating a period of thirty years during which the Mongols constantly crossed the Yalu to hold Korea to ransom.[102] After taking P'yong-yang and massacring its inhabitants, they reached the Koryo capital Kaeson at the end of December 1231. During the Mongol advance the local people were outrageously terrorized.[103] After the payment of a considerable amount of money the Mongols accepted the Korean request for peace, and in 1232 withdrew, although they continued to plunder on their way. The military governor resolved to take advantage of the return of peace to remove the seat of the Koryo government to the island of Kanghwa, which lay off the west coast.[104] As became apparent later, this was a clever move, making the governing authorities inaccessible to their Mongol enemies.

To collect the revenues they had exacted, the Mongols had left behind about 70 officials in the north-western part of the Korean Peninsula.[105] When a number of these were murdered, a new Mongol invasion took place in August and September 1232, again under the command of Sartaq. This attack progressed smoothly, and without much difficulty the invading troops reached the Han River. During the fighting Sartaq was killed; the Koreans, encouraged by this event, resisted with ever-increasing strength.[106]

At the quriltai in 1235 it was decided to end the constant resurgence of resistance in Korea. In September 1235 a Mongol army commanded by Tanqut Baghatur and Hong Pogwon again crossed the Yalu.[107] The army marched at first towards the east coast of the peninsula, but in the spring of 1236 the real attack began. The Mongols reached Kaeju via Anju in September and as the winter set in they were already south of the Han River. The Koreans made no attempt to face the Mongols with an army, their resistance taking the form of guerrilla activities. This method of dealing with the invaders was, however, of little use, mainly because the Korean population itself suffered heavy losses. A fresh request for peace achieved some success, insomuch as the Mongols acceded to it and withdrew some of their forces; but the troops that remained continued the regime of terror. The enslaved Korean people were obliged to try to remedy matters by resuming guerrilla activities,[108] but the toll that the people had to pay for this resistance was so high that the Korean leaders were forced in 1238 again to enter negotiations with their conquerors. For two years envoys were sent back and forth to Qaraqorum; after a relative of the king was sent as a hostage to the Mongol capital, peace was at last granted to the Koreans in 1241.[109]

14

The Mongol invader in Europe

THE END OF THE OLD RUSSIA

At the beginning of the tenth century the princedom of Kiev grew into the most powerful of the Russian states. During the rule of Sviatoslav (964–72) its territory increased considerably. After his death there were some disputes about the succession, but in 980 his son Vladimir ascended the throne. The most important event in his reign was his conversion to Christianity; by the end of the tenth century almost the whole of the Russian population had accepted this religion. At the time of Yaroslav (1036–54) Kiev entered the period of its largest growth; exactly where its boundaries ran is not known, but they included the region extending to Lake Ladoga in the north, Vladimir-Suzdal, Riazan and Kursk in the east, the Dniester in the south and Minsk in the west.[1]

After the death of Yaroslav in 1054 his princedom was divided among his sons into a number of autonomous regions. In the twelfth century and at the beginning of the thirteenth the most important of these were Kiev and Chernigov in the south, Galich and Volynia in the west, Smolensk in the centre, and Vladimir-Suzdal and Riazan in the north-east. In the north was the independent republic of Novgorod.[2] After this dismemberment Kiev did indeed keep its importance as a cultural and religious centre, but its political domination declined to some extent. The splitting up of Russia resulted in incessant jealousy and strife among the princedoms, and the Russian princes did not hesitate to call on other nations to help them in their disputes.

Among those who exploited this lack of unity were the

Turkish nomad tribes penetrating south Russia. The last to benefit in this way were the Cumans, who invaded the south Russian plains at the end of the eleventh century and set up a great kingdom there. Although the Cumans and the Russian princes often waged war against each other, the situation had changed so much by the end of the thirteenth century that Prince Mstislav of Galich married a daughter of Khan Kotian of the Cumans (see page 120). In the north-west also a danger had arisen in the twelfth century as the invading German Order of Knights drove the Letts and the Lithuanians of the Baltic Coast eastwards. Later the warlike Lithuanians attempted to compensate for their lost ground on the Baltic Coast at the expense of the Russian princes. However, nothing could stop the princes from engaging in endless quarrels among themselves. Even the Mongol assault of Jebe and Sübedei in 1222 could not bring about the unity they needed to face one of the most serious menaces in Russia's history: the second invasion of the Mongols.

After the quriltai of 1229 Ögödei sent the experienced General Sübedei to the west to carry out reconnaissances.[3] What the results of these were is not known. Presumably they aimed at collecting information for the great operation that was to start seven years later. During the quriltai of 1235 it was decided to send a large army to the west to conquer the Volga Bulgars, the Cumans and the Russians. The command of this army lay in the hands of Batu, Jochi's second son. His army of about 50,000 men formed the main group of the forces that marched to the west. At Ögödei's orders the other apanages sent reinforcements. The total strength of Batu's army must have been about 120,000 men.[4] In all probability these troops were largely Turkish, while the higher command was chiefly in the hands of the Mongols. The most important figure in this campaign was Sübedei, then about sixty years of age. Subordinate commanders under Batu were his brothers Orda, Berke and Shiban; two sons of Ögödei, Güyük and Qadan; a son and a grandson of Chaghatai, Baidar and Büri; finally, two sons of Tolui, Möngke and Böchek.[5] In addition to Sübedei there were a number of generals in the army. Not all the names of these former subcommanders of Genghis Khan are known; one of them was Boroldai.[6] Originally Ögödei intended to take supreme command of this operation himself.[7]

The campaign was prepared in advance by Batu and Sübedei with scrupulous care, as had always been done in any of Genghis Khan's actions. Scouts and spies were sent out to gather intelligence.[8] The first objective of the Mongols was Bulgar, the capital of the Volga Bulgars. This tribe played an important part for a number of centuries in trade between Central Asia and east and north Europe.[9] In the autumn of 1236 Bulgar was conquered by Batu and Sübedei;[10] the shattered town was quickly rebuilt.[11] Some of the Bulgars fled westwards, where they sought and were granted shelter in Russia.[12]

About the same time as the conquest of Bulgar, the Mongols attacked the Cumans (or Qipchaqs) who lived along the Volga. They also were defeated. Bachman, the chief of this group of the Cumans, escaped to an island in the Volga. In the winter of 1236–7, Möngke succeeded in taking him prisoner there, after which he was put to a cruel death.[13] A number of the Cumans fled to the west, but most of them bowed to Mongol domination. This Turkish people, a confederation of tribes, later formed the nucleus of the Mongol khanate in south Russia: it even gave it its name. One of the names by which the apanage (ulus) of Batu is known in history is Khanate Qipchaq.[14]

Although the Russian princes knew that the conquest of the khanate of the Volga Bulgars was the preliminary to the invasion of their own territory, they made no preparations to repulse the Mongol threat. There was no question of any united front. This territorial disruption made things easier for the Mongols. In December 1237 they began their first assault on a Russian princedom. When the prince of Riazan rejected out of hand the demand to surrender voluntarily, his capital was surrounded and captured on 21 December after a siege lasting only five days. Prince Yuri and his wife were executed.[15] The Mongols then moved on to Kolomna, where Prince Roman (Yuri's brother) resided. The prince of Vladimir-Suzdal tried unsuccessfully to relieve Kolomna. During this siege Kölgen, a son of Genghis Khan and his Merkit wife Qulan, was killed.[16] This town too fell after a short siege. Prince Roman was killed during the fighting.[17] In the princedom Riazan the Mongols destroyed a number of small towns so thoroughly that they disappeared for ever from the pages of history, their ruins remaining for years as a sad spectacle.[18]

Genghis Khan's custom of attacking an important town only after a number of the surrounding towns had been captured was followed by Batu and Sübedei in Russia. For the time being, therefore, they left Vladimir, the capital of Prince Yuri II, in peace. Batu went to Moscow, then of little importance. After a brief siege the town fell and after the usual plundering it was destroyed by fire.[19] Prince Yuri left Vladimir and moved north with his army. His capital was surrounded by the Mongols and on 8 February taken by storm. A typical atrocity then took place. Large numbers of the townspeople had fled into the churches in the hope of finding safety there. The Mongols, however, unfamiliar with the significance of churches, set them alight and the people inside died in the flames.[20] The family of the prince of Vladimir-Suzdal were put to death.[21] At the same time, Batu was surrounding Suzdal, and this town too fell after a short time.

The Mongols then turned north-west, where Prince Yuri II was camped with his army. In succession Perieaslavl, Yaroslavl and Tver (present-day Kalinin) fell into their hands. Yuri, who was near the Mologa River, was thus isolated from his own princedoms. On 4 March 1238 his army was defeated near the Sit River, and he himself died in the battle.[22] In the north there was now only the merchant republic of Novgorod. Nothing seemed able to stop the Mongol advance or to prevent the conquest of this Russian state. The town of Torzhok in this republic, however, did not capitulate without putting up a fight. It was only after two weeks that it surrendered on 23 March 1238. These two weeks were decisive for further operations in the north. The thaw set in, making the ground unsuitable for the Mongol cavalry. Novgorod was saved and would never suffer defeat at the hands of the Mongols.[23] Batu had to withdraw rapidly south to avoid being completely cut off. The town of Kozelsk also presented a serious obstacle: the Mongols besieged the town for seven weeks.[24]

Now that he had conquered some princedoms in north-east Russia, Batu decided to use the rest of 1238 and the following year to subdue the Cumans in south Russia and the tribes in north Caucasia.[25] The operations against the Cumans were conducted by Batu's brother Berke. After some fighting the Cumans in 1238 acknowledged the rule of the Mongols.[26] Khan Kotian fled with 40,000 compatriots to Hungary to seek asylum.[27] While Shiban and Büri went to the Crimea, Möngke and Qadan were ordered to reduce the tribes in Caucasia.[28] The Alans and Cherkesses (Circassians) who lived there had to accept the sovereignty of the Mongols in 1239.[29]

In the spring of 1240 Batu's armies, now reorganized and brought up to strength, resumed their westward march. The country of the Cumans offered a favourable springboard from which to mount an attack on the important princedom of Kiev. Although the exact facts and their sequence is not known, it is assumed that prior to the assault on the great town of Kiev, Chernigov and Perieaslav were first taken by the Mongols in the summer of 1240.[30] Prince Michael of Kiev and Chernigov escaped into Hungary and from there to Silesia.[31] The conduct of the defence of Kiev fell to the Boyar Dmitri. Möngke, who had been charged by Batu to attack Kiev, wanted to spare such an important town[32] and asked for its voluntary surrender. Not only was his request refused forthwith, but his envoys were put to death.[33] This deed sealed the fate of those who had committed it.

The largest part of the Mongol army, including all participating Genghisids, gathered before the great city.[34] The defenders, fighting valorously under the leadership of Dmitri, were unable to withstand the assault. After a siege of only a few days, Kiev fell on 6 December 1240.[35] The town that was so important to the Russians was plundered and destroyed. John of Plano Carpini, who passed by Kiev six years later on his journey to Mongolia, described what remained of the once so splendid city: 'Many valuable artistic relics and architectural monuments were reduced to rubble.'[36] The loss meant the end of Kiev as the seat of the most powerful prince and of the metropolitan bishop of Russia.[37] The heart had been torn out of the old Russia.

After this important success the Mongols marched further west. A number of towns fell, some by force of arms and others by cunning.[38] They were Kamenets (Podolsky), Vladimir (Volynia) and Galich. The country bordering Poland between Vladimir and Galich surrendered of its own accord, and it was here that Batu set up his winter military quarters. Most of the Russian princes, including Daniel of Galich, fled to Hungary and Poland,[39] a fact which turned the attention of the Mongols to these two countries. Hungary in particular, as the adopted country of the exiled Cumans, aroused the interest of the Mongols. The road to these central European states lay open to the Asiatic conquerors. Tradition has it that Batu was told by the prisoner Boyar Dmitri that the Mongols were wise to attack Hungary.[40]

CENTRAL EUROPE ON THE EDGE OF THE ABYSS

At the beginning of the thirteenth century central Europe was divided into a number of not very secure monarchies. These weak states often had a certain connection with the German empire. One of them, Bohemia, had in 1212 become, with the assistance of the German emperor, an autonomous state. King Wenceslas I of Bohemia was very favourably inclined towards his powerful neighbour, the more so on account of the marriage with a princess of the imperial family. Nevertheless Bohemia had not achieved real unity. Situated in the heart of Europe, it was a kingdom much enfeebled by internal difficulties.

On the plains of the Vistula the dukes of Piast had built up a state of some importance during the second half of the tenth century. With the annexation of Silesia, accomplished by Boleslaw Chrobry (992–1025), this dukedom had been greatly enlarged. After Duke Boleslaw Chrobry had succeeded in releasing himself from the suzerainty of the German emperor, he assumed the title of King of Poland. Unending quarrels about the succession weakened his authority. At the time of the Mongol invasion of Russia the power of King Boleslaw IV in fact did not extend beyond the dukedom of Sandomierz-Krakow. In Poland there were three dukes who no longer recognized Boleslaw as their sovereign. Of them Duke Henry II (the Pious) of Silesia was the most important. The other two were Conrad of Masovia and Miecislaw of Oppeln-Ratibor (present-day Opole and Raciborz). King Boleslaw IV made constant attempts to re-establish his authority over these three dukes, so that the country was continually disturbed by skirmishes, a situation which created in Poland precisely the kind of disintegration that had existed in Russia. To an even greater extent than in Russia, the aggressive German Order of Knights along the Baltic Coast formed a threat in Poland. Not only were the Poles driven from the coast by these knights, but the Lithuanians, who also had to flee before German colonization, attempted to make their territorial losses good at the expense of Poland.

More important than these two monarchies was the kingdom of Hungary, which had come into existence at the beginning of the eleventh century. Gradually the Hungarian kings managed to extend their territories to the Carpathians and the Transylvanian Alps. In the south they even reached the Adriatic Sea. As in Poland, every accession to the Hungarian throne gave rise to violent quarrels among the members of the royal family, a circumstance which offered the German and Byzantine emperors in turn an opportunity to interfere in Hungary. When King Béla III (1173–96) came to the throne a glorious period in Hungarian history began. Béla was an excellent leader, and when organizing his kingdom he made use of his knowledge of Byzantine and French cultures. It was a blow to Hungary that the rule of Andrew II (1205–35) lasted for thirty years. This frivolous and unprincipled monarch appeared to be totally unfitted to continue the work of Béla III. The great landowners in particular took advantage of the weakening authority of the king.[41] More and more the Hungarian crown had to capitulate before the power of the nobles. When King Béla IV came to the throne in 1235 he was confronted with a situation of almost utter anarchy, brought about by the independent attitude of the nobility.

Béla IV began his long reign full of good intentions. Unfortunately, although he achieved much as a prince of peace, in the main he had no ability as a leader in battle.[42] In 1239 Khan Kotian asked the Hungarian king to allow the Cumans, who had fled from south Russia, to enter his kingdom. Béla agreed on condition that the Cumans adopted the Roman religion and promised loyalty to the king. They had to settle in the central part of Hungary. One problem was that the integration of the Cumans appeared to be particularly difficult. The Hungarian population which in the thirteenth century supported itself mainly by agriculture was unable easily to accept the nomads from the south Russian steppes.[43] The king accepted them in the hope of strengthening his army with these nomad cavalrymen.[44]

Batu sent Béla an ultimatum. 'I have heard', he said, 'that you have taken the Cumans, who are my subjects, under your protection. I command you to send them away, for by taking them away from me you have become my enemy. It is easier for them to flee than it is for your people. They live in tents, while you live in houses and cities.' Batu also complained in this message that the envoys, probably about thirty of them, who he had sent to Béla, had never returned.[45] A number of these envoys had been taken prisoner by the Russian princes; some, however, did in fact arrive in Hungary.[46] The murder of their envoys was always strongly resented by the Mongols; Batu's accusation indicates therefore a serious miscalculation on the part of Béla. It is strange that such a man as King Béla IV made such a mistake. He was one of the few European kings who wished to learn something about the Mongols when they invaded Europe in 1236. He sent a number of messengers to Batu. One of them, the Dominican Julien, returned to Béla in 1237 after a visit to the Mongols.[47] By not sending the Cumans away, Béla ensured that a Mongol attack on his kingdom became inevitable. Possibly the king relied too much on the fact that the Hungarians had always been able to repel successfully the raiding nomad tribes from the south Russian steppes.[48]

Batu and Sübedei had to take into account the possibility of an attack from the north during their intended campaign against Hungary. The probability that this would occur was not great in view of their mutual relationship, but Poland's and Bohemia's intervention, perhaps supported by the German emperor, was not impossible. To counter such a threat, and to protect the northern flank of the main body marching against Hungary, a simultaneous attack on Poland had to be made. Sübedei, who was undoubtedly the spiritual leader of the Mongol plan of attack, here adapted one of Genghis Khan's principles: to protect a threatened flank by launching an offensive against the force presenting the threat.

Geographically Poland was more open than Hungary and Bohemia, both of which were to some extent guarded by a chain of mountains consisting of the Sudetic, Beskid and Carpathian mountains. Curiously, the three countries threatened in this way, each of which had only a small number of fortified places, did not begin to reinforce their armies until the Mongols were lined up on their frontiers.[49]

The region from which Batu's army began its march to the west lay between Vladimir and Galich, where he had set up his winter quarters. Early in February 1241 the troops assigned to Poland began their march. The commanders of this contingent of about 30,000 men[50] were Orda and Baidar, the latter being called in European history Peta. There were perhaps two Mongol columns in Poland; the one commanded by Orda was said to have made a wide turning movement through Masovia.[51] Although this is possible, it is unlikely.[52] To protect the main army by a flank cover, it was both undesirable and unnecessary to split up further the troops committed to the Polish campaign.

On 13 February 1241 the Mongols crossed the frozen Vistula. The town of Sandomierz was taken and plundered according to the time-honoured Mongol pattern. Further to the west, on 18 March near Chmielnik, Orda and Baidar met the Polish army under the command of King Boleslaw IV. The Poles were heavily defeated and Boleslaw with a part of his troops fled to Moravia.[53] On 22 March the Mongols stood before Krakow. Many of the inhabitants had already made their escape. On Palm Sunday the Mongols set the town on fire and took with them large numbers of the people who had remained.[54] Moving further west, Orda and Baidar reached a place east of Opole, where they forced Duke Miecislaw's army to retreat. Near Raciborz they crossed the Oder. Raciborz was burned by its inhabitants when they left the town. Breslau (present-day Wroclaw) fell into the hands of the Mongols, although the citadel itself did not surrender. Their first assault against the fortress having failed, the Mongols did not lose time with a siege. They bypassed the citadel of the town and pushed forward to the west.[55]

Orda's objective was the army of Duke Henry II of Silesia, which stood near Liegnitz (present-day Legnica). The Duke had about 30,000 men, including, in addition to his own Silesian troops, those of the Duke of Opole-Raciborz. Fugitive units from King Boleslaw's army joined themselves to these. Duke Henry was also supported by German knights who had possessions in Silesia. None of the neighbouring countries came to his assistance, however. His brother-in-law, the king of Bohemia, was indeed on his way, but his army made slow progress and did not arrive in time.[56] The combatants met each other on 8 April near Liegnitz;[57] the Mongols withdrew on 9 April. Henry started his pursuit with his heterogeneous army too hastily; after a short withdrawal Orda and Baidar went on to the attack. On the Katz-brook near Wahlstadt, about ten kilometres from Liegnitz, a battle took place that ended in a complete defeat for the Silesian-Polish army. Duke Henry attempted to escape but was killed, as were many of the German knights.[58] Duke Miecislaw sought protection in the citadel of Liegnitz, which, like that of Breslau, was putting up resistance.[59] It might have been thought that Orda and Baidar, after this victory, would have marched further to the west,[60] for the way lay open to them. They did not do so. Two days after the battle of Liegnitz Batu gained a decisive victory in Hungary; the flank cover in the north had fulfilled its task. The Mongols branched off south towards Batu's main force.

King Wenceslas of Bohemia, who realized that he could not alone fight the formidable army of Orda and Baidar, decided to retreat into the mountainous country of Bohemia and Moravia, where the Mongol cavalry would be unable to make full use of their mobility. This caution reflects upon Wenceslas's courage, but he at least ensured that Bohemia was not plundered by the invaders and that his army remained intact.

An assault on Glatz (now Klodzko) failed; the Mongols found that the narrow mountain passes lent themselves very well to attacks by the Bohemian army.[61] Orda and Baidar camped for about two weeks in the neighbourhood of Othmachau (between Opole and Klodzko). Early in May 1241 they entered Moravia. Various small, unprotected places were plundered. When an attempt to take the town of Olomouc came to nothing, they joined, via Brno, Batu's main army in Hungary. Although Bohemia remained unmolested, Moravia had much to endure. The destruction in Poland, Silesia and Moravia was all much of the same kind.[62]

Four weeks after Orda and Baidar had started their march in

Poland, Batu's main army departed. Presumably Batu and Sübedei wanted to await results in Poland before advancing on the main goal of their operation, Hungary, remembering the well-known principle of Genghis Khan that they had to be first sure of the safety of their threatened flank. They divided the troops left behind into three columns: a main force of about 40,000 men and a left and a right wing, each of about 10–20,000 men. This division was apparently made in order to facilitate a rapid penetration of the Carpathian passes.

The main army under Batu's command, to which Sübedei and Boroldai were also attached, forced the Carpathian passes south of Galich on 11 March 1241[63] and then proceeded south between Uzhgorod and Mukachevo.[64] There a Hungarian army awaited them; it suffered a great defeat on 12 March.[65] Large numbers of prisoners fell into the hands of the Mongols and were given the task of clearing the line of advance.[66] On 15 March Batu and Sübedei reached the Danube and disposed their troops before Pest. King Béla IV had gathered his army west of the river. Presumably the army of the Hungarian king was not up to strength; he left Batu, who had not yet been joined by Shiban's troops, unmolested.

The northern column of the advancing army was under the command of Shiban. He went along the upper Vistula and through the Jablunkovsky Pass to the basin of the Vah and the Morava rivers.[67] Shiban had orders to advance as rapidly as possible, for it was planned that he and Batu should arrive at Pest almost simultaneously. For this reason hardly any plundering was permitted during his march. With a speed that was remarkable for those days Shiban pushed on, forcing his column to cover about 75 kilometres a day. On 17 March he reached the Danube near Vac.[68] After he had taken this town by storm he chose his position north-west of Batu.

South of Batu a column commanded by Qadan was moving up via Moldavia and Transylvania to Hungary. Qadan's task was probably to play a security role as well as to make reconnaissances. At one point this column split up, Qadan taking the towns Bistrita and Grosswardein (now Oradea) and then following the Körös River;[69] and the troops advancing in the south, commanded by Böchek, moving through the old German settlements of Hermannstadt and Weissenburg (now

Alba Julia and Sibiu respectively) to the Mures River, where the towns of Arad and Szeged suffered greatly.[70] The troops of Qadan and Böchek committed many atrocities against the local people during their march.

While the Mongol army was advancing on Pest, the Hungarian people rose against the Cumans, partly because the nomads from south Russia showed little consideration for the inhabitants of their guest country and partly because they had reason to believe that the Cumans had fought alongside the Mongols in the battle between Hungarians and Mongols. It was customary in the heterogeneous Mongol army for the subdued tribes to be obliged to supplement losses and to march with the Mongols into battle. The Hungarians, already hostile towards the Cumans and finding their conduct treacherous, stormed Kotian's headquarters and killed him and his followers. After this incident a large number of Kotian subjects turned southwards, but not before they had exacted vengeance by putting as many Hungarians as possible to the sword.[71]

Batu and Sübedei found no opportunity to mount a successful attack on the Hungarian army, which lay behind the Danube. Entirely in accordance with their usual tactics, they withdrew slowly east.[72] King Béla followed them. Close to the place where the Hernad River flows into the Sajo, on the left bank of the Hernad, Batu and Sübedei chose their positions. On the plains of Mohi, south-west of Batu's position, Béla called a halt. Here he showed what a bad general he was; he allowed his army of about 65,000 men[73] to camp in an area that was much too small. Moreover, he surrounded his troops with a ring of wagons tied to each other with chains and ropes, probably intending it as a protection against Mongol attacks. He did not realize that he was also shutting his own troops in. This was the situation of both armies on the evening of 10 April 1241.[74]

In view of the route they followed it is unlikely that Qadan and Böchek linked up with Batu's troops on the plains of Mohi before the battle. In numbers the Mongols were fewer than the Hungarians; the latter, however, were at a disadvantage because of the inexperience of their commanders. Nor could the Hungarian army compare in discipline and courage with that of Batu.

On the evening of 10 April a Russian deserter from the

Mongol camp crossed over to the Hungarians. He told them that Batu and Sübedei would come into action in the night. It is further evidence of King Béla's carelessness that he took hardly any precautions but left his troops enclosed in their narrow camp. That night the Mongols did in fact start their attack. Batu, accompanied by his brother Shiban, turned north, passing the Hernad and the Sajo rivers. Sübedei and Boroldai went to a ford across the Sajo, east of its confluence with the Hernad; there they awaited the result of Batu's action. His attempt to reach the west bank of the Sajo over a bridge was discovered in time, and a Hungarian attack commanded by Béla's brother Coloman drove the Mongols back. The Hungarians were now in triumphant mood. Batu repeated his attempts to form a bridgehead west of the Sajo, and on his troops the Hungarian army concentrated its entire attention. Probably this was what Batu and Sübedei wanted. Sübedei, who had waited for his chance, was able to cross the Sajo in the south without meeting opposition and so could approach the plain of Mohi. In a short time King Béla's army was surrounded and for the most part enclosed in their narrow confines, from which there was no exit. In the morning of 11 April 1241 the issue was settled. The crowded Hungarians saw after some time that the struggle was hopeless and used an opening which the enemy made in their ranks to flee. This trick had the desired result: the Hungarians were pursued by the Mongols and slaughtered in large numbers. Many members of the Hungarian nobility fell. The king and his brother Coloman managed to escape – although Coloman, badly hurt, died later from his wounds. Five days after the battle on the Mohi plains the large town of Pest fell into the hands of the Mongols. When it had been plundered, it was set on fire.[75]

King Béla fled to Agram (present-day Zagreb). Until the winter of 1241–2 he was able to keep his territory west of the Danube free, partly because the river presented a serious obstacle and partly because the Mongols were using the summer to reorganize and rest their army. The inhabitants of the region occupied by Batu were subjected to the same terror as the people in China and Khwarazm had suffered. Large numbers of the male population were obliged to advance as the first echelon against the defenders of besieged towns. The

Mongols encouraged Hungarians who had fled to return to gather in the harvests. When this was done it did not, however, prevent the invaders from striking as mercilessly as ever; nor was any respect shown to women and children.[76] As they always did after their conquests, the Mongols quickly formed a government, which was naturally a rigid one, having as its primary aim the provision of the army. Nevertheless the normal life of the people was restored to some extent.[77]

The winter of 1241–2 was unusually severe; even the Danube froze over. Batu exploited this event during Christmas 1241 to cross the river near Esztergom. The Mongols did not shrink from invading even the German empire. In July 1242 they reached Neustadt, south of Vienna. Batu sent Qadan with his troops to the south to capture King Béla, who fled to a place on the coast of the Adriatic Sea when his pursuers approached. When it became apparent that he was not safe even there, he removed his court to an island off the coast.[78] Qadan followed him as far as Split, but made no attempt to take the king on the island. Instead he turned against Slovenia, Croatia and Bosnia, where the people fled to the safety of the mountains in their fear of the dreaded invaders.[79]

THE RETURN TO MONGOLIA

In March 1242 news reached the Mongol army that Ögödei had died in Mongolia on 11 December 1241. This was important information and prevented the Mongols from operating further west. The Genghisids in Europe had an interest in attending the quriltai which was to appoint the new Great Khan. Certainly Batu (who was then unaware of the manipulations of the Regent Töregene described in chapter 15) had good cause to return to Mongolia before the quriltai was held.

During the campaign in Europe a serious incident had occurred. Batu had quarrelled with two of his nephews: Güyük, the eldest son of Ögödei, and Büri, a grandson of Chaghatai. After the victory over the Russians in 1240 the Mongols held a banquet[80] at which Batu, as the supreme commander, was the first to drink one or two beakers of wine. Güyük and Büri thought that Batu was not entitled to this privilege, and Büri insulted Batu. Harqasun, a grandson of Genghis Khan's brother Qachi'un, spoke in favour of Büri and Güyük. The altercation became so furious that the three objectors threatened to strike Batu and tie him to a beam. The Mongols were extremely sensitive to questions of status and hierarchy, and matters of precedence frequently gave rise to feuds among them, particularly at their feasts and assemblies.[81] Batu complained about the behaviour of his three rebellious nephews to Ögödei who decided it would be wise to recall the trio to Mongolia.

Möngke went back with them, although there had been no difference of opinion between him and Batu. Why he went is not known, but in the light of the later developments of the quarrel it is not unlikely that Möngke journeyed to Qaraqorum as Batu's advocate. At first Ögödei was inclined to regard the behaviour of the three as a serious shortcoming. He made it known that he did not wish to receive his son Güyük; only after the death of his father did Güyük return to Mongolia.[82] Ögödei asked Chaghatai to investigate the behaviour of Büri. The Great Khan himself wished to punish the other two heavily for their breach of discipline. Ögödei thought that Harqasun especially had committed a grave offence. This distant cousin had insulted a grandson of Genghis Khan. Later he adopted a milder attitude, and eventually he personally pardoned the three men.[83] This quarrel was to have far-reaching consequences; it was the direct cause of the splitting of the Genghisids into two mutually hostile groups: Jochi's and Tolui's branches of the family began a feud against those of Ögödei and Chaghatai.

After the decision to return to Mongolia, Batu, Orda and Qadan began the journey in late March and early April 1242, each starting from the region where he was encamped at that moment. The Mongols left Hungary never to return. Batu went along the south bank of the Danube to Walachia.[84] Orda made for the south-east via Transylvania; some of the German settlements had to endure much cruel treatment during his withdrawal.[85] Qadan led his troops through Bosnia and Serbia to Bulgaria. In the northern part of the Balkan Peninsula the Mongols caused a great deal of destruction, notwithstanding the bitter resistance they experienced in many places.[86] In

Walachia the three armies reunited. The large numbers of prisoners they had brought with them from the conquered countries hindered their movement. Some of these slaves were given permission to return to their native land, but when they had travelled a short distance, they were treacherously cut down by cavalry who rode after them.[87] The Mongols retreated via south Russia, spending the winter 1242–3 on the lower Volga. After an absence of seven years the army reached Mongolia in 1243.

Although it is often accepted that the Mongols left Hungary in 1242 in connection with the quriltai which Ögödei's successor had to arrange, it is remarkable that they did not withdraw from the south Russian steppes. It is not impossible that the evacuation of Hungary was motivated by Batu's logistical difficulties and recognition that the Hungarian pastures were insufficient to provide for his army's needs. The grazing capacity of these pastures could not sustain the Mongol army for a prolonged period and it was the recognition of this basic fact that prompted Batu to withdraw east of the Carpathian mountains to a land five times the size of Hungary.[88]

The European states were much relieved when the Asiatic armies turned east. Originally the danger had been under-estimated, but after the annihilation which the European armies suffered at Liegnitz and Mohi the danger of the situation began to be appreciated. The misery suffered by the defeated states was largely due to the reluctance to unite against the invaders. As Genghis Khan had done, Batu and Sübedei made good use of the rivalries existing between the various kingdoms in Europe. Not only in Russia, but also in central Europe, there had been no attempt to join forces against the Mongols.

That Hungary was so humiliated had an internal as well as a European reason. This monarchy was not united: the king, the nobility and the clergy were divided into mutually hostile groups, and this led the country more readily to disaster.[89] That the European powers of 1240 failed to assist the threatened monarchies was the result of the long-standing feud between the Germano-Italian empire and the Vatican. The difficulties had begun in 1215, when Frederic II became emperor. During the pontificate of Pope Gregory IX (1227–41) this dispute reached

its climax; the attention of these two influential rulers was
during the period 1239–41 focused on their own quarrels. They
took hardly any notice of the drama that was unfolding close to
their frontiers. In mid-February 1241 the pope even went so far
as to order prayers in Hungary for a crusade against the
emperor – and not, as might have been expected, against the
Mongols.[90] Frederic especially must be blamed for concentrating exclusively on events in Italy. Perhaps it is true that the
rapid success of the Mongols could not have been anticipated,
but the emperor failed entirely to discern the consequences of
the Mongol invasion; Frederic foresaw no danger from the
Mongol advance. Moreover, it formed no part of his policy to
offer assistance to Béla, who remained neutral in his struggle
with the pope.[91] One of Frederic's subjects, the duke of Austria,
did not even think twice about exploiting the hopeless situation
in which his neighbour Hungary found itself; after the battle of
Mohi this duke forced the defeated King Béla to pay off an old
claim. There is no doubt that if the Mongols had attempted to
reach the Atlantic coast, they would have done so. No
European army could have resisted the victorious Mongols.[92]

The achievements of the Asiatic invaders, which seemed
improbable, were the result of their daring, their battle
experience and their discipline, but first and foremost of their
superb skill in using their military capacity. Here there is no
doubt that Sübedei's great talents as a general played an
important part: the intelligent handling of the campaign in
Russia and central Europe was almost entirely his work – old as
he was. It is possible that Batu was only the supreme
commander in name and that the real command lay in the
hands of Sübedei.[93] This might explain the indignation of
Güyük and Büri at Batu's claim to have the right to drink the
first beaker at the victory feast. Ögödei insisted that the
successes of the Mongol army in Europe were due to Sübedei
and the other experienced generals.[94] This was undoubtedly a
correct judgement. Just as in China during the period 1236–41
(see pages 157–61), it is primarily the names of the Genghisids
which one associates with the victories won in Russia and
central Europe; during the campaigns in Russia and central
Europe the actual leadership in all areas probably rested

primarily in the hands of the generals chosen and trained by Genghis Khan.

Russia was to suffer the effects of the Mongol invasion for centuries. The south Russian plains, where the Cumans had ruled, remained a Mongol possession, under the rule of Batu, whose ulus extended already as far as the Ural River. The defeated Russian princes thus became more or less vassals of Batu: it was the beginning of a dark period in the history of Russia.

15
The last phase of unity

In government Ögödei contented himself with continuing the work of his father, usually permitting Genghis Khan's officials to finish or perfect what they had started. There were no innovations with regard to the countries that fell to the conquerors under the new leadership. The penetration into Europe was more or less prepared by Genghis Khan; the raid of Jebe and Sübedei in the years 1221–2 may be regarded as a model for the campaign of Batu and Sübedei during the period 1236–42.

The main difference between his father's methods and those of Ögödei was that Ögödei attacked on several fronts at once. Genghis Khan had been obliged to eliminate his opponents one by one; during Ögödei's time Mongol armies often operated simultaneously in China, Korea, South-west Asia and Europe. This became possible when troops could be recruited in various parts of the enormous empire. The Mongol soldiers in the army then became a minority, the majority being formed of Turkish, Tangut, Khitan, Jurchen and Tajik recruits. Later, use was also made of Cumans, Alans and Cherkesses. The Mongols remained the strongest element in the command.

It is thought that Ögödei drank himself to death.[2] At the end of his life he was so enslaved by alcohol that Chaghatai appointed someone to see that his brother was rationed to a certain number of beakers of drink – a problem Ögödei solved by using bigger beakers.[3] In the spring of 1241 he became seriously ill, but quickly recovered. On 7 December 1241 Ögödei took part in a big battue. As usual there was a drinking party when the hunters returned. During the night of 10 December he collapsed and died at dawn,[4] probably of a paralysis.[5] So, in the year of the Tiger ended the 12-year rule of the first successor of Genghis Khan.

How many sons Ögödei had, is not known.[6] It was the sons of Töregene who came to be considered for succession. Like his father, Ögödei had named a successor; originally this was his third son Köchü, but he died in 1236, during the campaign in China. Ögödei then chose the young and intelligent Shiremün, Köchü's eldest son,[7] but apparently did not make his wish sufficiently clear. The resulting confusion gave Töregene an opportunity to put forward her own candidate. In this matter Ögödei showed that he had not learnt from his father the importance of leaving precise instructions about the succession.

Like his son and successor Güyük, Ögödei was not buried in the 'great forbidden precinct' (the last resting place of Genghis Khan), but near his own ulus. We do not know exactly where this was, but it must have been some distance away from the Kara Irtish River.[8]

After the death of Ögödei, Töregene assumed the regency. This woman, who came from the Naiman tribe, had been married to a headman of the Merkit who was killed in battle with the Mongols.[9] Although it was possible for a woman to be head of the Mongol state, there were certain objections against Töregene.[10] She succeeded in coming to power with the support of Chaghatai and by her own manipulations.[11] The aim of this energetic and self-willed regent was to influence opinion among the Genghisids so that when the quriltai was convened, her eldest son Güyük would be chosen as ruler. Güyük's quarrel with Batu was, however, a reason why a number of Genghisids could not find him acceptable. In order to make the choice of her eldest son certain, Töregene required a number of years in which to prepare the ground. She therefore postponed the quriltai for as long as possible.

Töregene, who was influenced by a highly intelligent and clever servant-woman from Khurasan named Fatima,[12] soon fell foul of a group of experienced ministers,[13] against whom she had had serious objections even when Ögödei had been alive.[14] The first to feel the regent's displeasure was the Kereit Chinqai, an official who had been chosen by Genghis Khan, and served

Ögödei loyally. Töregene disapproved of him so strongly that she decided to have him murdered.[15] Chinqai fled to Köten, the second son of Ögödei and Töregene. Köten, who had an apanage in the former Tangut kingdom of Hsi-Hsia, refused to surrender Chinqai[16] and began to adopt an increasingly independent attitude towards his mother. Later he joined the faction which opposed his brother Güyük.[17] The two Yalavachs were the next to suffer Töregene's dislike. Mahmud, who held a governmental post in Peking, also fled to Köten and was given the same asylum as Chinqai. Mahmud's son, Masud, the governor of Transoxiana went to Batu for protection. Not everyone managed to escape the wrath of Töregene. Körgüz, the governor of Khurasan and a friend of Chinqai, became involved in difficulties with Chaghatai and was put to death. Arghun, a member of the Oirat tribe, became the new governor of Khurasan and Mazandaran.[18] In the place of Mahmud Yalavach the regent appointed Abd al-Rahman, who had promised to gain more income by raising taxes.

Another minister with whom the regent came into conflict was the capable Yeh-lü Ch'u-ts'ai. This Khitan had busied himself mainly with the finances since his appointment as Genghis Khan's adviser in 1215. The struggle between the various factions and cliques at the Mongol court during the latter part of Ögödei's reign helped to weaken the already precarious administrative structure established by Yeh-lü Ch'u-ts'ai. The pro-Chinese party that he headed was replaced in power by the pro-Muslim section of the court. Yeh-lü Ch'u-ts'ai kept his title of chief of the secretariat and continued to perform his astrological duties; however, he lost most of his influence in government affairs. Yeh-lü Ch'u-ts'ai retired from office in 1242 and a short time later, in 1243, he died.[19] After Chaghatai's death in 1242 the opposition of the Genghisids to the regent's arbitrariness increased. Genghis Khan's youngest brother Temüge even advanced on Qaraqorum with an army. However, after Güyük had returned from Europe Temüge was beguiled by Töregene into abandoning his plan.[20]

It should be remembered that this description of Töregene originates from the two Persian historians, Juvaini and Rashid al-Din, who were supporters of the later Mongol rulers of Persia, descendants of Genghis Khan's youngest son, Tolui. These two writers idealize Sorqaqtani, Tolui's widow, and probably represent her competitor, Töregene, unfavourably because she pleaded the case for her own son.[21]

At the end of 1245, when Töregene considered that the choice of Güyük was assured, she called a quriltai together. It took place in the summer of 1246 close to a small lake probably situated near the source of the Orkhon River not far from Qaraqorum. A number of vivid contemporary descriptions of this quriltai survive.[22] The most valuable is, however, undoubtedly that of the Franciscan monk John of Plano Carpini, who was present at the meeting.[23] We do not possess such a detailed description even of later quriltais.[24]

The selection of the new Great Khan took place in a huge tent that could accommodate some 2,000 people. Surrounded by a wooden fence, the tent had been erected in a large camp, the 'Sira-Ordu'. Nearly all the Genghisids were present. The first to arrive were Sorqaqtani, Tolui's widow, and her sons. The other family members were Temüge with his sons, Elchidei the son of Qachi'un, the sons and grandsons of Chaghatai and the sons of Jochi. The sons and grandsons of Ögödei, as the foremost candidates for the position of Great Khan were of course also present. Batu failed to appear:[25] presumably he had been sufficiently informed of Töregene's intrigues to push Güyük as the most favoured candidate. Under the pretext of an attack of gout[26] he remained in his ordu on the lower Volga. Pointing out that as the doyen of the Genghisids he should not absent himself, Sübedei tried in vain to persuade him to change his mind.[27]

The guests came from all parts of the great empire. Governors who were directly controlled by the central authority, represented the conquered countries. The vassals were either present themselves or sent deputies. The gathering was a magnificent spectacle and gave a good impression of the power of the Mongols. Among the most important guests were Prince Yaroslav of Vladimir-Suzdal (who died during the quriltai); the later Sultan Qilij Arslan of the Rum-Seljuqs; the chief qadi of the caliph of Baghdad; Sempad the brother of King Hethun I of Cilicia; both claimants to the throne of Georgia (David Lacha, son of the late King Giorgi III, and David Narin, son of Queen Rusudan); representatives of the rulers of Aleppo, Mosul, Fars,

Kirman, Erzerum and Alamut. All the guests were housed in 2,000 tents and according to John of Plano Carpini did not have to pay for the hospitality they received.

At an early stage it became clear that there were three candidates for the position of Great Khan: Köten, who may have been approved of by Genghis Khan as Ögödei's possible successor;[28] Shiremün, who was Ögödei's own choice; and Güyük, proposed by his mother. One point that weighed against Köten was his poor health. Although much was expected from Shiremün, he was considered to be still too young to stand at the head of the mighty empire. Plano Carpini says that the chances of Köten and Güyük were at first equal, but the final choice fell on the latter. Güyük insisted on a proviso that future Great Khans should only be chosen from his family.[29]

The inauguration of the new Great Khan took place, as Plano Carpini tells us, on the feast of St Bartholomew, 24 August 1246. Conforming to the ceremonial at Ögödei's installation, those present removed their hats and placed their belts over their shoulder when the choice had been made. Orda and another relative (probably Yesü Möngke) took Güyük by his hands and led him to his throne. The assembly then went outside and genuflected towards the south. John of Plano Carpini refused to do this, not knowing whether it was a form of incantation or a gesture of submission to God or some other deity.[30]

THE APOSTOLIC NUNCIO

The first news to reach Europe about the conquests of Genghis Khan was of the fall of the Khwarazm sultanate. The European Christians thought they had found in the still unknown conqueror an ally in their conflict with Islam.[31] Once again the legend of Prester John was told by the crusaders in the Holy Land (see page 83n) supported now by rumours about central Asiatic tribes which had been converted to Nestorian Christianity.[32] However, enthusiasm for the new conqueror waned considerably when stories about the conduct of Jebe and Sübedei in Russia during the years 1221 and 1222 became

known. Until their second invasion of Russia the legendary
Asiatic barbarians attracted little more interest in Europe, but
indifference changed to fear when the Mongol armies penetrated deep into Europe and in 1241 won great victories at
Liegnitz and Mohi.

Innocent IV, made pope in 1243, showed in more than one
way that he was one of the most able of those called to the Holy
See. The new pope resolved to persuade the Mongols to live in
peace with Europe by converting them to Christianity. To do
this he first set about learning as much as possible about this
unknown people from Central Asia, by seeking information
from the countries which had been overrun by them in
1240–2.[33] From the king of Hungary especially he learned much
that was of value to him.[34] King Béla IV seems in this respect
to have been one of the best-informed European monarchs: after
Batu left his country in 1242, he continued to follow Mongol
achievements closely.[35]

In 1245 Pope Innocent IV sent a number of envoys to the
feared rulers in Asia.[36] The most important of these were the
Dominicans Andrew of Longjumeau and Ascelin of Lombardy,
and the Franciscans Laurence of Portugal and John of Plano
Carpini. Little is known of the journey of Laurence of
Portugal.[37] For various reasons the two Dominicans did not go
further than the Middle East; to what extent they intended or
had been given the task of going to Mongolia is not clear.[38]

When he returned, John of Plano Carpini wrote an
invaluable account of his journey referred to repeatedly in this
book. He had presumably been given a commission similar to
that of the other apostolic nuncios. According to his own
statement, he went to Mongolia on his own initiative: 'We
decided voluntarily to go first to the Tatars,* for we feared that
danger would threaten the church of God in the near future
from that quarter.'[39] John of Plano Carpini was 63 years of age
when he began his difficult and dangerous journey from Lyons
on 16 April 1245. The old monk was well aware of the
inevitable risks, privations and weariness he would experience
on the long road: 'We did not spare ourselves, but tried to carry
out the pope's assignment according to the will of God.'[40]

---

* In Europe the Mongols were then called Tatars (see pages 4–5).

In the letter which Innocent IV gave Plano Carpini, the pope told the Great Khan that the Creator of this world had put all earthly elements together so that they should live peacefully with each other. The pope was therefore shocked to hear of the destruction which the Mongols had caused; he hoped that the Mongol khan would give brother John the opportunity of explaining the holy writ.[41] The letter was addressed to the king and people of the Tatars; the name of the sovereign was not given as it was not known in Europe.[42] In this letter, which dealt with political matters, the pope did not urge the Great Khan to join Christendom.[43]

Unlike the other nuncios of Innocent IV, who made their way along the mediterranean to the Middle East, Plano Carpini travelled via Poland and Russia. In so doing he followed the route which the envoy of the Hungarian King Béla IV, the Dominican Julien, had travelled in 1237 when returning from a visit to Batu.[44] Among John of Plano Carpini's companions was Stephen of Bohemia, who also started from Lyons, and Benedict of Poland, who joined the party in Breslau. Benedict was to act as interpreter.[45]

The winter of 1245–6 was particularly severe – the Dnieper and the Sea of Azov froze. After leaving Kiev on 4 February the party reached the ordu of Batu on the lower Volga on 4 April. Before John of Plano Carpini could pay his respects to Batu, he had a problem to solve: the Mongols expected him to offer a gift. Plano Carpini's reply was brief: 'The pope did not give presents.'[46] This dilemma also confronted the other nuncios, who had not gone further than South-west Asia.[47] Batu, seated in a tent taken from the Hungarian king,[48] told the group to move to Qaraqorum. North of the Aral Sea, south of Lake Balkash and through the country of the Naiman, Plano Carpini made his way to the Mongol capital. On 22 July 1246 he arrived at the 'Sira Ordu'.

It was only after the inauguration of Güyük that the monk could attempt to hand over the pope's letter. Once again he was faced with the difficulty that the pope had sent no gifts. This was probably the reason why the party had to wait until November before they were admitted to the Great Khan's presence. Chinqai, who had been restored to favour after Güyük's elevation, was, with Qadaq (one of Güyük's Nestorian confidential agents), the spokesman with whom Plano Carpini negotiated.

From Chinqai the pope's representatives learned that the Great Khan planned to send an embassy with them to Europe. This idea was not well received by the visitors. They feared – justifiably – that this ambassador would be a spy, who could not fail to become aware of the deep political conflicts in Europe. He might therefore advise the Great Khan to venture once again into the western countries. Moreover, John of Plano Carpini feared that in proud and arrogant Europe the Mongol ambassador might be murdered, encouraging the Mongols to take vengeance.

On 11 November 1246 Güyük gave his answer in a letter written in Mongol. This was then translated into Persian. With the help of an interpreter John of Plano Carpini translated it into Latin.[49] Later he handed over to the pope the Persian text (of which the opening was written in Turkish) with its imperial seal, and the Latin version. The letter shows how powerful the Great Khan felt himself to be. He demanded that the pope and all the European kings should come to Qaraqorum to do him honour. The subjection of the whole world had been entrusted to Genghis Khan and Ögödei by the will of God; Güyük wondered therefore what grounds the pope had for believing that he spoke in the name of God. The message ended with the threat that if the kings of Europe would not submit voluntarily, they would henceforward be regarded as the enemies of the Mongols.[50]

On 13 November John of Plano Carpini and his comrades were permitted to depart. Passing the domicile of Töregene they set off to face the central Asiatic winter: 'We travelled throughout the winter, often sleeping in the desert on snow except when we were able to clear a place with our feet. When there were no trees but only open country, we found ourselves many a time completely covered with snow driven by the wind.'[51] On 9 May 1247 they arrived again in Batu's ordu. A month later they were enthusiastically welcomed on their arrival in Kiev.[52] Although it is not recorded in the account of his travels, there are indications that John of Plano Carpini went through Hungary to Cologne,[53] and was still there on 3 October 1247.[54] After an absence of two and a half years the

65-year-old Franciscan monk returned to Lyons on 18 November 1247.

In appreciation of his nuncio's devotion to his task, Pope Innocent IV named the elderly monk bishop of Antivari (now Bar) in Dalmatia. The exact date of John of Plano Carpini's death is not known,[55] but it is thought to be 1252.[56]

TWILIGHT OF THE ÖGÖDEIDS

Plano Carpini, who met Güyük personally, left a reliable description of this Great Khan. 'The present emperor may be forty or forty-five years old or more; he is of medium height, very intelligent and extremely shrewd and most serious and grave in his manner. He is never seen to laugh for a slight cause nor to indulge in any frivolity, so we were told by the Christians who were constantly with him.'[57] Güyük's health was not good and he was constantly ill. He suffered from heavy attacks of rheumatism. Yet this did not prevent him from indulging freely in drink. Nor would he control his appetite for women.[58]

Güyük soon reversed his mother's treatment of Chinqai by restoring him to the dignity of minister. The most eminent of his helpers was, however, Qadaq, who had already given Güyük long service. The new Great Khan was prevented from playing any great part in governmental duties by his ill health; he left such matters mainly to Qadaq and Chinqai. Influenced by these two Nestorians, increasingly he came to favour Nestorianism.[59] It was not only in his relationship with Chinqai that Güyük showed that he took little account of the likes and dislikes of his mother. Masud Yalavach was restored to his position as governor of Transoxiana. Abd al-Rahman, who had been made responsible for the finances of the conquered territories in China by Töregene, was found guilty of neglecting his duties and put to death. He was replaced by Mahmud Yalavach.[60]

Shortly after Güyük's elevation, two important people died. The first was Töregene, who survived her son's election by only a few months.[61] Of more concern to the Mongol Empire was the death of Sübedei. After his return to Mongolia in 1246 he settled in the homelands of his native tribe, the Uriangqat (east of Lake Baikal), where he died in the same year at the age of 70.[62] Sübedei, with Yeh-lü Ch'u-ts'ai, had been chiefly responsible for continuing the principles of leadership laid down by Genghis Khan, and the work of these two men had resulted in much being accomplished during Ögödei's period of rule, both in civil and military affairs. As a general Sübedei, like Jebe, may be considered one of the greatest in the history of the world.

The unexpected death of Köten offered Qadaq and Chinqai a chance of getting rid of the servant-woman Fatima. It was suspected that Töregene's confidante was responsible for Köten's death: after torture she confessed to the deed. Nobody was surprised when she was condemned to death; she was thrown into a river.[63]

The new Great Khan, finding that the central authority had weakened during his mother's regency, decided to restore its former power. He repeated his grandfather's instructions that the Yasa must be followed scrupulously. Güyük could only rely on a limited number of Genghis Khan's chosen right-hand men; he was sensible enough to reappoint as soon as possible those who had been thrown out of office by his mother. In the meantime, however, many of the supremely able men who had helped his grandfather were dead, and he lacked the judgement necessary to enable him to choose sound and loyal replacements for the vacant offices.

In family matters Güyük did not neglect his responsibilities. He appointed a special court consisting of Orda and Möngke to enquire into the attempt of his uncle Temüge to depose Töregene. His uncle was found guilty and put to death.[64] Güyük introduced a reform in the khanate of Chaghatai. In 1242 Chaghatai had been succeeded by his grandson Qara Hülagü, a son of Mö'etüken who had been killed in 1221 at Bamian. In 1246 Güyük put his personal friend Yesü Möngke at the head of this khanate, under the pretext that a grandson may not inherit as long as a son is living.[65]

A change was also made in South-west Asia. A confidential agent of Güyük, Eljigidei, was asked in 1247 to look after the regions south and south-west of the Caspian Sea.[66] Exactly what his function there was, is not clear; nor is it known what his relationship was with the governor, Baiju, who remained the military commander. It must be assumed that Eljigidei was a kind of high commissioner and Baiju's superior.[67]

In the kingdom of Georgia a solution was found for the disputes about the succession. Queen Rusudan had returned to Tiflis and soon afterwards she was formally deposed. A short time later she died, some said from grief. The kingdom was divided between the rival nephews: David Lacha, the son of King Giorgi III, received the larger part; and David Narin, the son of Queen Rusudan, had to be satisfied with a comparatively small territory.[68]

One king who strengthened his ties with the Mongol Empire was King Hethun I of Cilicia in south-east Anatolia. Hethun made skilful, frequent and often far-sighted use of this alliance to protect his Christian kingdom against his mighty Islamic neighbours. His brother, the constable Sempad, who was present at Güyük's inauguration, noted the influence of Nestorianism in Central Asia. In a letter which he sent in February 1248 from Samarkand to his brother-in-law, the king of Cyprus, he discussed the significance of the Christian influence upon the Mongols.[69]

The choice of Güyük as Great Khan meant an unavoidable confrontation with Batu. The quarrel which arose in 1240 in Russia had not been forgotten. To make matters worse, Batu had been conspicuous by his absence at Güyük's installation. Güyük now decided to use force to settle the feud in his favour. Pretending to pay a visit to his own apanage, he started out westwards from Qaraqorum. The degree of dissension that already existed among the Genghisids soon became very clear. Sorqaqtani, a sister of Batu's mother, who knew Güyük's real intent, secretly dispatched a courier to Batu to warn him that the Great Khan was marching at the head of an army to settle matters with him.[70] Batu decided not to evade his cousin: marching eastwards he reached the Ili River. An encounter with Güyük seemed inevitable when the latter passed Beshbaliq in April 1248. The exact position of the two cousins is not known, when the 43-year-old Great Khan suddenly died.[71]

A battle between the armies of Güyük and Batu would perhaps not have had fatal consequences for the Mongol Empire, but it would certainly have seriously endangered its confidence. As it was, this mutual challenge did not pass off without stirring up trouble. The suppressed discord in the Genghisid ranks suddenly manifested itself in all its intensity. Batu and Sorqaqtani, as representatives of the families of Jochi and Tolui, saw their opportunity to contest the sovereignty of Ögödei's family. In order to prepare their bid for power, they offered no objection to the regency of Güyük's wife, the insignificant Oghul Qaimish.[72]

The struggle for supremacy which flared up after the death of Güyük caused a permanent rift in the Golden Family. The unity which the Mongol Empire achieved for some decades was only a surface unity. The apanages of the Genghisids began to develop more and more as separate khanates. These chances had grave results for Ögödei's successors. Their chances of becoming Great Khan had been thrown away by the alliance of Batu and Sorqaqtani. In the Mongol Empire they began to play an increasingly minor role. The sudden death of Güyük marked the beginning of the Ögödeids' demise.

Maps

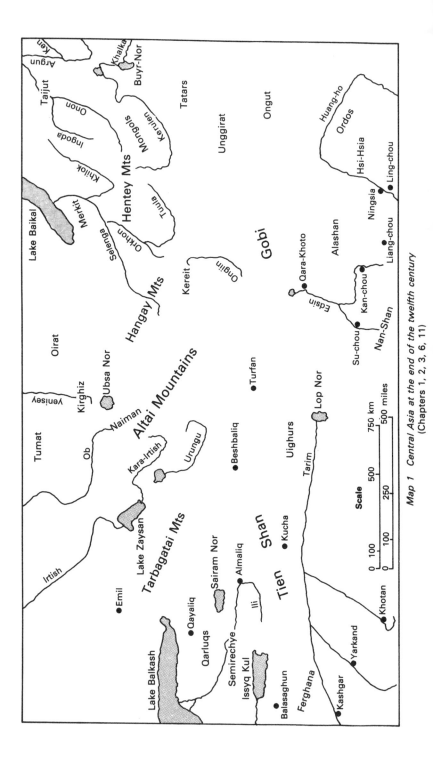

Map 1   Central Asia at the end of the twelfth century
(Chapters 1, 2, 3, 6, 11)

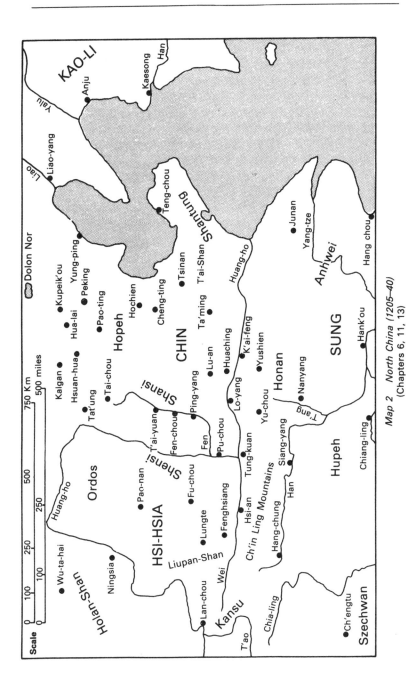

Map 2 *North China (1205–40)*
(Chapters 6, 11, 13)

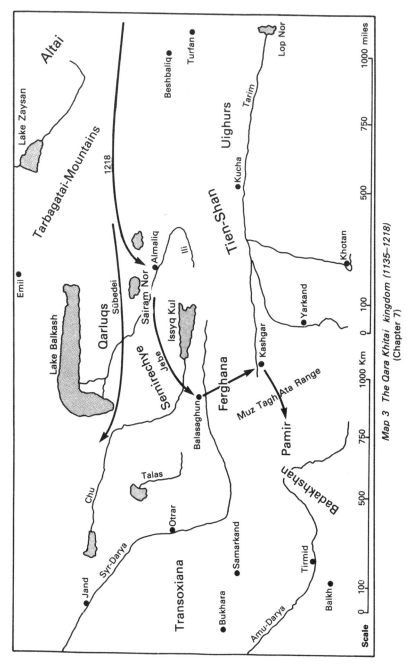

Map 3 The Qara Khitai kingdom (1135–1218)
(Chapter 7)

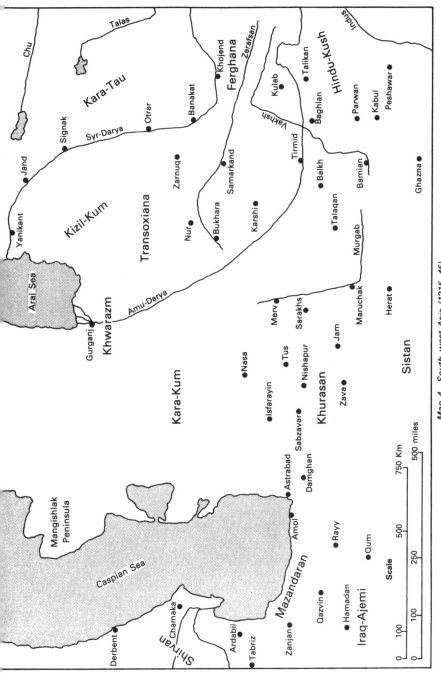

Map 4 *South–west Asia (1215–45)*
(Chapters 7, 8, 10, 13)

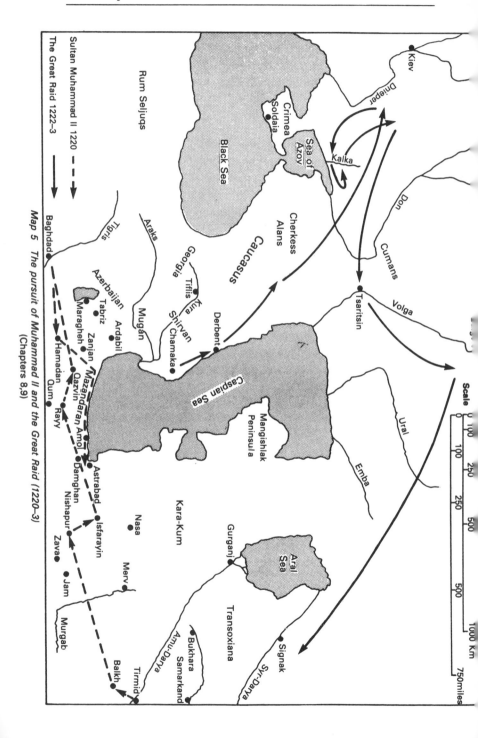

Map 5   *The pursuit of Muhammad II and the Great Raid (1220–3)*
(Chapters 8,9)

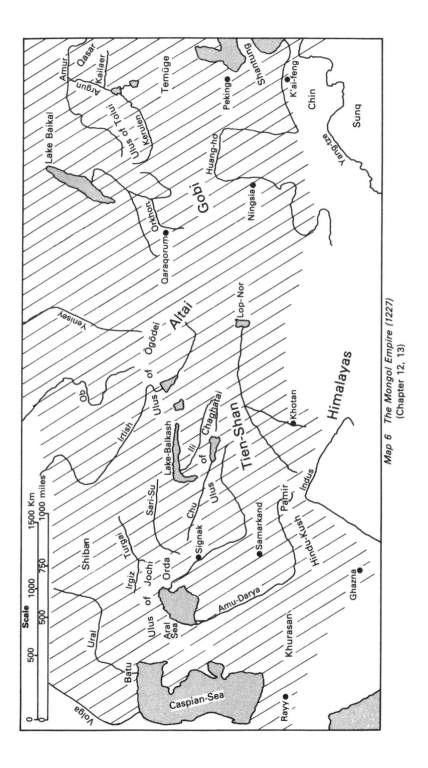

Map 6 *The Mongol Empire (1227)*
(Chapter 12, 13)

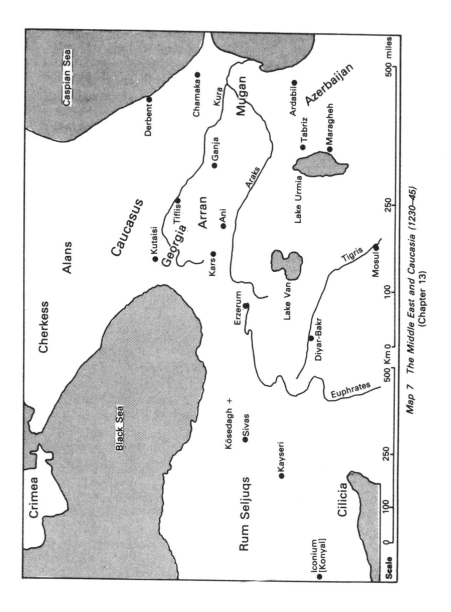

Map 7 The Middle East and Caucasia (1230–45)
(Chapter 13)

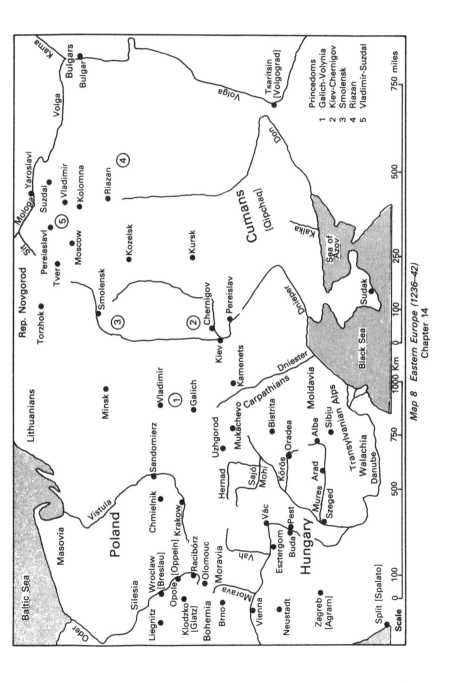

Map 8   Eastern Europe (1236–42)
Chapter 14

Notes

CHAPTER 1

1 Risch, 1930, p. 236.
2 Jahn, 1954, p. 46.
3 Pelliot, 1920, p. 146.
4 Sinor, 1963, p. 306.
5 Grousset, 1939, p. 248.
6 Vladimirtsov, 1948b, pp. 39–40.
7 Grousset, 1939, p. 250.
8 Vladimirtsov, 1948b, p. 43.
9 Ibid., p. 46.
10 Ibid., p. 43.
11 Ibid., p. 47.
12 Grousset, 1939, p. 250.
13 Ibid., p. 250.
14 Vladimirtsov, 1948b, p. 56.
15 Vernadsky, 1953, p. 13.
16 Vladimirtsov, 1948b, p. 60; Boyle, 1958, p. 60; Jackson, 1978, p. 193.
17 Grousset, Auboyer et Buhot, 1941, p. 278.
18 Pelliot, 1914, p. 627; Grousset, 1939, p. 245.
19 Barthold, 1935, p. 151.
20 Grousset, 1939, p. 244.
21 von Erdmann, 1862, p. 563; Grousset, 1939, p. 244.
22 Pelliot, 1920, p. 146.
23 Pelliot et Hambis, 1951, pp. 273–8.
24 Barthold, 1935, p. 51; Pelliot, 1929, p. 125.
25 Boyle, 1958, p. 20.
26 Dawson, 1955, pp. 72, 123–4.
27 Barthold, 1935, p. 151.
28 Grousset, 1941, p. 55.
29 Ibid., p. 25.
30 Pelliot, 1920, p. 146; Pelliot et Hambis, 1951, pp. 402–9.
31 Grousset, 1939, p. 248.
32 Barthold, 1935, p. 127; Pelliot, 1914, p. 629.
33 Vladimirtsov, 1948b, p. 40.
34 Spuler, 1966, p. 151.
35 Barthold, 1935, p. 48.
36 Ibid., p. 49.
37 Vladimirtsov, 1948a, p. 49.
38 Jahn, 1954, p. 19.
39 Ibid., p. 18; Spuler, 1966, p. 153.
40 Barthold, 1935, p. 52.
41 Grousset, 1939, p. 276.
42 Ibid., p. 277.
43 D'Ohsson, 1834, vol. 1, p. 409.
44 Pelliot, 1930, p. 33; Spuler, 1972, p. 31.
45 Jagchid and Bawden, 1965, p. 246.
46 Risch, 1930, p. 80.
47 Spuler, 1972, p. 176.
48 Moule and Pelliot, 1938, p. 168.
49 Haenisch, 1933, p. 145; Boyle, 1965, p. 145.
50 Spuler, 1966, pp. 142–3.
51 Grousset, 1939, p. 251.
52 Ibid.
53 Dawson, 1955, p. 94.
54 Ibid.
55 Spuler, 1972, p. 31.
56 Boyle, 1963, p. 201.
57 D'Ohsson, 1834, vol. 2, p. 618.
58 Boyle, 1963, p. 201.
59 D'Ohsson, 1834, vol. 1, p. 369, vol. 2, pp. 30, 42.
60 Hambis, 1970, p. 129.
61 Dawson, 1955, p. 96.
62 Risch, 1930, p. 95.
63 Boyle, 1958, p. 21.
64 D'Ohsson, 1834, vol. 2, p. 59, 86, 107, 204.
65 Vladimirtsov, 1948b, p. 69.

66 Ibid.
67 Dawson, 1955, p. 103.
68 Vladimirtsov, 1948a, p. 35.
69 Dawson, 1955, p. 107.
70 D'Ohsson, 1834, vol. 1, p. 19.

CHAPTER 2

1 Valdimirtsov, 1948a, p. 12;
Grousset, 1939, p. 253.
2 Pelliot et Hambis, 1951, p. 231.
3 Haenisch, 1948, par. 54; Cleaves,
1982, sect. 54.
4 Haenisch, 1948, par. 54–6; Cleaves,
1982, sect. 56.
5 Haenisch, 1948, par. 60.
6 Ibid., par. 101.
7 Ibid.; Pelliot et Hambis, 1951,
p. 186; Ratchnevsky, 1983, p. 150.
8 Vladimirtsov, 1948a, p. 12.
9 Krause, 1922, p. 41; Pelliot, 1959,
pp. 282–6; Schmidt, 1829, p. 63.
10 Pelliot et Hambis, 1951, p. 126.
11 Heissig, 1964, p. 43.
12 Pelliot, 1959, p. 289.
13 Haenisch, 1948, par. 59; Cleaves,
1982, sect. 59; Krause, 1922, p. 11.
14 Grousset, 1941, p. 51.
15 Haenisch, 1948, par. 61; Cleaves,
1982, sect. 61; Ratchnevsky,1983,
p. 19.
16 Haenisch, 1948, par. 63.
17 Ibid., par. 70–3.
18 Ibid., par. 60; Pelliot et Hambis,
1951, p. 173.
19 Haenisch, 1948, par. 79–87;
Cleaves, 1982, sect. 82–7.
20 Haenisch, 1948, par. 90–3; Cleaves,
sect. 90–3.
21 Haenisch, 1948, par. 116.
22 Ibid., par. 40.
23 Ibid., par. 94; Cleaves, 1982, sect.
94.
24 Haenisch, 1948, par. 96.
25 Ibid., par. 97; Cleaves, 1982, sect.
97.
26 Haenisch, 1948, par. 100; Boyle,
1971, p. 228.
27 Haenisch, 1948, par. 99, 101.
28 Ibid., par. 103.
29 Ibid., par. 104–10.
30 Ibid., par. 112.

31 Pelliot, 1949, p. 26; Boyle, 1971,
pp. 97–8.
32 Haenisch, 1948, par. 117.
33 Vladimirtsov, 1948a, p. 29.
34 Haenisch, 1948, par. 118–19;
Cleaves, 1982, sect. 118–19.
35 Haenisch, 1948, par. 123.
36 Pelliot, 1959, p. 297;
Ratchnevsky,1983, pp. 82–3.
37 Pelliot, 1959, p. 301; Boyle, 1958,
p. 39.
38 Vladimirtsov, 1948a, p. 34.
39 Haenisch, 1948, par. 125; Cleaves,
1982, sect. 125.
40 Vladimirtsov, 1948a, pp. 34–5.
41 Krause, 1922, p. 12; Haenisch,
1948, par. 129; Pelliot et Hambis,
1951, p. 37.
42 Pelliot et Hambis, 1951, p. 135.
43 Ibid., p. 231; Krause, 1922, p. 15.
44 Krause, 1922, p. 15; Haenisch,
1948, par. 151, 155, 177; Pelliot et
Hambis, 1951, p. 231.
45 Haenisch, 1948, par. 132.
46 Krause, 1922, p. 14; Pelliot et
Hambis, 1951, p. 192.
47 Pelliot et Hambis, 1951, p. 192.
48 Ibid.; Krause, 1922, p. 15.
49 Haenisch, 1948, par. 134; Pelliot et
Hambis, 1951, p. 192.
50 Haenisch, 1948, par. 135.
51 Ratchnevsky, 1965, pp. 90–1.
52 Pelliot et Hambis, 1951, p. 192.
53 Krause, 1922, p. 15; Pelliot et
Hambis, 1951, pp. 214, 257; Boyle,
1977, p. 75.
54 Pelliot et Hambis, 1951, p. 309.
55 Grousset, 1941, p. 99; Hambis,
1973, p. 62.
56 D'Ohsson, 1834, vol. 1, p. 75.
57 Haenisch, 1948, par. 159; Pelliot et
Hambis, 1951, p. 295; Cleaves
1982, sect. 159.
58 Krause, 1922, p. 16; Haenisch,
1948, par. 161.
59 Krause, 1922, p. 16; Haenisch,
1948, par. 161; Pelliot et Hambis,
1951, p. 295.
60 Haenisch, 1948, par. 163; Pelliot et
Hambis, 1951, p. 296; de
Rachewiltz, 1977, p. 46.
61 Krause, 1922, p. 17.
62 D'Ohsson, 1834, vol. 1, p. 60.

63 Krause, 1922, p. 17.
64 Ibid., p. 18; Haenisch, 1948, par. 141; Cleaves, 1982, sect. 141.
65 Barthold, 1935, p. 123; Barthold, 1956, vol. 1, p. 28.
66 Haenisch, 1948, par. 129.
67 Ibid., par. 142–3; Krause, 1922, p. 19.
68 Vladimirtsov, 1948, p. 39.
69 Haenisch, 1948, par. 145.
70 Pelliot et Hambis, 1951, p. 155.
71 Ibid., pp. 155–6; Haenisch, 1948, par. 147; Cleaves, 1982, sect. 147.
72 Haenisch, 1948, par. 154; Hambis, 1973, pp. 72–3; Cleaves, 1982, sect. 154.
73 Vladimirtsov, 1948, p. 40.
74 Haenisch, 1948, par. 155; Cleaves, 1982, sect. 155.
75 Krause, 1922, p. 19.
76 Haenisch, 1948, par. 153; Cleaves, 1982, sect. 153.
77 Grousset, 1939, p. 264.

CHAPTER 3

1 Haenisch, 1948, par. 164; Cleaves, 1982, sect. 164.
2 Vladimirtsov, 1948a, p. 42.
3 Krause, 1922, p. 20; Haenisch, 1948, par. 165; Cleaves, 1982, sect. 165.
4 Krause, 1922, p. 20.
5 Ibid., p. 21; Haenisch, 1948, par. 168; Cleaves, 1982, sect. 168.
6 Krause, 1922, p. 21; Haenisch, 1948, par. 169; Boyle, 1958, p. 37.
7 Krause, 1922, p. 21; Haenisch, 1948, par. 170.
8 Haenisch, 1948, par. 170.
9 Ibid., par. 171; Cleaves, 1982, sect. 171.
10 Haenisch, 1948, par. 172–3; Cleaves, 1982, sect. 172–3.
11 D'Ohsson, 1834, vol. 1, p. 73
12 Haenisch, 1948, par. 178.
13 Pelliot et Hambis, 1951, pp. 41–2.
14 Ibid., pp. 45–7; Cleaves, 1955, pp. 357–421; Boyle, 1958, p. 37.
15 Krause, 1922, p. 23–4; Cleaves, 1955, p. 357–421.
16 Krause, 1922, p. 24.
17 Ibid., p. 23.
18 Ibid., p. 24; Haenisch, 1948, par. 183–5; de Rachewiltz, 1977, p. 47.
19 Krause, 1922, p. 24.
20 Hambis, 1973, p. 84.
21 Haenisch, 1948, par. 187; Cleaves, 1982, sect. 187.
22 Krause, 1922, p. 25; Haenisch, 1948, par. 190.
23 Krause, 1922, p. 25; Haenisch, 1948, par. 193.
24 Haenisch, 1948, par. 193.
25 Krause, 1922, p. 26.
26 Haenisch, 1948, p. 194; Cleaves, 1982, sect. 194.
27 Krause, 1922, p. 26.
28 Haenisch, 1948, par. 195; Cleaves, 1982, sect. 195.
29 Krause, 1922, p. 26.
30 Ibid.
31 Haenisch, 1948, par. 196.
32 Krause, 1922, p. 26.
33 Haenisch, 1948, par. 196; Cleaves, 1982, sect. 196.
34 Haenisch, 1948, par. 196; Cleaves, 1982, sect. 196.
35 Haenisch, 1948, par. 189.
36 Ibid., par. 197; Cleaves, 1982, sect. 197.
37 Krause, 1922, p. 28.
38 Valdimirtsov, 1948a, p. 65.
39 Krause, 1922, p. 29.
40 Haenisch, 1948, par. 239.
41 Ibid., par. 198.
42 Barthold, 1928, p. 361.
43 Haenisch, 1948, par. 200–1; Cleaves, 1982, sect. 200–1.
44 Vladimirtsov, 1948a, p. 65.
45 Haenisch, 1948, par. 235; Cleaves, 1982, sect. 235.
46 Barthold, 1928, p. 362.
47 Krause, 1922, p. 29; Ratchevsky, 1983, p. 92.
48 Haenisch, 1948, par. 238; Boyle, 1958, pp. 44–6.
49 Haenisch, 1948, par. 238; Vladimirtsov, 1948a, p. 65.
50 Haenisch, 1948, par. 240–1.
51 Ibid., par. 202; Krause, 1922, p. 29.
52 Vladimirtsov, 1948b, p. 108.
53 Krause, 1922, p. 28.

54 Grousset, 1941, p. 181; Boyle, 1958, p. 39.
55 Haenisch, 1948, par. 177.
56 Pelliot, 1930, p. 32.
57 Valdimirtsov, 1948a, p. 54.
58 Haenisch, 1948, par. 202; Cleaves, 1982, sect. 202.
59 Haenisch, 1948, par. 202; de Rachewiltz, 1977, p. 49.
60 Haenisch, 1948, par. 244; Cleaves, 1982, sect. 244.
61 Haenisch, 1948, par. 245; Cleaves, 1982, sect. 245.

CHAPTER 4

1 Vladimirtsov, 1948a, p. 55.
2 Ibid., p. 36.
3 Barthold, 1928, p. 386; Ratchnevsky, 1983, p. 162.
4 Vladimirtsov, 1948a, p. 61; Ratchnevsky, 1983, p. 162.
5 Morgan, 1986a, p. 163.
6 Ratchenevsky, 1983, p. 87.
7 Vernadsky, 1938, pp. 339, 360; Ayalon, 1971a, p. 135.
8 Valdimirtsov, 1948a, p. 61; Ratchnevsky, 1983, p. 87, 165.
9 Barthold, 1928, pp. 391–2; Boyle, 1958, p. 42; Ayalon, 1971b, pp. 154–5.
10 Ayalon, 1971b, pp. 127, 132, 140.
11 Ratchnevsky, 1983, pp. 165–6.
12 Ibid., p. 87.
13 Riasanovsky, 1931, pp. 402–4.
14 Raisanovsky, 1937, p. 33.
15 Ayalon, 1971b, pp. 151–2.
16 Boyle, 1958, p. 40.
17 Riasanovsky, 1937, p. 33.
18 Vernadsky, 1953, p. 30.
19 Pelliot, 1930, pp. 193, sq.; Olbricht, 1954, pp. 36–40.
20 Olbricht, 1954, pp. 66, 87.
21 Ibid., pp. 40–1.
22 Vernadsky, 1953, p. 127.
23 Spuler, 1985, p. 350.
24 Olbricht, 1954, p. 20; Spuler, 1985, p. 349.

CHAPTER 5

1 Vladimirtsov, 1948b, p. 132.
2 Spuler, 1960, p. 36.
3 Barthold, 1928, p. 386; Boyle, 1958, p. 32.
4 Valdimirtsov, 1948a, p. 59.
5 Boyle, 1958, p. 150; Boyle, 1971, p. 30.
6 Barthold, 1928, p. 385.
7 Grousset, 1939, p. 282; Boyle, 1958, p. 37.
8 Vernadsky, 1938, p. 351.
9 Vladimirtsov, 1948a, p. 59.
10 Haenisch, 1948, par. 220; de Rachewiltz, 1977, p. 47.
11 Pelliot, 1930, p. 33.
12 Haenisch, 1948, par. 209.
13 Ibid., par. 224–9; Barthold, 1928, pp. 383–4; Pelliot, 1930, p. 26.
14 Barthold, 1928, p. 384; Haenisch, 1948, par. 224.
15 Haenisch, 1948, par. 226.
16 Vladimirtsov, 1948a, p. 57.
17 Haenisch, 1948, par. 224.
18 Grousset, 1939, p. 282.
19 Vladimirtsov, 1948a, p. 58.
20 Haenisch, 1948, par. 192.
21 Ibid., par. 228.
22 Risch, 1930, pp. 161–9; Grenard, 1935, p. 76.
23 Martin, 1950, p. 19.
24 Poucha, 1956, p. 144.
25 Barthold, 1928, p. 421; Sinor, 1981, p. 137.
26 Moule and Pelliot, 1938, p. 173.
27 von Erdmann, 1862, p. 364.
28 Grousset, 1939, p. 284.
29 de Hartog, 1979b, p. 479.
30 Grousset, 1939, p. 284; Sinor, 1976, p. 251; Sinor, 1981, p. 137.
31 de Hartog, 1979b, p. 480.
32 Altunian, 1911, p. 74.
33 Risch, 1930, p. 175.
34 Ibid., p. 174.
35 Haenisch, 1948, par. 193; Boyle, 1958, p. 373.
36 Altunian, 1911, pp. 76–7.
37 Franke, H., 1974, pp. 169–72.
38 Risch, 1930, p. 17.
39 de Hartog, 1979b, p. 482.
40 Moule and Pelliot, 1938, p. 173.
41 Martin, 1950, p. 17.

42 Vernadsky, 1953, p. 116.
43 Sinor, 1971, pp. 239, 241.
44 de Hartog, 1979b, p. 482.
45 Vernadsky, 1938, p. 354; Sinor, 1981, p. 135.
46 Vernadsky, 1938, p. 351.
47 Riasanovsky, 1937, p. 164.
48 Boyle, 1958, p. 40.
49 Dawson, 1955, pp. 100–1; Boyle, 1958, pp. 27–8.
50 Boyle, 1958, p. 28.
51 Vernadsky, 1953, p. 118–19.
52 Boyle, 1971, p. 53.
53 Westermann Lexicon der Geographie, vol. 3, 1970, pp. 392–4.
54 de Hartog, 1979b, p. 484.
55 Barthold, 1928, p. 404.
56 Vladimirtsov, 1948a, p. 72.

CHAPTER 6

1 Duyvendak, 1935, pp. 170–201; Fitzgerald, 1942, pp. 373–417; Eberhard, 1960, pp. 187–230.
2 Pelliot, 1914, p. 631; Grousset, 1941, pp. 210–12.
3 Haenisch, 1948, par. 249.
4 Krause, 1922, p. 27; Ratchnevsky, 1983, p.93.
5 Hambis, 1973, p. 91.
6 Krause, 1922, p. 28; Grousset, 1941, p. 213; Ratchnevsky, 1983, p. 94.
7 Hambis, 1973, pp. 98–9.
8 Krause, 1922, p. 29.
9 Haenisch, 1948, par. 265.
10 Krause, 1922, p. 29.
11 Ibid.; Ratchnevsky, 1983, p. 94.
12 Krause, 1922, p. 29; Haenisch, 1948, par. 249; Ratchnevsky, 1983, p. 95.
13 Grousset, 1941, p. 215.
14 Ibid.
15 Krause, 1922, p. 30.
16 Ibid.
17 Pelliot et Hambis, 1951, pp. 181–2.
18 D'Ohsson, 1834, vol. 1, p. 213.
19 Grenard, 1935, p. 109.
20 Vladimirtsov, 1948a, pp. 76–7.

21 Martin, 1950, p. 126.
22 Krause, 1922, pp. 30–1; Pelliot et Hambis, 1950, p. 62.
23 Waley, 1931, pp. 62–3.
24 Krause, 1922, p. 30.
25 Ibid., p. 31.
26 Ibid.
27 Ibid.
28 Grousset, 1939, p. 288.
29 Haenisch, 1948, par. 247; Grousset, 1941, p. 218.
30 Krause, 1922, p. 31.
31 Ibid.
32 Waldron, 1983, p. 656.
33 Grousset, 1944, p. 244.
34 Krause, 1922, p. 32.
35 Grenard, 1935, p. 118.
36 Krause, 1922, p. 32.
37 Martin, 1950, p. 165.
38 Grousset, 1941, p. 219.
39 Grousset, 1944, p. 245.
40 Martin, 1950, p. 165.
41 Grousset, 1944, p. 247.
42 Krause, 1922, p. 32.
43 Pelliot et Hambis, 1951, p. 173.
44 Krause, 1922, p. 32; Vladimirtsov, 1948a, p. 80.
45 Martin, 1950, p. 169.
46 Vladimirtsov, 1948a, p. 81.
47 Krause, 1922, p. 32.
48 Ibid., p. 33.
49 Martin, 1950, p. 170.
50 Krause, 1922, p. 33.
51 Grousset, 1941, p. 220.
52 Krause, 1922, p. 33.
53 Haenisch, 1948, par. 251; Boyle, 1971, p. 34.
54 Vladimirtsov, 1948a, p. 81.
55 Krause, 1922, p. 33.
56 Ibid.; Vladimirtsov, 1948a, p. 81.
57 Krause, 1922, p. 33; de Rachewiltz, 1977, p. 49.
58 Krause, 1922, p. 33.
59 Ibid., p. 34.
60 Ibid., p. 33.
61 Grousset, 1944, p. 249.
62 Martin, 1950, p. 176.
63 Hambis, 1973, p. 103.
64 Krause, 1922, p. 34.
65 von Erdmann, 1862, p. 328.
66 Krause, 1922, p. 33.
67 Barthold, 1928, pp. 393–4.
68 Haenisch, 1948, par. 252.

69 Martin, 1950, p. 180;
   Kwanten,1979, p. 118.
70 Krause, 1922, p. 34.
71 Ibid., p. 35.
72 Ibid.; Martin, 1950, p. 190.
73 Walker, 1939, p. 68.
74 Grousset, 1944, p. 252.
75 Grousset, 1939, p. 292.
76 Krause, 1922, p. 35.
77 Martin, 1950, p. 161.
78 Barthold, 1936, p. 882; Martin,
   1950, p.242; de Rachewiltz, 1977,
   p. 50; Ratchnevsky, 1983, p. 110.
79 Grousset, 1944, p. 252.
80 Grousset, 1939, p. 293.
81 Krause, 1922, p. 35.
82 Ibid.
83 Ibid., p. 36.
84 Ibid., p. 37; de Rachewiltz, 1977,
   pp. 51–2.
85 de Rachewiltz, 1977, p. 52–3.
86 Krause, 1922, p. 38.
87 Ibid.
88 Pelliot, 1930, p. 49; Pelliot et
   Hambis, 1951, p. 371; de
   Rachewiltz, 1977, p. 54.
89 Vladimirtsov, 1948a, p. 87.
90 Ibid.
91 Ibid., p. 89.
92 Ibid., p. 85; Bretschneider, 1910,
   vol. 1, p. 10; de Rachewiltz, 1962,
   p. 193.
93 Grousset, 1944, p. 255; de
   Rachewiltz, 1962, p. 194.
94 Grousset, 1941, p. 265.
95 Vladimirtsov, 1948a, p. 84.
96 Ibid.
97 Ibid.

CHAPTER 7

1 Sinor, 1954, p. 84.
2 Barthold, 1956, vol. 1, p. 27;
   Hambis, 1953, p. 56; Bosworth,
   1968, p. 148.
3 Barthold, 1956, vol. 1, pp. 27–8.
4 Ibid., p. 28.
5 Ibid., p. 29.
6 Bosworth, 1968, p. 147.
7 Spuler, 1965, p. 346; Hambis,
   1953, p. 56.
8 Barthold, 1928, p. 324.
9 Ibid., p. 327; Barthold, 1956,
   vol. 1, p. 29.
10 Barthold, 1945, p. 109; Spuler,
   1966, p. 196.
11 Barthold, 1928, p. 339.
12 Bosworth, 1968, p. 167.
13 Hartman, 1975, p. 70.
14 Ross and Elias, 1895, p. 125.
15 Spuler, 1966, p. 197; Hartman,
   1975, p. 75.
16 Barthold, 1928, p. 348; Hartman,
   1975, pp. 75–8.
17 Barthold, 1928, p. 348; Bosworth,
   1968, p. 182; Hartman, 1975, p. 78.
18 Barthold, 1928, p. 348.
19 Ibid., p. 349.
20 Bosworth, 1968, p. 191.
21 Spuler, 1966, p. 199; Hartman,
   1975, p. 80.
22 Barthold, 1928, p. 367;
   Ratchnevsky, 1983, p. 107.
23 Barthold, 1935, p. 150.
24 Barthold, 1945, p. 109.
25 Barthold, 1935, p. 155.
26 Barthold, 1928, pp. 365–6; Boyle,
   1958, p. 395.
27 Barthold, 1928, p. 364; Barthold,
   1935, p. 150; Hartman, 1975, p. 80.
28 Barthold, 1928, p. 369.
29 Barthold, 1956, vol. 1, p. 35.
30 Barthold, 1928, p. 369.
31 Barthold, 1956, vol. 1, p. 34.
32 Barthold, 1928, p. 368; Boyle,
   1958, p. 65.
33 Boyle, 1958, p. 64.
34 Ibid., pp. 66, 73.
35 Boyle, 1968, p. 303.
36 Barthold, 1928, p. 393.
37 Boyle, 1968, p. 303.
38 Barthold, 1928, p. 394.
39 Boyle, 1968, p. 303.
40 Ibid., p. 304.
41 Barthold, 1928, p. 396.
42 Boyle,1968, p. 304.
43 Barthold, 1928, p. 396.
44 Ibid., p. 397.
45 Boyle, 1968, p. 304.
46 Barthold, 1928, p. 397.
47 Ibid., p. 394; Spuler, 1966, p. 205.
48 Spuler, 1966, p. 205.
49 Barthold, 1928, p. 395.
50 Spuler, 1966, p. 205.
51 Lech, 1968, p. 19.

52 Barthold, 1928, p. 394.
53 Barthold, 1956, vol. 1, p. 71.
54 Vladimirtsov, 1948a, p. 93.
55 Barthold, 1928, p. 395.
56 Vladimirtsov, 1948a, p. 93.
57 Barthold, 1928, p. 397.
58 Boyle, 1968, p. 304.
59 Haenisch, 1948, par. 254; Cleaves, 1982, sect. 253.
60 Boyle, 1958, p. 79; Pelliot, 1930, pp. 52–3.
61 Boyle, 1968, p. 305.
62 Barthold, 1928, p. 399.
63 Vladimirtsov, 1948a, p. 94; Boyle, 1958, p. 367.
64 Boyle, 1958, p. 80.
65 Bretschneider, 1910, vol. 1, p. 277; Barthold, 1928, p. 399.
66 Grousset, 1944, p. 263; Boyle, 1958, p. 75.
67 Barthold, 1928, p. 401; Boyle, 1958, p. 65.
68 Grousset, 1944, p. 264.
69 Grousset, 1941, p. 224.
70 Ibid., p. 197; Boyle, 1968, p. 305.
71 Vladimirtsov, 1948a, p. 89; Boyle, 1963, p. 305.
72 Marquart, 1914, p. 136; Barthold, 1928, p. 371; Spuler, 1960, p. 89.
73 Haenisch, 1948, par. 202, 237.
74 D'Ohsson, 1834, vol. 1, p. 172; Bretschneider, 1910, vol. 1, p. 233.
75 Barthold, 1928, pp. 401, 402; Martin, 1950, p. 231; Ratchnevsky, 1983, p. 107.
76 Barthold, 1928, p. 402; Vladimirtsov, 1948a, p. 91.
77 Barthold, 1928, p. 402; Grousset, 1944, p. 265.
78 Boyle, 1958, p. 67.
79 Ibid.
80 Ibid.
81 Ibid.; Pelliot, 1930, p. 55.
82 Boyle, 1958, p. 68.
83 Barthold, 1928, p. 403; Grousset, 1944, p. 266.
84 Boyle, 1958, p. 143.
85 Barthold, 1928, p. 403; Vladimirtsov, 1948a, p. 98.
86 Barthold, 1956, vol. 1, p. 38; Hartman, 1975, p. 82.
87 Barthold, 1935, p. 148; Spuler, 1960, p. 8; Spuler, 1966, p. 205.
88 Hartman, 1975, pp. 83–4.
89 Barthold, 1928, p. 399; Boyle, 1958, p. 390.
90 Hartman, 1975, p. 84.
91 Barthold, 1928, p. 400.
92 Ibid.
93 Haenisch, 1948, par. 254.
94 Ibid., par. 243.
95 Boyle, 1971, pp. 17, 164.
96 Haenisch, 1948, par. 255.
97 Ibid.; Boyle, 1971, p. 17.
98 Haenisch, 1948, par. 255.

CHAPTER 8

1 Barthold, 1935, p. 123.
2 Barthold, 1928, p. 377.
3 Ibid.
4 Ibid., p. 378.
5 Boyle, 1958, p. 466; Spuler, 1966, p. 199.
6 Barthold, 1928, p. 379.
7 Spuler, 1972, p. 32.
8 Barthold, 1956, vol. 1, p. 71; Ratchnevsky, 1983, p. 154.
9 Barthold, 1928, p. 404.
10 Boyle, 1958, p. 376; Boyle, 1968, p. 306.
11 Barthold, 1928, p. 405; Barthold, vol. 1, p. 39.
12 Grenard, 1935, p. 139.
13 Spuler, 1985, p. 22.
14 Barthold, 1928, p. 160.
15 Barthold, 1928, pp. 371–2; Boyle, 1968, p. 306.
16 Barthold, 1928, p. 406.
17 D'Ohsson, 1834, vol. 1, p. 212.
18 Barthold, 1928, pp. 409, 411.
19 Haenisch, 1948, par. 257.
20 Bretschneider, 1910, vol. 1, p. 10; Vladimirtsov, 1948a, p. 96.
21 Haenisch, 1948, par. 257.
22 Bretschneider, 1910, vol. 1, 277; Boyle, 1958, p. 82.
23 Barthold, 1928, p. 403; Martin, 1950, p. 237.
24 Barthold, 1928, p. 404.
25 Ibid., p. 407.
26 Barthold, 1935, p. 161.
27 Haenisch, 1959, p. 87.
28 Waley, 1931, p. 78.

29 Boyle, 1958, p. 83; Boyle, 1968, p. 307.
30 Barthold, 1928, p. 407.
31 Boyle, 1958, pp. 100–2.
32 Barthold, 1928, pp. 408–9.
33 Boyle, 1968, p. 307.
34 Barthold, 1928, p. 409.
35 Grousset, 1944, p. 284; Boyle, 1958, p. 106.
36 Barthold, 1928, p. 410.
37 Grousset, 1944, p. 286.
38 Spuler, 1985, p. 22.
39 Boyle, 1958, p. 117; Boyle, 1968, p. 308.
40 Barthold, 1928, p. 411.
41 Boyle, 1958, p. 108; Boyle, 1968, p. 308.
42 Barthold, 1928, p. 412.
43 Ibid., p. 419; Boyle, 1958, p. 378.
44 Barthold, 1928, p. 419.
45 Boyle, 1958, p. 143.
46 Barthold, 1935, p. 161.
47 Waley, 1931, p. 93.
48 Bretschneider, 1910, vol. 1, p. 278; Barthold, 1928, p. 412; Boyle, 1958, p. 85.
49 Barthold, 1928, p. 414.
50 Bretschneider, 1910, vol. 1, p. 278; Boyle, 1958, pp. 86–90.
51 Barthold, 1928, p. 417.
52 Boyle, 1958, p. 143.
53 Barthold, 1928, pp. 417, 419.
54 Ibid., pp. 417–18; Boyle, 1958, p. 93.
55 Boyle, 1968, p. 308.
56 Barthold, 1928, p. 427.
57 Ibid., p. 420.
58 Boyle, 1958, p. 143.
59 Haenisch, 1958, par. 257.
60 Barthold, 1928, p. 420.
61 Ibid., p. 421; Boyle, 1968, p. 307.
62 Barthold, 1928, p. 422.
63 Boyle, 1958, p. 144.
64 Ibid., p. 145; Boyle, 1968, p. 310.
65 Boyle, 1958, p. 146.
66 Ibid., p. 384; Barthold, 1928, pp. 422, 425.
67 Bretschneider, 1910, vol. 1, p. 280; Barthold, 1928, p. 426.
68 Spuler, 1985, p. 24.
69 Boyle, 1968, p. 311.
70 Haenisch, 1948, par. 257.
71 Barthold, 1928, p. 424; Boyle,

1958, pp. 174–5.
72 Boyle, 1958, p. 175.
73 Barthold, 1928, p. 446.
74 Ibid., p. 428.
75 Grousset, 1944, p. 291.
76 Barthold, 1928, pp. 430–1.
77 Ibid., p. 432.
78 Boyle, 1958, pp. 399–401.
79 Ibid., p. 402; Boyle, 1968, p. 317.
80 Bretschneider, 1910, vol. 1, p. 280; Barthold, 1928, p. 432.
81 Barthold, 1928, p. 437; Boyle, 1958, pp. 402–4.
82 Boyle, 1958, p. 131; Boyle, 1968, p. 312.
83 Barthold, 1928, p. 433.
84 Boyle, 1958, p. 126.
85 Barthold, 1928, p. 434; Boyle, 1958, pp. 124, 126.
86 Haenisch, 1948, par. 254.
87 Barthold, 1928, p. 435; Boyle, 1971, p. 118.
88 Barthold, 1928, pp. 436–7.
89 Boyle, 1968, p. 313.
90 Boyle, 1958, p. 159.
91 Barthold, 1928, p. 446.
92 Spuler, 1960, p. 9.
93 Boyle, 1971, p. 165.
94 Boyle, 1958, p. 162; Boyle, 1968, p. 313.
95 Grousset, 1939, p. 301.
96 Grousset, 1944, p. 306.
97 Boyle, 1968, p. 314.
98 Ibid.
99 Grousset, 1939, p. 302; Boyle, 1958, pp. 177–8.
100 Bretschneider, 1910, vol. 1, p. 281; Grousset, 1939, p. 302.
101 Boyle, 1958, p. 152; Boyle, 1971, p. 165.
102 Boyle, 1958, p. 132; Boyle, 1968, pp. 312, 317.
103 Barthold, 1928, p. 441.
104 Boyle, 1958, pp. 406–7; Boyle, 1968, p. 319.
105 Barthold, 1928, p. 443.
106 Boyle, 1958, p. 132.
107 Boyle, 1971, p. 137.
108 Boyle, 1958, pp. 132–3.
109 D'Ohsson, 1834, vol. 1, pp. 294–6.
110 Boyle, 1968, p. 320.
111 Grousset, 1939, p. 303.
112 Barthold, 1928, pp. 445–6; Boyle,

1968, p. 320.
113 Boyle, 1958, pp. 134, 411.
114 Barthold, 1928, p. 446.
115 Haenisch, 1933, p. 529; Krause, 1922, p. 38; Barthold, 1928, p. 446.
116 Barthold, 1928, p. 449.
117 Vladimirtsov, 1948a, p. 106.
118 Bretschneider, 1910, vol. 1, p. 282; Boyle, 1958, p. 135.

CHAPTER 9

1 Altunian, 1911, p. 21.
2 Grousset, 1941, p. 258.
3 Grousset, 1944, p. 341.
4 Grenard, 1935, p. 165.
5 Grousset, 1944, p. 341.
6 Grousset, 1941, p. 516.
7 Schütz, 1973, p. 256.
8 Ibid.
9 Grousset, 1944, p. 341.
10 Ibid., p. 342.
11 Grousset, 1939, p. 307.
12 Grousset, 1941, p. 517.
13 Schütz, 1973, p. 257.
14 Grousset, 1939, p. 307.
15 Altunian, 1911, p. 21.
16 Schütz, 1973, p. 258.
17 Bretschneider, 1910, vol. 1, p. 295; Marquart, 1914, p. 142; Grousset, 1941, p. 517.
18 Bretschneider, 1910, vol. 1, p. 295; Marquart, 1914, p. 143; Grekov et Iakoubovski, 1939, p. 54; Spuler, 1965, p. 12.
19 Bretschneider, 1910, vol. 1, p. 296; Vernadsky, 1948, p. 39.
20 Grekov et Iakoubovski, 1939, p. 191.
21 Ibid., p. 190; Bezzola, 1974, p. 41.
22 Bretschneider, 1910, vol. 1, p. 296; Grekov et Iakoubovski, 1939, p. 191.
23 Grousset, 1939, p. 208.
24 Grekov et Iakoubovski, 1939, p. 193.
25 Grousset, 1941, pp. 518–19.
26 Bretschneider, 1910, vol. 1, p. 297; Grekov et Iakoubovski, 1939, p. 193.
27 Grenard, 1935, p. 168; Grousset, 1939, p. 308.

28 von Erdmann, 1862, pp. 434–5; Grekov et Iakoubovski, 1939, p. 194.
29 Marquart, 1914, p. 145; Barthold, 1956, vol. 1, p. 41.
30 Grenard, 1935, p. 168.
31 Marquart, 1914, p. 146; Grousset, 1939, p. 308.
32 Haenisch, 1933, p. 534; Haenisch, 1948, par. 257; Cleaves, 1982, sect. 257.
33 Wolff, 1872, p. 110; Howorth, 1876, vol. 2, p. 97.
34 Spuler, 1960, p. 10.

CHAPTER 10

1 Bretschneider, 1910, vol. 1, p. 35.
2 Waley, 1931, p. 51.
3 Bretschneider, 1910, vol. 1, p. 42; Waley, 1931, p. 48.
4 Waley, 1931, p. 44.
5 D'Ohsson, 1834, vol. 1, p. 416.
6 Waley, 1931, p. 54.
7 Ibid., p. 69.
8 Ibid., p. 92.
9 Ibid., pp. 93–110.
10 Ibid., p. 112.
11 Ibid., p. 117.
12 Ibid., p. 118.
13 Ibid., p. 133.
14 Ibid., p. 135.
15 Boyle, 1958, pp. 137–8.
16 Barthold, 1928, p. 453.
17 D'Ohsson, 1834, vol. 2, pp. 319–23.
18 Barthold, 1928, p. 453.
19 Boyle, 1958, pp. 137–8.
20 Ibid., p. 139.
21 Bretschneider, 1910, vol. 1, p. 283; Barthold, 1928, pp. 454–5.
22 Boyle, 1968, p. 321.
23 Vladimirtsov, 1948a, p. 108.
24 Barthold, 1928, p. 455; Boyle, 1968, p. 322.
25 Vladimirtsov, 1948a, p. 109.
26 Spuler, 1966, p. 208.
27 Bretschneider, 1910, vol. 1, p. 283; Barthold, 1928, p. 456; Boyle, 1968, p. 322.
28 Barthold, 1928, p. 456.
29 Ibid.; Boyle, 1958, p. 96.
30 Barthold, 1928, p. 457.

31 Yule, 1916, vol. 2, pp. 287–8.
32 Waley, 1931, pp. 34–8, 72, 112.
33 Boyle, 1958, p. 97.
34 Haenisch, 1948, par. 263.
35 Pelliot, 1930, pp. 47–8.
36 Barthold, 1956, vol. l, p. 71.
37 Grousset, 1939, p. 304.
38 Barthold, 1928, p. 163.
39 Spuler, 1960, p. 9.
40 Grousset, 1939, pp. 304–5.
41 Barthold, 1928, p. 163; Schurman, 1956, p. 304.

CHAPTER 11

1 Haenisch, 1948, par. 256.
2 Krause, 1922, p. 39.
3 Boyle, 1971, p. 147.
4 Vladimirtsov, 1948a, p. 113.
5 Haenisch, 1948, par. 265.
6 Krause, 1922, p. 39.
7 Grenard, 1935, p. 309.
8 Walker, 1939, p. 294.
9 Grenard, 1935, p. 174.
10 Haenisch, 1948, par. 267.
11 Vladimirtsov, 1948, p. 115.
12 Grousset, 1939, p. 309.
13 Grenard, 1935, p. 175.
14 Krause, 1922, p. 39.
15 Ibid., p. 40.
16 Ibid.
17 Haenisch, 1948, par. 265.
18 Krause, 1922, p. 40.
19 Spuler, 1972, p. 43.
20 Barthold, 1928, p. 458; Boyle, 1971, p. 118.
21 Haenisch, 1948, par. 268; Cleaves, 1982, sect. 268.
22 Pelliot, 1959, vol. 1, p. 305.
23 Haenisch, 1933, p. 547.
24 Pelliot, 1959, vol. 1, p. 327.
25 Krause, 1922, p. 40; Boyle, 1958, p. 183.
26 Pelliot, 1959, vol. 1, p. 308; Ratchnevsky, 1983, p. 127.
27 Krause, 1922, p. 41; Schmidt, 1829, p. 105.
28 Vladimirtsov, 1948a, p. 115.
29 Krause, 1922, p. 40.
30 Haenisch, 1948, par. 267; Cleaves, 1982, sect. 267.

31 Haenisch, 1933, p. 546.
32 Haenisch, 1948, par. 268; Cleaves, 1982, sect. 268.
33 Haenisch, 1933, pp. 546–7.
34 Spuler, 1972, p. 44.
35 Haenisch, 1948, par. 268.
36 Grousset, 1941, p. 273.
37 Spuler, 1972, p. 44.
38 Pelliot, 1959, vol. 1, pp. 335–6; Spuler, 1972, p. 44.
39 Pelliot, 1959, vol. 1, p. 342; Krause, 1922, p. 41; Haenisch, 1933, p. 549.
40 Spuler, 1972, p. 44.
41 Ibid., p. 145; Kwanten, 1979, p. 124.
42 Boyle, 1958, p. 189; Boyle, 1971, p. 31.
43 Boyle, 1968, p. 45.
44 Pelliot, 1959, vol. 1, p. 353; Boyle, 1971, p. 228.

CHAPTER 12

1 Barthold, 1928, p. 459; Pelliot, 1929, p. 166; Pelliot, 1930, p. 13.
2 Barthold, 1928, p. 459.
3 Vladimirtsov, 1948a, p. 133; Ratchnevsky, 1983, p. 132.
4 Barthold, 1928, p. 461.
5 Grousset, 1939, p. 314; Ratchnevsky, 1983, p. 133.
6 Boyle, 1971, p. 17.
7 Vladimirtsov, 1948a, p. 124; Ratchnevsky, 1983, p. 145.
8 Vladimirtsov, 1948a, p. 133; Ratchnevsky, 1983, pp. 136–7.
9 Barthold, 1928, p. 461; Ayalon, 1971b, pp. 163–4; Ratchnevsky,1983, p. 147.
10 Barthold, 1928, p. 461.
11 Ibid., p. 462.
12 Ibid.; Ayalon, 1971b, p. 163.
13 Stübe, 1908, p. 532.
14 Vladimirtsov, 1948a, p. 131; Vernadsky, 1953, p. 2; Ratchnevsky, 1983, p. 147.
15 Vladimirtsov, 1948a, p. 131.
16 Krause, 1924, p. 6.
17 Grousset, 1939, p. 316.
18 Vernadsky, 1953, p. 127.

19 Jansma, 1959, p. 10.
20 Barthold, 1956, vol. 1, p. 43.
21 Vernadsky, 1953, p. 131; de Rachewiltz, 1966, p. 132; Sinor, 1982, p. 307; Ratchnevsky, 1983, pp. 161–2.
22 Vladimirtsov, 1948a, p. 121; Vernadsky, 1953, p. 130; Ratchnevsky, 1983, p. 158.
23 Voegelin, 1941/2, pp. 404–5, 409; de Rachewiltz, 1973, pp. 23–4; Franke, H., 1978, pp. 17–18; Ratchnevsky, 1983, p. 141.
24 Haenisch, 1948, par. 230; Sagaster, 1973, p. 225; Franke, H., 1978, p. 16; Ratchnevsky, 1983, p. 142.
25 Vladimirtsov, 1948a, p. 117; Schurman, 1956, p. 304.
26 Vladimirtsov, 1948a, p. 118.
27 Ibid., p. 119; Schurman, 1956, p. 309.
28 Vladimirtsov, 1948a, p. 123.
29 Ayalon, 1971b, p. 164; Ratchnevsky, 1983, pp. 162–4.

CHAPTER 13

1 Boyle, 1971, p. 163.
2 Barthold, 1935, p. 180.
3 Ibid.
4 Pelliot, 1949, p. 29.
5 Grousset, 1939, p. 469.
6 Pelliot, 1949, p. 28.
7 Ibid., p. 44.
8 Grousset, 1939, p. 469.
9 Grousset, 1941, p. 285; Boyle, 1958, p. 43.
10 Barthold, 1935, p. 180.
11 Bretschneider, 1910, vol. 1, p. 160; Boyle, 1958, p. 43.
12 Grousset, 1939, p. 319.
13 Henthorn, 1963, p. 195.
14 Grousset, 1941, p. 277.
15 Ibid., p. 537.
16 Krause, 1922, p. 41.
17 Haenisch, 1948, par. 269; Boyle, 1977, p. 75.
18 Boyle, 1958, pp. 183–4; Boyle, 1971, p. 30.
19 Boyle, 1958, p. 185.
20 Ibid., pp. 186–7; Boyle, 1971,

pp. 30–1; Ayalon, 1971b, p. 153.
21 Pelliot, 1920, p. 157.
22 Boyle, 1971, p. 16.
23 Ibid., p. 17.
24 Ibid., p. 61.
25 Ibid., pp. 18–19.
26 Boyle, 1958, p. 549.
27 Ibid., pp. 204–8; Boyle, 1971, pp. 76–94.
28 Franke, O., 1948, vol. 4, p. 161.
29 de Rachewiltz, 1962, pp. 189, 210–11.
30 Pelliot, 1914, p. 628.
31 D'Ohsson, 1834, vol. 2, p. 63; Kwanten, 1979, pp. 128–9.
32 Haenisch, 1941, p. 43.
33 Spuler, 1985, p. 349.
34 Olbricht, 1954, p. 40; Spuler, 1985, p. 350.
35 Olbricht, 1954, pp. 40–1.
36 Haenisch, 1948, par. 279–80.
37 Pelliot, 1930, pp. 193–5; Olbricht, 1954, p. 41.
38 Haenisch, 1948, par. 279.
39 D'Ohsson, 1834, vol. 2, p. 63.
40 Haenisch, 1948, par. 281; Cleaves, 1982, sect. 281.
41 Grousset, 1941, pp. 538–9.
42 Pelliot, 1959, vol. 1, p. 165; Boyle, 1971, pp. 61–2; Dawson, 1955, p. 156.
43 Dawson, 1955, pp. 183–4.
44 Bretschneider, 1910, vol. 1, p. 123.
45 Grousset, 1941, p. 289.
46 Boyle, 1972, pp. 125–31.
47 Grousset, 1939, p. 324.
48 Ibid., p. 325; Boyle, 1958, p. 424.
49 Minorsky, 1953, pp. 149–56; Spuler, 1985, p. 30.
50 Grousset, 1939, p. 325.
51 Spuler, 1985, p. 30.
52 Minorsky, 1953, p. 154; Boyle, 1958, p. 438; Hartman, 1975, pp. 85–6.
53 Boyle, 1958, pp. 452–3.
54 Boyle, 1971, p. 46.
55 Boyle, 1958, pp. 453–7.
56 Ibid., p. 459; Spuler, 1985, p. 31.
57 Pelliot, 1924, p. 301; Grousset, 1939, p. 326.
58 Pelliot, 1914, p. 634.
59 Boyle, 1958, pp. 489–500.
60 Spuler, 1985, p. 34.

61 D'Ohsson, 1834, vol. 2, p. 70.
62 Altunian, 1911, p. 35 sq.; Grousset, 1939, p. 327.
63 Pelliot, 1924, p. 247.
64 Houtsma, 1892, pp. 14–15.
65 Matuz, 1973, 182–3.
66 Turan, 1970, p. 249.
67 Matuz, 1973, p. 189.
68 Turan, 1970, p. 249.
69 Matuz, 1973, pp. 195–6.
70 Altunian, 1911, p. 38; Grousset, 1939, p. 328.
71 Grousset, 1939, p. 328.
72 Franke, O., 1948, vol. 4, p. 284.
73 Krause, 1922, p. 40.
74 Franke, O., 1948, vol. 4, p. 284.
75 Ibid., p. 285.
76 Ibid.
77 Grousset, 1939, p. 322.
78 Ibid.
79 Boyle, 1971, p. 34.
80 Grousset, 1939, p. 322.
81 Franke, O., 1948, vol. 4, p. 287.
82 Ibid.
83 Ibid., p. 288.
84 Boyle, 1958, p. 549.
85 Haenisch, 1948, par. 272; Cleaves, 1982, sect. 272.
86 D'Ohsson, 1834, vol. 2, p. 59.
87 Boyle, 1958, p. 551; Ayalon, 1971b, pp. 153–5.
88 Franke, O., 1948, vol. 4, p. 288.
89 Ibid., p. 288.
90 Krause, 1924, p. 90.
91 Franke, O., 1948, vol. 4, p. 289.
92 Ibid., p. 291.
93 Grousset, 1939, p. 323.
94 Ibid.
95 Grousset, 1941, p. 293.
96 Franke, O., 1948, vol. 4, p. 303.
97 Ibid.
98 Henthorn, 1963, p. ix.
99 Ibid., p. 14.
100 Ledyard, 1964, p. 2.
101 Henthorn, 1963, p. 195.
102 Franke, O., 1948, vol. 4, p. 302.
103 Henthorn, 1963, p. 64.
104 Ibid., p. 70.
105 Grousset, 1939, p. 323.
106 Henthorn, 1963, p. 74.
107 Ibid., p. 102.
108 Ibid., pp. 103–4.
109 Ledyard, 1964, p. 4.

CHAPTER 14

1 Vernadsky, 1938, pp. 28–31.
2 Ibid., pp. 36–7; Grekov et Iakoubovski, 1939, pp. 184–5.
3 Bretschneider, 1910, vol. 1, p. 300; Grekov et Iakoubovski, 1939, p. 196; Spuler, 1965, p. 15.
4 Vernadsky, 1953, p. 49.
5 Grousset, 1941, p. 296; Boyle, 1958, p. 269; Boyle, 1971, p. 56.
6 Haenisch, 1948, par. 277; Boyle, 1971, pp. 56–7.
7 Spuler, 1965, p. 16.
8 Vernadsky, 1953, p. 49.
9 Spuler, 1960, p. 11.
10 Bretschneider, 1910, vol. 1, p. 309; Spuler, 1965, p. 17.
11 Barthold, 1935, p. 167.
12 Spuler, 1965, p. 17.
13 Bretschneider, 1910, vol. 1, p. 311; Pelliot, 1920, pp. 166–7; Boyle, 1971, p. 58.
14 Grousset, 1939, p. 329; Sinor, 1959, p. 66.
15 Spuler, 1965, p. 17.
16 Boyle, 1958, p. 269; Boyle, 1971, p. 59.
17 Grousset, 1939, p. 330.
18 Grekov et Iakoubovski, 1939, p. 200.
19 Vernadsky, 1953, p. 51.
20 Grousset, 1939, p. 330.
21 Vernadsky, 1953, p. 51.
22 Bretschneider, 1910, vol. 1, p. 313; Spuler, 1965, p. 18.
23 Spuler, 1965, p. 18.
24 Bretschneider, 1910, vol. 1, p. 313; Grekov et Iakoubovski, 1939, p. 202.
25 Spuler, 1965, p. 19.
26 Grousset, 1939, p. 329; Saunders, 1971, p. 82.
27 Bretschneider, 1910, vol. 1, p. 322.
28 Boyle, 1971, p. 60.
29 Bretschneider, 1910, vol. 1, p. 316; Grousset, 1939, p. 297.
30 Bretschneider, 1910, vol. 1, p. 307; Grekov et Iakoubovski, 1939, p. 204.
31 Spuler, 1965, p. 19.
32 Grekov et Iakoubovski, 1939, p. 305.

33 Vernadsky, 1953, p. 52.
34 Bretschneider, 1910, vol. 1, pp. 318–19.
35 Vernadsky, 1953, p. 52.
36 Dawson, 1955, p. 30.
37 Spuler, 1960, p. 12.
38 Spuler, 1965, p. 20.
39 Bretschneider, 1910, vol. 1, p. 323; Vernadsky, 1953, p. 52.
40 Bretschneider, 1910, vol. 1, p. 319.
41 Sinor, 1959, pp. 48–64.
42 de Ferdinandy, 1958, p. 144.
43 Strakosch-Grassmann, 1893, p. 2; Sinor, 1959, pp. 68–9.
44 de Ferdinandy, 1958, p. 139; Sinor, 1959, p. 70.
45 Strakosch-Grassman, 1893, p. 42; Sinor, 1956, pp. 42–3.
46 Strakosch-Grassmann, 1893, p. 9.
47 Sinor, 1952, p. 600; Sinor, 1956, p. 42; Bezzola, 1974, p. 52.
48 Sinor, 1959, p. 68; Bezzola, 1974, p. 66.
49 Strakosch-Grassmann, 1893, p. 29.
50 de Hartog, 1979a, p. 171.
51 Strakosch-Grassmann, 1893, p. 42; de Ferdinandy, 1958, p. 142.
52 Spuler, 1960, p. 13; Spuler, 1965, p. 22.
53 Grousset, 1939, p. 331.
54 Strakosch-Grassmann, 1893, p. 39.
55 Sinor, 1971, p. 245.
56 Strakosch-Grassmann, 1893, pp. 43–4.
57 Ibid., p. 45.
58 Ibid.
59 Ibid., p. 46.
60 Spuler, 1965, p. 22.
61 Strakosch-Grassmann, 1893, p. 50.
62 Ibid., p. 67.
63 von Hammer-Purgstall, 1840, p. 120.
64 Ibid.
65 Ibid.
66 Strackosch-Grassmann, 1893, pp. 67–71.
67 Ibid.
68 Ibid.
69 von Hammer-Purgstall, 1840, p. 122.
70 Strakosch-Grassmann, 1893, pp. 92–6; Bezzola, 1974, p. 88.
71 Strakosch-Grassmann, 1893,

pp. 72–5; Bretschneider, 1910, vol. 1, p. 323; de Ferdinandy, 1958, p. 140; Sinor, 1959, p. 72.
72 Bretschneider, 1910, p. 141.
73 de Ferdinandy, 1958, p. 141.
74 Strakosch-Grassmann, 1893, pp. 78–9.
75 Ibid., pp. 84–7.
76 Grousset, 1939, p. 322; Bezzola, 1974, pp. 87–8.
77 Vernadsky, 1958, p. 70.
78 Bretschneider, 1910, vol. 1, p. 325; Sinor, 1959, p. 75.
79 Strackosch-Grassmann, 1893, pp. 161–7.
80 Boyle, 1958, p. 588.
81 Jackson, 1978, p. 195.
82 Boyle, 1958, p. 240.
83 Haenisch, 1948, par. 257–77.
84 Strakosch-Grassmann, 1893, p. 173.
85 de Ferdinandy, 1958, p. 149.
86 Strakosch-Grassmann, 1893, p. 168; Bretschneider, 1910, vol. 1, p. 326.
87 Strakosch-Grassmann, 1893, p. 173.
88 Sinor, 1977, pp. 181–3.
89 Strakosch-Grassmann, 1893, p. 18; Sinor, 1956, p. 44.
90 Sinor, 1959, pp. 70, 74; Bezzola, 1974, p. 76.
91 Sinor, 1959, p. 70.
92 Sinor, 1956, p. 45.
93 Haenisch, 1948, par. 270.
94 Ibid., par. 277.

CHAPTER 15

1 Boyle, 1958, p. 240.
2 Haenisch, 1948, par. 281; Cleaves, 1982, sect. 281.
3 Boyle, 1971, p. 65.
4 Franke, O., 1948, vol. 4, p. 305; Boyle, 1958, p. 200.
5 Boyle, 1971, p. 120.
6 Hambis, 1945, pp. 3–4.
7 Boyle, 1971, p. 180.
8 Boyle, 1968, pp. 45 sq.
9 Pelliot, 1931/2, p. 55 (193).
10 Spuler, 1985, p. 37.

11 Grousset, 1939, p. 334; Boyle, 1958, p. 240; Boyle, 1971, p. 176.
12 Boyle, 1958, p. 245.
13 Boyle, 1971, p. 176.
14 Boyle, 1958, p. 241.
15 Spuler, 1985, p. 37.
16 Ibid.; Boyle, 1958, p. 241.
17 Hambis, 1945, p. 71; Boyle, 1971, p. 21.
18 Boyle, 1958, pp. 241, 503; Boyle, 1971, p. 177.
19 Bretschneider, 1910, vol. 1, p. 10; de Rachewiltz, 1962, p. 208.
20 Boyle, 1958, p. 244; Boyle, 1971, p. 178, 182; Jackson, 1978, p. 198.
21 Ayalon, 1971b, pp. 155–6, 162–3.
22 Boyle, 1958, pp. 249–54; Boyle, 1971, pp. 180–2.
23 Risch, 1930, pp. 237–43.
24 Spuler, 1985, pp. 217–18.
25 Boyle, 1958, p. 249.
26 Boyle, 1971, p. 180.
27 Bretschneider, 1910, vol. 1, p. 332; Grousset, 1941, p. 305.
28 Boyle, 1958, p. 251.
29 Boyle, 1971, p. 182.
30 Risch, 1930, p. 241.
31 Richard, 1949, p. 292.
32 Krause, 1925, p. 353.
33 Bezzola, 1974, pp. 110–13.
34 Sinor, 1956, p. 47.
35 Sinor, 1957, pp. 205–6.
36 Bezzola, 1974, p. 113.
37 Pelliot, 1922/3, p. 8 (6).
38 Ibid. (1924), pp. 225–335 (29–139); Sinor, 1956, p. 47; Bezzola, 1974, p. 124.
39 Risch, 1930, p. 49.
40 Ibid.
41 Ibid., pp. 43–5.
42 Pelliot (1924), p. 302 (106).

43 Ibid. (1922/3), p. 6.
44 Sinor, 1952, pp. 599–600; Sinor, 1956, p. 47; Sinor, 1957, p. 206.
45 Pelliot (1924), p. 283 (87).
46 Risch, 1930, p. 226.
47 Pelliot (1924), p. 308 (112).
48 Risch, 1930, p. 227.
49 Pelliot (1922/3), pp. 11, 29.
50 Ibid., pp. 18–23; Risch, 1930, p. 259.
51 Risch, 1930, p. 259.
52 Ibid., p. 260.
53 Sinor, 1956, p. 47; Sinor, 1957, pp. 204–5.
54 Pelliot, 1924, p. 256 (60).
55 Risch, 1930, p. 41.
56 Pelliot, 1924, p. 332 (156).
57 Risch, 1930, p. 256.
58 Boyle, 1971, pp. 180, 188.
59 Boyle, 1958, p. 259.
60 Boyle, 1971, p. 183; Spuler, 1985, p. 39.
61 Pelliot, 1931/2, p. 57 (195); Grousset, 1939, p. 325.
62 Bretschneider, 1910, vol. 1, p. 332; Grousset, 1941, p. 305.
63 Boyle, 1958, p. 245; Boyle, 1971, p. 179.
64 Ayalon, 1971b, pp. 157–9, 164–5.
65 Boyle, 1958, p. 255; Boyle, 1971, pp. 182–3.
66 Boyle, 1958, pp. 256–7.
67 Pelliot, 1924, p. 315 (119); Bezzola, 1974, p. 155.
68 Spuler, 1985, pp. 41–2; Grousset, 1939, p. 337.
69 Pelliot, 1924, p. 326 (130).
70 Boyle, 1971, pp. 99, 185.
71 Pelliot, 1931/2, pp. 57–8, 61 (195–6, 199); Boyle, 1958, p. 261.
72 Boyle, 1958, p. 263.

Bibliography

Alinge, C., *Mongolische Gesetze* (Leipzig, 1934).

Altunian, G., *Die Mongolen und ihre Eroberungen in kaukasischen und kleinasiatischen Ländern im XIII. Jahrhundert* (Berlin, 1911).

Ayalon, D., 'The Great Yasa of Chingiz Khan, a reexamination', in *Studia Islamica*, vol. 33 (1971a), pp. 97–140, vol. 34 (1971b), pp. 151–80.

Barthold, W., *Turkestan down to the Mongol Invasion* (London, 1928).

——, '12 Vorlesungen über die Geschichte der Türken Mittelasiens', in *Die Welt des Islams*, Beiband (1935).

——, 'Cingis Khan', in *Encyclopaedia of Islam*, vol. 1 (Leiden, 1936), p. 882.

——, *Histoire des Turcs d'Asie Centrale* (Paris, 1945).

——, *Four Studies on the History of Central Asia*, vols 1 & 3 (Leiden, 1956).

Bausani, A., 'Religion under the Mongols' in *Cambridge History of Iran*, vol. 5, *The Saljuq and Mongol Periods* (Cambridge, 1968), pp. 538–49.

Bawden, C. R., *The Mongol Chronicle Altan Tobci* (Wiesbaden, 1955).

Beazley, C. R., *The Texts and Versions of John of Plano Carpini and William Rubruquis* (London, 1903).

Becquet, J. et Hambis, L., *Jean de Plan Carpin: Histoire des Mongols* (Paris, 1965).

Bezzola, G., *Die Mongolen in abendländischer Sicht (1200–1270)* (Bern, 1974).

Bretschneider, E., *Mediaeval Researches from Eastern Asiatic Sources*, vols 1 & 2 (London, 1910).

Bosworth, C. E., 'The political and dynastic history of the Iranian world (A.D. 1000–1217)', in *Cambridge History of Iran*, vol. 5, *The Saljuq and Mongol Periods* (Cambridge, 1968), pp. 1–203.

Boyle, J. A., 'On the titles given in Juvaini to certain Mongolian princes', in *Harvard Journal of Asiatic Studies*, vol. 19 (1956), pp. 146–54.

——, *The History of the World-Conqueror by Ala-ad-din Malik Juvaini*, vols 1 & 2 (Manchester, 1958).

——, 'Juvaini and Rashid al-Din as sources on the history of the Mongols', in *Historians of the Middle East*, ed. B. Lewis and P. M. Holt (London, 1962), pp. 133–7.

——, 'Kirakos of Ganjak on the Mongols', in *Central Asiatic Journal*, vol. 8 (1963a), pp. 199–214.

——, 'The Mongol commanders in Afghansitan and India according to Tabaqat-i-Nasiri of Juzjani', in *Islamic Studies*, vol. 2 (1963b), pp. 235–47.

——, 'A form of horse sacrifice amongst the 13th- and 14th-century Mongols', in *Central Asiatic Journal*, vol. 10 (1965), pp. 145–50.

——, 'Dynastic and political history of the Il-Khans', in *Cambridge History of Iran*, vol. 5, *The Saljuq and Mongol Periods* (Cambridge, 1968a), pp. 303–421.

——, 'The burial place of the Great Khan Ögödei', in *Acta Orientalia*, vol. 32 (1968b), pp. 45–50.

——, *The Successors of Genghis Khan*, translated from the Persian of Rashid al-Din (New York and London, 1971).

——, 'The seasonal residence of the Great Khan Ögödei', in *Central Asiatic Journal*, vol. 16 (1972), pp. 125–31.

——, 'Sites and localities connected with the history of the Mongol Empire', in *The Mongol World Empire 1206–1370*, chapter 16 (London, 1977).

Chavannes, E., 'Inscriptions et pièces de chancellerie chinoise de l'époque mongole', in *T'oung Pao*, vol. 5 (1904), pp. 357–447, vol. 6 (1905), pp. 1–42, vol. 9 (1908), p. 297–428.

Cheshire, H. T., 'The Tatar invasion of Europe', in *Slavonic Review*, vol. 5, pp. 89–105.

Cleaves, F. W., 'Sino-Mongolian inscriptions of 1362', in *Harvard Journal of Asiatic Studies*, vol. 12 (1949), pp. 1–133.

——, 'Sino-Mongolian inscriptions of 1346', in *Harvard Journal of Asiatic Studies*, vol. 15 (1952), pp. 1–123.

——, 'The historicity of the Baljuna covenant', in *Harvard Journal of Asiatic Studies*, vol. 18 (1955), pp. 357–421

——, *The Secret History of the Mongols* (translation), vol. 1 (Cambridge, Mass., 1982).

Cordier, H., 'L'invasion mongole au Moyen-Age et ses conséquences', in *Mélanges d'histoire et géographie orientales*, vol. 2 (Paris, 1920), pp. 254–69.

Dawson, Chr., *The Mongol Mission: Narratives and Letters of the Franciscan Missionaries in Mongolia and China* (London and New York, 1955).

Doerfer, G., 'Zur Datierung der Geheime Geschichte der Mongolen', in *Zeitschrift des deutschen Morgenländischen Gesellschaft*, vol. 113 (1964), pp. 87–111.

Douglas, R. K., *The Life of Jenghiz Khan* (London, 1877).

Duyvendak, J. J. L., *Wegen en gestalten der Chineesche geschiedenis* ('s Gravenhage, 1935).

Eberhard, W., *A History of China* (London, 1960).

von Erdmann, F., *Temudschin der Unerschütterliche* (Leipzig, 1862).

Euler, E., 'Die Begegnung Europas mit den Mongolen in Spiegel abendländischer Reiseberichte', in *Saeculum*, vol. 23 (1972), pp. 47–58.

de Ferdinandy, M., *Tschingis Khan – Der Einbruch der Steppenmenschen* (Hamburg, 1958).

Fitzgerald, C. P., *China* (London, 1942).

Franke, H., 'Asien und Europa im Zeitalter des Mongolensturms', in *Saeculum Weltgeschichte*, vol. 5 (1965), pp. 1–68.

——, 'Siege and defence of towns in medieval China', in *Chinese Ways in Warfare,*' ed. F. A. Kierman and J. K. Fairbank (Cambridge, Mass., 1974), pp. 151–201.

——, *From Tribal Chieftain to Universal Emperor and God: the Legitimation of the Yüan Dynasty* (München, 1978).

Franke, O., *Geschichte des chinesischen Reiches*, vols 4 & 5 (Berlin, 1948, 1952).

Gibb, H. A. R., *The Travels of Ibn Battuta (A.D. 1325–1354)* (Cambridge, 1958).

Grekov, B. et Iakoubovski, A., *La Horde d'Or* (Paris, 1939).

Grenard, F., *Gengis-Khan* (Paris, 1935).

Grousset, R., *Histoire de l'Asie*, vol. 3 (Paris, 1922).

——, *L'Empire des Steppes* (Paris, 1939).

——, *L'Empire mongol (1er phase)* (Paris, 1941).

——, *Le Conquérant du Monde (Vie de Gengis Khan)* (Paris, 1944).

Grousset, R., Auboyer, J. et Buhot, J. 'L'Asie orientale des origines au xvᶜ siècle', in *Histoire du Moyen-Âge*, vol. 10 (Paris, 1941).

Haenisch, E., 'Die letzten Feldzüge Cinggis Hans und sein Tod', in *Asia Major*, vol. 9 (1933), pp. 503–51.

——, 'Kulturbilder aus Chinas Mongolenzeit', in *Historische Zeitschrift*, vol. 164 (1941), pp. 21–48.

——, *Die Kulturpolitik des mongolischen Weltreiches* (Berlin, 1943).

——, 'Der Stand der Yüan-ch'ao-pi-shi Forschung', in *Zeitschrift des deutschen Morgenländischen Gesellschaft*, vol. 98 (Neue Folge vol. 23) (1944), pp. 107–20.

——, *Die Geheime Geschichte der Mongolen* (Leipzig, 1948).

——, 'Die Jagdgesetze im mongolischen Ostreich', in *Deutsche Akademie der Wissenschaften zu Berlin*, Veröffentlichung 48 (Berlin, 1959).

——, 'Weiterer Beitrag zum Text der Geheime Geschichte' in *Zeitschrift des deutschen Morgenländischen Gesellschaft*, vol. 111 (Neue Folge vol. 36) (1962), pp. 137–49.

Halperin, Ch. J., 'Russia in the Mongol Empire in comparative perspective', in *Harvard Journal of Asiatic Studies*, vol. 43 (1983), pp. 239–61.

Hambis, L., 'Le Chapitre CVII du Yuan Che (les généalogies impériales mongoles dans l'histoire officielle de la dynastie mongole)', in *T'oung Pao*, Supplément au vol. 38 (1945).

——, *La Haute-Asie* (Paris, 1953).

——, 'L'Histoire des Mongols avant Gengis-Khan d'après les sources chinoises et la documentation conservée par Rasidu-d'-din', in *Central Asiatic Journal*, vol. 14 (1970), pp. 125–33.

——, *Gengis Khan* (Paris, 1973a).

——, 'L'Asie Central et les études mongoles' in *Journal Asiatique* (numéro spécial) (1973b).

von Hammer-Purgstall, J., *Geschichte der Goldenen Horde in Kiptschak* (Pesth, 1840).

Hartman, A., *An-Nasir li-Din Allah (1180–1225). Politik, Religion, Kultur in der späten 'Abbasidenzeit'* (Berlin, New York, 1975).

de Hartog, L., *Djenghis Khan, 's Werelds grootste veroveraar* (Amsterdam, Brussels, 1979a).

——, 'The army of Genghis Khan', in *Army Quarterly and Defence Journal*, vol. 109 (1979b), pp. 476–85.

——, *Europese reizigers naar de Grote Khan. De reizen van de franciscaner monniken en de familie Polo naar de opvolgers van Djenghis Khan* (Baarn, 1985).

Heissig, W., *Ein Volk sucht seine Geschichte* (Düsseldorf, Wien, 1964).

——, 'Mongolenreiche', in *Propyläen Weltgeschichte*, vol. 6 (1964), pp. 345–72.

Henthorn, W. E., *Korea: the Mongol Invasions* (Leiden, 1963).

Houtsma, M. Th., *Over de geschiedenis der Seljuken van Klein-Azië* (Amsterdam, 1892).

Howorth, H. H., *History of the Mongols*, vols 1, 2a, 2b, 3 (London, 1876, 1880, 1888).

Hung, W., 'The transmission of the book known as the Secret History of the Mongols', in *Harvard Journal of Asiatic Studies*, vol. 14 (1951), pp. 443–92.

Jackson, P., 'The dissolution of the Mongol Empire', in *Central Asiatic Journal*, vol. 22 (1978), pp. 186–244.

Jagchid, S. and Bawden, C. R., 'Some notes on the horse-policy of the Yüan dynasty', in *Central Asiatic Journal*, vol. 10 (1965), pp. 246–68.

Jahn, K., *Enkele beschouwingen over de geschiedenis en beschaving der oud-Turkse volkeren*, (Leiden, 1954).

Jansma, T., *Oost-westelijke verkenningen in de dertiende eeuw* (Leiden, 1959).

Jenkins, G., 'A note on climatic cycles and the rise of Chinggis Khan', in *Central Asiatic Journal*, vol. 18 (1974), pp. 217–26.

Khachikyan, L. S., 'Mongols in Transcaucasia', in *Cahiers d'Histoire Mondiale*, numéro spécial (1958), pp. 98–125.

Krader, L., 'The cultural and historical position of the Mongols', in *Asia Major*, vol. 3 (1953).

——, 'Qan – Qayan and the beginning of the Mongol Kingship', in *Central Asiatic*

Journal, vol. 1 (1955), pp. 17–35.

——, 'Feudalism and Tatar polity of the Middle Ages', in *Comparative Studies in Society and History*, vol. 1 (1958/9), pp. 74–94.

Krause, F. E. A., *Cingis Han. Die Geschichte seines Lebens nach den chinesischen Reichsannalen* (Heidelberg, 1922).

——, *Die Epoche der Mongolen* (Berlin, 1924).

——, *Geschichte Ostasiens*, vol. 1 (Göttingen, 1925).

Kwanten, L., 'Chingis Khan's conquest of Tibet. Myth or reality?', in *Journal of Asian History*, vol. 8 (1974), p. 1–20.

——, *Imperial Nomads: a History of Central Asia, 500–1500* (Philadelphia, 1979).

Lattimore, O., 'Chingis Khan and the Mongol conquests', in *Scientific American*, vol. 209 (1963), pp. 55–68.

Lech, K., *Das mongolische Weltreich. Al-'Umari's Darstellung der mongolische Reiche* (Wiesbaden, 1968).

Ledyard, G., 'The Mongol campaigns in Korea and the dating of the Secret History of the Mongols', in *Central Asiatic Journal*, vol. 9 (1964), pp. 1–22.

Martin, H. D., *The Rise of Chingis Khan and his Conquest of North China* (Baltimore, Md, 1950).

Marquart, J., 'Über das Volkstum der Komanen', in *Osttürkische Dialekstudien* (Abhandlungen der Königl. Gesellschaft der Wissenschaft zu Göttingen), vol. 13 (Berlin, 1914).

Masson Smith, J., 'Mongol manpower and the Persian population', in *Journal of the Economic and Social History of the Orient*, vol. 18 (1975), pp. 271–99.

Matuz, J., 'Der Niedergang der anatolischen Seldschuken: die Entscheidungsslacht am Kösedag', in *Central Asiatic Journal*, vol. 17 (1973) pp. 180–99.

Minorsky, V., *Studies in Caucasian History* (London, 1953).

Morgan, D. O., 'The Mongol armies in Persia', in *Der Islam*, vol. 56 (1979), pp. 81–96.

——, 'Who ran the Mongol Empire?', in *Journal of the Royal Asiatic Society* (1982), pp. 124–36.

——, 'The "Great Yasa of Chingiz Khan' and the Mongol Law in the Ilkhanate', in *Bulletin of the School of Oriental and African Studies*, vol. 49 (1986a), pp. 163–76.

——, *The Mongols* (Oxford, 1986b).

Moule, A. C., 'Table of the emperors of the Yüan dynasty', in *Journal of the North China Branch of the Royal Asiatic Society* (1914).

Moule, A. C. and Pelliot, P., *Marco Polo: the Description of the World*, vol. 1 (London, 1938).

Olbricht, P., *Das Postwesen in China unter der Mongolenherrschaft in 13. und 14. Jahrhundert* (Wiesbaden, 1954).

d'Ohsson, M. C., *Histoire des Mongols*, vols 1, 2, 3, 4 (Amsterdam, 1834).

Pelliot, P., 'Chrétiens d'Asie Centrale et d'Extrême-Orient', in *T'oung Pao*, vol. 15 (1914), pp. 623–44.

—— 'À propos des Comans', in *Journal Asiatique*, vol. 208 (1920), pp. 125–85.

——, 'Les Mongols et la Papauté', in *Revue de l'Orient Chrétien*, vol. 23 (1922/3), pp. 3–30, vol. 24 (1924), pp. 225–335, vol. 28 (1931/2), pp. 3–84.

——, 'Les Systèmes d'écriture en usage chez les anciens Mongols', in *Asia Major*, vol. 2 (1925) pp. 286–9.

——, 'L'édition collective des oeuvres de Wang Kouo-wei', in *T'oung Pao*, vol. 26 (1929), pp. 113–82.

——, 'Notes sur le "Turkestan" de W. Barthold', in *T'oung Pao*, vol. 27 (1930), pp. 12–56.

——, *Notes sur l'histoire de la Horde d'Or* (Paris, 1949).

——, *Notes on Marco Polo*, vol. 1, 2, 3 (Paris, 1959, 1963, 1973).

Pelliot, P. et Hambis, L., *Histoire des campagnes de Gengis Khan* (Leiden, 1951).

Phillips, E. D., *The Mongols* (London, 1969).

Poucha, P., *Die Geheime Geschichte der Mongolen* (Prague, 1956).

de Rachewiltz, I., 'Yeh-lü Ch'u-ts'ai (1189–1243): Buddhist idealist and Confucian statesman', in *Confucian Personalities*, ed. A. F. Wright and D. Twitchett (Stanford, 1962), pp. 189–216.

——, 'Personnel and personalities in north China in the early Mongol period', in *Journal of the Economic and Social History of the Orient*, vol. 9 (1966), pp. 88–144.

——, 'Some remarks on the ideological foundation of Chingis Khan's empire', in *Papers on Far Eastern History*, vol. 7 (1973), pp. 21–36.

——, 'Muqali, Bol, Tas and An-t'ung', in *Papers on Far Eastern History*, vol. 15 (1977), pp. 45–62.

Ratchnevsky, P., 'Sigi-Qutuqu, ein mongolischer Gefolgsmann im 12.–13. Jahrhundert', in *Central Asiatic Journal*, vol. 10 (1965), pp. 87–113.

——, *Činggis-Khan, sein Leben und Wirken* (Wiesbaden, 1983).

——, 'Die Rechtsverhältnisse bei den Mongolen im 12.–13. Jahrhundert', in *Central Asiatic Journal*, vol. 31 (1987), pp. 64–110.

Riasanovsky, V. A., 'The influence of Chinese law upon Mongolian law', in *Chinese Social and Political Science Review*, vol. 15 (1931), pp. 402–21.

——, 'Mongol law and Chinese law in the Yüan dynasty', in *Chinese Social and Political Science Review*, vol. 20 (1936), pp. 266–89.

——, *Fundamental principles of Mongol law* (Tientsin, 1937).

Richard, J., 'Le Début des relations entre la Papauté et les Mongols de Perse', in *Journal Asiatique*, vol. 237 (1949), pp. 291–7.

——, 'L'Etrême-Orient légendaire au Moyen-Âge: Roi David et Prêtre Jean', in *Annales d'Éthiopie*, vol. 2 (Paris, 1957), pp. 225–42.

——, 'Les Causes des victoires mongoles d'après les historiens occidentaux du 13e siècle, in *Central Asiatic Journal*, vol. 23 (1979), pp. 104–17.

——, 'Le Christianisme dans l'Asie centrale', in *Journal of Asian History*, vol. 16 (1982), pp. 101–24.

Risch, F., *Johann de Plano Carpini: Geschichte der Mongolen und Reisebericht* (Leipzig, 1930).

Rockhill, W. W., *The Journey of William of Rubruck to the Eastern Parts of the World* (London, 1900).

Ross, E. D. and Elias, N., *A History of the Moghuls of Central Asia* (London, 1895).

Sagaster, K., 'Herrschaftsideologie und Friedensgedanke bei den Mongolen', in *Central Asiatic Journal*, vol. 17 (1973), pp. 223–42.

Sakharov, A. M., 'Les Mongols et la civilisation russe', in *Cahiers d'Histoire Mondiale*, numéro special (1958), p. 77–97.

Saunders, J. J., *The History of the Mongol Conquests* (London, 1971).

Schmidt, I. J., *Geschichte der Ost-Mongolen und ihres Fürstenhauses, verfasst von Ssanang Ssetsen Chungtaidschi der Ordus'* (St Petersburg, Leipzig, 1829).

Schurman, H. F., 'Mongolian tributary practices in the thirteenth century', in *Harvard Journal of Asiatic Studies*, vol. 19 (1956), pp. 304–89.

Schütz, E., 'Tatarenstürme in Gebirgsgelände', in *Central Asiatic Journal*, vol. 17 (1973), pp. 253–73.

Sinor, D., 'Un voyageur du 13e siècle: le dominicain Julien de Hongrie', in *Bulletin of the School of Oriental and African Studies*, vol. 14 (1952), pp. 589–602.

——, 'Central Eurasia', in *Orientalism and History* (Cambridge, 1954), pp. 82–103.

——, 'Les Relations entre les Mongols et l'Europe jusqu'à la mort d'Arghoun et de Béla IV', in *Cahiers d'Histoire Mondiale*, vol. 3 (1956), pp. 39–62.

——, 'John of Plano Carpini's return from the Mongols', in *Journal of the Royal Asiatic Society* (1957), pp. 193–206.

——, *History of Hungary* (London, 1959).

——, *Introduction à l'étude de l'Eurasie centrale* (Wiesbaden, 1963).

——, *Inner Asia* (The Hague, 1969).

——, 'On Mongol strategy', in *Proceedings of the fourth East Asian Altaistic Conference* (Taipei, 1971), pp. 238–49.

——, 'What is Inner Asia?', in *Altaica Collecta: Berichte und Vorträge des XVII Permanent Altaistic Conference* (Wiesbaden, 1976), pp 245–58.

——, 'Horse and pasture in Inner Asian history', in *Inner Asia and its Contacts with Medieval Europe* (London, 1977), pp. 171–84.

——, 'The Inner Asian Warriors', in *Journal of the American Oriental Society*, vol. 101 (1981), pp. 133–44.

——, 'Interpreters in medieval Inner Asia', in *Journal of the Israel Oriental Society*, vol. 16 (1982), pp. 293–320.

Spuler, B., 'Die Mongolen und das Christentum', in *Internationale Kirchliche Zeitschrift* (1938), pp. 156–75.

——, 'Die Goldene Horde und Russlands Schicksal' in *Saeculum*, vol. 6 (1955), pp. 397–406.

——, *The Muslim World*, Part II, *The Mongol Period* (Leiden, 1960).

——, *Die Goldene Horde: Die Mongolen in Russland (1223–1502)* (Wiesbaden, 1965).

——, 'Geschichte Mittelasiens seit dem Aufreten der Türken', in *Handbuch der Orientalistik*, vol. 5 (Leiden, 1966), pp. 123–310.

——, 'The disintegration of the caliphate in the East', in *Cambridge History of Islam*, vol. 1, *The Central Islamic Lands* (London and New York, 1970), pp. 143–74.

——, *History of the Mongols* (London, 1972).

——, *Die Mongolen in Iran* (Leiden, 1985).

Strakosch-Grassmann, G., *Der Einfall der Mongolen in Mitteleuropa in den Jahren 1241–1242* (Innsbrück, 1893).

Stübe, R., 'Tschingiz-Chan seine Staatsbildung und seine Persönlichkeit', in *Neue Jahrbücher für das klassische Altertum, Geschichte und deutsche Literatur* (Leipzig, 1908).

Turan, O., 'Anatolia in the period of the Seljuks and the Beyliks', in *Cambridge History of Islam*, vol. 1, *The Central Islamic Lands* (London and New York, 1970), pp. 231–62. ,

Vernadsky, G., 'The scope and contents of Chingis Khan's Yasa', in *Harvard Journal of Asiatic Studies* (December 1938), pp. 337–60.

——, *A History of Russia* (New Haven, Conn., 1948).

——, *The Mongols and Russia* (London and New Haven, Conn., 1953).

Vladimirtsov, B., *Gengis-Khan* (Paris, 1948a).

——, '*Le Régime social des Mongols: le féodalisme nomade* (Paris, 1948b).

Voegelin, E., 'The Mongol orders of submission to European Powers, 1245–1255' in *Byzantion*, vol. 15 (1941/2), pp. 378–413.

Waldron, A. N., 'The problem of the Great Wall of China', in *Harvard Journal of Asiatic Studies*, vol. 43 (1983), pp. 643–63.

Waley, A. *The Travels of an Alchemist: the Journey of the Taoist Ch'ang-Ch'un* (London, 1931).

Walker, C. C., *Jenghiz Khan* (London, 1939).

Werner, E. T. C., 'The burial place of Gengis Khan', in *Journal of the North China Branch of the Royal Asiatic Society* (1925), pp. 80–6.

Wolff, O., *Geschichte der Mongolen oder Tataren* (Breslau, 1872).

Wylie, T. V., 'The first Mongol conquest of Tibet reinterpreted', in *Harvard Journal of Asiatic Studies*, vol. 37 (1977), pp. 103–33.

Yule, H., *Cathay and the Way Thither*, vols 1 & 2 (London, 1913, 1916).

Index